Critical acclaim for Celling America's Soul

"As a criminologist I am repeatedly reminded that every opportunity to put a human face on the statistics of correction is a move away from stereotypic thinking…Prisoners are not monsters who must be locked away forever in sterile environments for the protection of society. I'd like to add this book to my courses as a recommended book."

—Julia Hall, Ph.D.
Drexel University

"*Celling America's Soul* is easily the most popular book in this Oklahoma prison unit's library. All the black guys rave about how good it is and can't get it passed along fast enough. At first they flocked around it, reading it in a group, but now are back to reading it two at a time inside their cages. With all of us pulling and the word spreading, we will get recognition eventually."

—James Bauhaus
Oklahoma State Penitentiary

"Everyone who is connected to the correctional system needs to own a copy."

—Bryan A. McMichael
Pennsylvania Prison Society
State Correctional Institution, Dallas PA

"Tears welled as I read about life within these walls…I hope people read this book and see what prisons are really like. Thank you for being courageous in telling these stories. **Dianna L. Hollis**
President, Lobbyist Coalition, PA

"Judith, the other SageWriters, *Celling, Contemplations of a Convict, Healing Our Imprisoned Minds* and whatever we may produce next are the answer to one of this prisoner's prayers."
—Leonard Jefferson
State Correctional Institution, Albion PA

"An insightful, compelling book about the negative effects of America's criminal justice system…The brutally honest, heartfelt testimony gives insight into the challenges, abuse, trauma, indignities, and turmoil that many prisoners face on a daily basis…This book showcases the intellect and artistic talents of many prisoners.…All police, prosecutors, and judges should make *Celling America's Soul* required reading so they remember that there is a person, spirit, and loving family behind that easy conviction…The book brings into focus what we all know, and wish to change. Prison does not rehabilitate, it does not heal, and it certainly does not make our society a safer place to live."
—Darrell J. van Mastrigt
InnocenceDenied.com

"*Celling* is like a 'broadside' as in colonial times, a declaration of war against the penal system…It says all those things that any conscious and conscientious person must know."
—the late Carl Hirsch, PhD

Pennsylvania State University

"The book's journey through Shadow America is authentic and intimate, with the voices of the incarcerated used to articulate the experiences, the issues and the transformations. *Celling* shows the reader's role as a stakeholder in a degenerating prison process which contributes to increased risk to the community…The call is for rehabilitation rather than retribution."

—Errol McClean
Organization development consultant

"What goes on in America's prisons is America's best-kept secret…Prisoners say it is the best book in print that captures the horror, pathos, violence and ambiguity of prison life from most every perspective. As a white Republican lawyer, reading the truth of prisoners that the book captures has opened my eyes and I am horrified. These compelling, dramatic stories, exceptionally well-written, expose the brutality inflicted upon those we incarcerate…There are uplifting and heart-searing stories of men and women beaten down but yet transforming themselves, and the healing power of writing is on display on every page…This book had been deemed 'dangerous' by some prison officials and, until recently, was confiscated as 'putting the security of the institution at risk.' Prisoners were denied access to the book. Trustone, working with the Department of Correction, got the ban on the book lifted…It is a must-read for people of conscience.

—Robert Surrick, Esq.
Author of Lawyers, Judges and Journalists: The Corrupt and the Corrupters

(Editor's note: Robert Surrick, appointed in 1980 by former PA governor Thornburgh to investigate corruption at the highest level, documented his twenty years of whistleblowing against corrupt judges, lawyers and politicians in his book. His appeal for the return of his law license was denied after he publicly called Supreme Court justices "long on greed and short on scholarship" during one of his two runs for State Supreme Court.)

Celling America's Soul has been recommended by NPR's "Radio Times" and NAMI, the National Association for the Mentally Ill.

CELLING AMERICA'S SOUL:
Torture and Transformation in Our Prisons and Why We Should Care

by
Judith Trustone

with *SageWriters*

Anton Forde/Trevor Mattis
Danny Haggard
"Jameel Salahuddin"
Muti Ajamu-Osagboro
Robert "Muhkam" Hagood
Tony Harper

and
Joan Gauker
LaChae Singletary
PF Lazor
Anne-Marie Cusac
Bobbie Harvey
Iron Thunderhorse
Tom Big Warrior
Richard Tut Carter
Dianna Hollis
and many, many prisoners

ISBN-13: 978-1512227529

Published by:

Sagewriters Publishing
Box 215
Swarthmore, PA 19081
Info@Trustonekindness.com
Local phone: 610-328-6101

Printed in US on recycled paper
First edition published February 2003; Third edition January 2015

SageWriters

SageWriters is a community of free and imprisoned writers, artists, musicians, filmmakers, playwrights and activists working together to give artistic voice to movements for justice and healing; reawakening compassion in our elected officials; supporting effective re-entry programs; ending prisons as we know them and developing community-based houses of healing.

About the Art

Because cameras are not permitted in the prison, the art in the book is from color copies of prison-approved Polaroids of oil paintings that have been scanned into black and white photographs. The art and photographs are intended to soften some of the harsh intensity of prisoners' stories. The cover is of the Eastern State Penitentiary Historical site. The two SageWriters who chose anonymity are not included in the pictures on the back cover. The pictures of Muti, Anton/Trevor and Muhkam are stills from a documentary, "Unbelievable Isolation" by Glen Holsten of WHYY-TV in Philadelphia. Tony's picture is from his graduation from a G.E.D. class when he first came to prison twenty years ago.

Cover Art by Judith Trustone & James Lloyd

This Book is Dedicated to:

- the 8.9 million Americans currently in the grip of a corrupt and inhumane criminal justice system and those who love them.

- all those who participated in this book's birth, openly or anonymously, and those who love them.

- the caring people working inside the incarcerated community for justice, reform, kindness and decency.

- those falsely accused and criminally imprisoned.

- the victims of crimes, especially those crimes that would never have happened if their perpetrators had received treatment and rehabilitation.

- all the political prisoners around the world who dared to speak out against oppression.

- those whose spirits have been crushed by racism, sexism, classism, poverty and war.

- our ancestors, whose wisdom flows through us; and those who will come after us: all of our children, that they may know and keep freedom in their lives. May they know a more just and humane world.

Acknowledgements

Special thanks to Peter Brigham, Brian Jennings, Douglas Jennings, Rosalyn Payne, Phyllis Cross, Joan Gauker, Phyllis Redman, Brenda Emrick, Jack Liza, Atta Arghandiwal, Nikki Forston, Lindee Rochelle, Bea Dallet, Evelyn Lynch, John Harnish, Sarah Lauenborg, the late Robert Seidenberg, M.D., Gale Muhammad and Women Who Never Give Up, Lifers, Inc., Pennsylvania Prison Society, Lifers, Inc., AFSC's Prison Project, The Lionheart Foundation, *Graterfriends,* and the families of the imprisoned who inspired us with their devotion and determination.

Other books by Judith Trustone

The Cats' Secret Guide to Living with Humans
How To Train Your Mind To Be Kind All the Time (availably early 2015)
Where Rainbows Go At Night: poems, pondering and politics (early 2015)

Eighteen Years On Death Row
by Larry "Rocky" Harris

Documentaries by Judith Trustone

How To Create a Kindness Circle

Soothing and Nurturing the Human Spirit

Healing Justice: a journey into Shadow America

Films

Out of the Shadows

TV Series

Who Deserves to Be Freed?

Contents

PART VII: *Transformation*

Hidden Innocence
Holmesburg Prison
Oil on canvas   *Muti Ajamu-Osagboro*

Introduction

Charles Dickens was right. When he came to Philadelphia back in the 1840's to visit the brand new Eastern Penitentiary, he pronounced that the Quaker-inspired penitentiary was a model that would never work. He said, "Those who devised this system...and those benevolent gentlemen who carry it into execution, do not know what they are doing...I hold this slow and daily tampering with the brain to be immeasurably worse than any torture of the body."

Despite his prophetic warning, we continue to build prisons at a rapid rate as a response to our acceptance in this country of a high level of poverty, the lack of health care, an inadequate social safety net, and an obsession with guns and the military in a culture that loves violence. This cultural obsession with guns, human killing guns not squirrel rifles, reflects masculinity gone mad, where politicians can't get elected if they're not tough on crime.

Just as Bush maintained his blind stance in Iraq, so too the prison industrial complex blindly grows at an insane rate, totally ignoring its ineffective focus solely on punishment and an almost 70% failure to rehabilitate. Despite the noble efforts of many dedicated staff to create positive change within the criminal justice system, this 19th Century model continues to flourish despite overwhelming evidence of how prisons create violence in our communities.

What price do we pay as a people for institutions that grind up almost all who enter? Where our Thrown-Away People are warehoused? What does it say about us that we'll pay for an average of $30,000 a year to lock up a criminal ($65,000 for older inmates) and just $3,900 to educate a child? States have been forced to choose between building and improving schools or building prisons.

The results of mass incarceration and mandatory sentencing have resulted in a growing caste system of the formerly incarcerated, now numbering 16 million, who find it impossible to find jobs, housing, treatment, or education, driving them back to prison.

Why does America incarcerate more of its citizens than any other country in the world, to the consternation of the rest of the planet?

Like most Americans, despite decades of human rights activism, I hadn't given much attention to prisons, perceiving them as impenetrable. In 1993, I read about James Taylor, a lifer at Graterford (PA) Prison who had transformed himself by establishing an inmate-created self-help course called PAR, People Against Recidivism. He was attempting his fifth unsuccessful appeal for clemency during his 35 years behind bars.

The only way out of prison for a lifer in Pennsylvania, one of four states with such a Draconian law, is through a pardon recommended by the Board of Pardons. If Taylor had been convicted across the river in New Jersey, he would have been paroled years ago. Unfortunately, the Board, which makes recommendations to the governor for clemency, has only recommended two lifers in16 years. It's costing the state $325 million a year to keep almost 5,000 lifers behind bars and without hope, more than any other state. In other states where lifers are eligible for parole, the recidivism rate is just 2%. Are Pennsylvania prisoners worse than those in New Jersey, New York, and Delaware? Is death by incarceration truly a more humane alternative to the death penalty?

I wrote in support of Taylor's appeal for clemency, and when he wrote and invited me to Graterford to do a workshop, I was curious. Soon I was mentoring writers in the PAR group and eventually was hired as an artist-in-residence to teach creative writing.

When four of the fifteen students claimed innocence, at first I cynically said, "*Sure* you are. Show me." I was cracked wide open when I showed their cases to a lawyer, who confirmed that only a technicality or a mandatory sentencing law kept them locked up. I became determined to bring their stories to the public and SageWriters was born. I later learned that an estimated ten- to fifty-thousand innocent people are sent to prison each year.

As word got out that we were working on *Celling America's Soul*, I became subjected to increasing harassment by guards, and I resigned when I was ordered to strip for a full-body search. But the work continued by mail and expensive collect phone calls (The PA Department of Corrections gets a $7-million-per-year kickback from the overcharging phone company). When the book first came out, it and I were banned, though eventually I was able to convince prison officials to unban it when I threatened to expose them to Oprah Winfrey! (I haven't yet been on Oprah...)

It's not that people working in prisons are bad people. It's just that it's a bad, unfixable system that, by its nature, brings out the worst in many. This dynamic was verified back in the seventies with the Stanford study, where psychologically-screened volunteer students were divided into two groups, prisoners and guards. They had to stop the experiment after just three days as the student guards began to be abusive to the student prisoners, showing that it is the situation of one person having power over another that evokes torture and abuse, as we saw with Abu Ghraib, Charles Graner, one of the soldiers who was convicted of torture and sent to prison, was on leave as a Pennsylvania prison guard. (He had a reputation and record for abusing PA prisoners as well.)

Many social scientists conclude that prisons cause crime, where 70% of the 700,000 non-violent offenders come out every year with Post-Traumatic Stress Disorder, and according to Stop Prison Rape, an estimated 140,000 a year have been raped. Those coming home from prison find few jobs, little available low-income housing, and the stigma of being a person who's been to prison. The formerly-incarcerated have become our 'new lepers'.

They also bring multiple health challenge, as 40% of people in prison suffer from HIV, Hepatitis C, and TB, often never diagnosed and with little follow-up once they're released. A shocking percentage die within two weeks of leaving prison from homicide, suicide, overdosing, and the results of poor prison health care and diet.

With one out of three black men facing incarceration, racism obviously plays a major role in the prison industry.

This huge, profitable business employs hundreds of thousands from judges, lawyers, guards and policemen to court employees, doctors, dentists, office staff, nurses, clerks, "counselors", commissary suppliers, paper and cleaning supply providers, and many other related occupations. Pennsylvania's former Speaker of the House sat on the board of a private prison corporation that paid him $30,000 per year, while he was the Speaker. This corporate business relies on defining as many activities as possible as "criminal" in order to keep as many people behind bars as they can in order to keep profits up. There is no real rehabilitation taking place except in a few more enlightened places. To keep everyone in order, a system of severe repression and absolute control is essential. Clearly prisons are a threat to public safety.

Certainly there are those who are too damaged and violent and who are a danger to society; they need confinement and treatment for their violence. Despite progressive programs here and there, punishment in the form of physical abuse and psychological torture, which is all many of our prisons offer, makes inmates even more frustrated and violent.

Studies show that 70% of prisoners have drug addictions, 35% are mentally ill or retarded, and practically all suffer from various degrees of poverty, lack of education and health care, neglect, and abuse. Despite the stereotype that everyone in prison is getting a free college education, in reality there are only a few programs available, and it's estimated that 70% of the incarcerated can't read or write well enough to fill out an application for a driver's license. Several of the men in this book could only write their names when they first came to prison as teens. Many of the previously non-violent come out of prison filled with rage, a new "super criminal".

A Senate subcommittee once surveyed all of the wardens and superintendents in the country and 92% said we have to look at alternatives and most said we could release half of the people in prison today with no risk to the community. So what are we doing?

Then there's the slavery issue. When I first taught in prison, the guys would claim that prisons are one huge slave plantation. It took years before I actually looked at the 13th Amendment and saw that there's a clause excluding prisoners from emancipation, so we do actually still have slavery in prison!

'Section 1. Neither slavery nor involuntary servitude, **except as a punishment for crime whereof the party shall have been duly convicted,** shall exist within the United States, or any place subject to their jurisdiction. **Section 2. Congress shall have the power to enforce this article by appropriate legislation.**

Pennsylvania DOC pays prisoners 19 cents per hour. Colorado, in response to the flight of immigrants due to their anti-immigrant legislation, is proposing to have prisoners harvest their crops at the rate of 50 cents per day.

A new civil rights movement is beginning to emerge demanding the exclusion of the slavery clause allowing from the 13th Amendment. It would solve many of the problems in prisons if inmates were treated like American citizens, paid minimum wage to help them once released and allowed to vote as they are in Europe. Imagine politicians campaigning to prisoners!

The main flaw (besides maintaining slavery) is that prisons are based on a patriarchal, pseudo-militaristic model that foments a form of toxic masculinity that pervades and weakens the most positive efforts on the part of staff and inmates. The system does not discriminate between those arrested for pot (70% of drug arrests) and serial killers. In these days of Homeland Insecurity, all are treated as serial killers, which can force the non-violent into accelerated learning in the College for Criminals, again posing new threats to the community just for the sake of jobs for the prison industrial complex and salvation for economically-depressed rural communities where teachers resign to take higher paying jobs as prison guards. Where else in America can you earn, with overtime, $70,000 per year with just a high school education?

Many prisoners have been in there since they were teens, and due to politicians' testosterone-driven tough-on-crime laws and a fearful, manipulated, uninformed populace, most of them will never get out.

The cost of maintaining a prisoner in Pennsylvania is $47,000 a year; $65,000 for older inmates. The epidemic of Hepatitis C in those prisons offering diagnosis and treatment can run $100,000 a year per patient. Just the six SageWriters whose stories appear in this book have cost us over $6,160,000 so far. Where possible in the interviews, I list the amount we've paid so far to keep each person behind bars.

In 2006, after two years of meeting with prisoners, prison staff, and administrators, the blue-ribbon Commission on Safety and Abuse in American Prisons (www.prisoncommission.org), published *Confronting Confinement: A Report on Safety and Abuse in America's Prisons* (available free online). These prominent Americans came to the same conclusions found in this book. It appears that their suggestions, like those of the Warren Commission and the Gates Commission, will also be ignored by our government.

What does it do to America's soul to continue to ignore, as the American Bar Association has stated, that our criminal justice system is "broken"? Why should we care, even if the costs of prisons cuts into funds for education, housing, and health care? Few do care until someone they care about is incarcerated. Then it's shock and disbelief that such a 19th Century behemoth is the dominant model in 21st Century America, much to the consternation of the rest of the planet.

Newspapers report that Graterford Prison may be sold, as it sits on land prime for McMansions, and replaced by three new smaller prisons built elsewhere. What an opportunity for citizens to get involved in the planning and implementation of new kinds of institutions, Houses of Healing rather than Houses of Punishment!

Unfortunately, the taxpayers who bear the burden are not allowed into the process, for if the truth about prisons is revealed, prisons as we know them will come to an end at the demand of an awakened, rational and compassionate citizenry who have come to realize that as Blues group The Blind Boys of Alabama sing, "long as one of us is chained, all of us are chained, none of us is free."

In 2006, in an effort to awaken America, Philadelphia City Council passed a Resolution declaring March as "Justice Month", stating, "Whereas a society there is a necessity for us to look more closely and critically at who make up this prison population. For instance, the 'war on drugs' has created a situation where 70% of the incarcerated are non-violent offenders. Likewise, with one in three black men serving time in penal institutions at some point in their lives, this should be regarded as an acute situation; and whereas it is time for us to look collectively at some of the alternatives."

"Justice Month" brings together the organizations and individuals working toward prison change to form an alliance, a Justice Community, to educate the public about the issues, legislation, and alternatives. (www.justicemonth.org), SageWriters co-sponsored "Locked Up: Keys to Prison Change", a conference in Philadelphia on alternatives. The idea is being explored in other parts of the country for "Sister Cities for Justice." Prisoners at Graterford have created a "Public Safety Initiative" to address violence in their communities. A recent simulcast form the prison drew 1500 citizen, mostly young black men, to hear them at Philadelphia Community College. Are we reaching a critical mass to work for real change?

Creating SageWriters has enabled me to grow in ways I never could have imagined. In that creative writing class, I, like many others, was cracked wide open due by the suffering, injustice, degradation and corruption of the criminal justice business. I am in awe of those who've transformed themselves while behind bars. I am filled with gratitude for my privilege, my freedom, and my choices, and I'm thankful for the inspiration I've received and the brilliance I've found in my brothers and sisters and their families living in Shadow America.

Judith Trustone
Swarthmore, PA

"The fact is that more than 95% of the people now in prison are getting out some day. If we don't try hard to make a difference with the inmate while they're with us, we're jeopardizing public safety." Pennsylvania Secretary of Corrections, Jeffrey A. Beard,Ph.D.

Forward One
WHY YOU SHOULD CARE

By Anton Forde/Trevor Mattis, author,
Contemplations of a Convict:
A Journey to Freedom When Innocence Isn't Enuf

Ladies and gentlemen of this Republic, prison reform and other related issues lie buried n the public's consciousness. Few pay attention to this social issue or think it's important, and most don't want to hear about it. Lock them up and throw away the key is all there is to it. Why should we care?

Most middle-class and rich people live under the illusion that crime is far removed from them. Feeling relatively safe in their isolated enclaves, they're irrationally confident in law enforcement and the justice system to protect them. And their rights.

Prisons, criminals, prison reform, these are society's dirty laundry and soiled underwear that no one wants to touch or hear about. Hide it, throw t away, destroy it, do anything but expose it. Who wants the public embarrassment?

Why should you care? You should care because your confidence in the justice system and the Department of Corrections, society's sanitizers, is completely misplaced. Instead of "rehabilitating" society's miscreants, these institutions are factories of a social contagion set to destroy the fabric of American society in the near future. They've failed miserably in their mission.

What is going on in prisons today is the bio-engineering of a new breed of Super Criminals. Contrary to the public's perception, 90% of all prisoners will re-enter society someday. The justice system is now sweeping vast numbers of wayward youth into prisons. The DOC then molds and shapes them into Super Criminals by subjecting them to a program of degradation, brutalization, and dehumanization, and then spews them back to the community.

Why should you care? Because these Super Criminals who are re-emerging back into society will target you and your family without remorse. Like suicide bombers, full of hatred, fearless, depraved and impervious to the threat of prison, they won't just rob or rape you, they'll murder and maim you for no other reason than because they can, the same way prison guards brutalized and abused them for no other reason than because they could. Who is to blame? You. You stood by, apathetic to the calls and cries and warnings: Guantanamo, Sing Sing, and Camp Hill, to name a few.

Unlike before when these Super Criminals would target mainly those within their own community, this new breed will operate outside their social boundaries with impunity, killing at random. They are equal-opportunity murderers; it's happening right now. They're smart, ruthless, and they don't care if they live or die, and they're pre-conditioned to spend the rest of their lives incarcerated. The next wave of Super Criminals being conditioned in prisons across the country right now will no longer target the poor and the working class. The economic divide and other socioeconomic dysfunctions create the climate for the rich and middle class to be targeted.

The justice system's folly of over-reliance on punishment and the antiquated Department of Corrections' policies of abuse are the social pressures forcing this evolution into criminality. You can ignore the need for prison change at your own peril now, but rest assured that one day it will come knocking at your door. Then you'll share the pain of those of us behind these cruel walls.

This is why you should care.

* * *

(Anton has spent almost 24 years in prison for a crime he did not commit. His story appears later in this book.)

Forward Two
Joan Gauker

Joan Gauker, Coordinator of Volunteers at Graterford Prison, is the founder and editorial writer of Graterfriends. Created in the 1980s, Graterfriends is a monthly newspaper devoted to prisoners' issues and justice. Now published by the Pennsylvania Prison Society, it is circulated around the country.

Terrorism is not a new thing to those who live in American prisons. Yet it continues daily because we who are free on the outside stay outside those walls physically, emotionally, mentally and spiritually. Too "busy" with our lives, we rationalize not getting involved in meaningful ways until someone close to us gets caught up in the system. Though quick to move to stop atrocities anywhere else in the world, or to protest when an animal is abused, we are slow to even notice those same atrocities in our own prisons and jails. Fortunately, this book opens yet another door to the truth about the American prison system, and begs us to come inside and look around.

This will be hard. Reading this book makes us uncomfortable since we don't really believe our progressive society has such a degrading prison system. Many think our prisons are "country clubs." Yet those who DO know the system is degrading believe it should be that way. We in the United States assume that a prisoner becomes a person without a family or community, and that treatment for that "alien" is expensive and is "coddling." As if blind to the fact that most prisoners will return to their former communities, American prison officials (with our silent blessings) generally see it as their mission to inflict additional punishment above what the courts deemed adequate, often on a daily basis. Unmindful and uncaring that the real punishment for anyone is **being** in prison, many correctional officers, who are full of their power, become new judges and juries each day for their unwilling charges. Because of America's backwardness, Europeans come to our country constantly with the sole purpose of befriending our prisoners, our own people, whom we abandon. This fact, alone, should call us to a higher plane in our dealings with our fellow citizens.

In the midst of our inhumanity to prisoners, here and there imprisoned men and women rise above the mayhem and violence in which they are forced to live. They find a way to become serene. They take up reading, writing, painting, and music, and find themselves and a piece of a life. They become model prisoners. You'll meet several of them, some artists and poets, in this book. Yet the American prison system, whose mission is to punish, often cannot abide model prisoners. So they soon find a way to make it difficult for such positive prisoners to write, to paint, to read, and to make music. Then it becomes difficult to exist without being accused of some imagined infraction, which will finally put the model prisoner into solitary confinement in The Hole.

After being immersed in this book, one can no longer turn away from the truth that sensitive, intelligent, thoughtful, decent, perceptive and too many innocent people are rotting away in a system which could put their talents to use in so many enriching ways for the good of society. After reading the experiences, insights and observations in *Celling America's Soul*, shame and common sense should propel us to change our system into one that recognizes the redemptiveness of each offender; one that finds a way to probe the intellect and stir the heart of each of its charges; one that encourages forgiveness; and one that promotes restoration – so that offenders can return to society ready to enhance their families, themselves, their communities, and ultimately their nation.

Not just an exposé of the horrors of American prisons, the book also celebrates those prisoners who have managed to transcend their environment to become thoughtful artists and writers, dedicated to giving voice to the incarcerated.

In the second half of the book, *Transformation*, prisoners, activists, teachers, visionaries, and correctional staff describe what other countries are doing, and what we could do in this country if we had no political limitations and could think of true treatment and rehabilitation outside the cellblock.

* * *

"Blessed indeed are we who live among those who hate, hating no one; amidst those who hate, let us dwell without hatred."

"Hatreds never cease through hatred in this world; through love alone they cease. This is an eternal law."

Dhammapada, 197, 5

PART I
The View from Shadow America

Imagine

Imagine being fed hatred and being fed by hatred.
Imagine spending hours at a time contemplating revenge.
Imagine constantly being prodded, poked, and provoked
to the brink of uncontrollable anger,
but you continuously fight to contain that fury.

What you've just imagined is the life I live.

Imagine the only comfort and solace you have is you.
Imagine the only company and companion you have
is you.
Imagine the only person who loves you is you.
Imagine dying a second at a time for fifty years.
And every second you die, you know it and feel it.

What you've just imagined is the life I live.

Imagine not having any hopes or dreams.
Imagine not having any visions or a future.
Just staring, looking, watching, sometimes thinking,
but you stare at nothing, look at nothing, think of
nothing.
Imagine just being in here, existing.

What you've just imagined is me.

by Anton Forde/Trevor Mattis

Chapter One

The Creative Writing Class

The course started in July in a sweltering room with a feeble fan that was too noisy to use. The fifteen men, several of them Lifers, were mostly black and Hispanic and a couple of whites. After determining their skill levels and interests, I decided I could best serve them by expanding their minds and bringing a little bit of beauty and normalcy into their grim lives.

They spoke often of the horrible smells in prison where 3,300 men eat, smoke, ejaculate, sweat and shit in open toilets. One night in class, I asked them to sit in a circle with their eyes closed while I played meditative music (audiotapes are considered contraband, one of the many ways I got into trouble). I walked around the circle and placed a drop of essential rose oil on each of their left wrists, instructing them to breathe in the fragrance and then begin writing whatever came up for them.

Here are just a few of their five-minute responses:

"Freedom to inhale the scented vapor of life beyond this small room. So strong it will be with me the rest of the night and well into my dreams. Comforting and soothing, a pleasure that cannot be tainted or touched by the harsh surroundings of my personal hell, a place I prefer not to return to, but I must. Only now I'm a little stronger and revived, with the vapors of Freedom deep in my lungs, infecting every pore of my being."

"My mind went to the first time I made love to a woman after almost sixteen years in prison. I remember just wanting to smell her body from head to toe. I felt alive again. I felt my senses return. I was free and whole, most of all complete. Oh what a smell!"

"It's as if I was circled by rose bushes out in open space, relaxing without a care in the world."

"The color of light I've seen produced
from the mild fragrance of a rose,
perhaps less real or more imagined.
Blue, lime, deep green, yellow and purple.
The rainbow of my mind?
Or something more or less creative than a moment
of enhanced illusion?"

"Lush, soft, deep, bright, fresh, wild, free, sensual, energetic, enveloping, opening, motivating. Biting, expanding. Outdoors. Nose candy. Excitement. Anticipation. Unpeeled fruit."

They were all visibly brightened and excited at what the olfactory stimulation had opened up in them. When the guard came to escort me out, he sniffed the air suspiciously, and the students had a good laugh, a nanosecond of joy.

During one of the class assignments, which focused on finding beauty in such a place, Anton wrote the following piece, which was published in the Philadelphia Inquirer.

"Last spring, I participated in the horticultural program here at Graterford (now disbanded). I was given an assignment to plant a packet of seeds. I chose a packet that was supposed to be extremely hard to grow outside optimum conditions. The seeds were those of the genus *Calceolaria*. I took on the challenge and carefully nurtured the seeds to seedlings. I watched as the seedlings grew into small plants. These plants then bore some of the most beautiful flowers I've ever seen. The common name of the plant is pocketbook plant, because the delicate blossoms are shaped like a lady's pocketbook. There were soft pink, blue, yellow and red flowers, and they all sold the first day of our annual plant sale.

This experience taught me a valuable lesson that I think society should heed. Proper nurture and care are Nature's prerequisites for maximizing the potential of all life. It showed me what prison is all about. In here, I see a lot of seeds that grew up without proper nurture and care, and they survived, but now they are wild and hardy. These many young seedlings, mostly Black and Hispanic, are now being further exposed to much harsher conditions and environments. I wonder what type of plants they are going to develop into as we challenge Nature's laws within prisons. Not withstanding that, have you ever seen a cactus bloom?"

* * *

One week Muti came to class excited about having seen the first rainbow ever in his life the night before one of the many prisoner events, a Runathon, to raise funds for charity.

A Real Rainbow

It was late afternoon-early evening
and the sea of captured bodies filtered into the night
yard.
I shared the obligatory greetings of Freedom.
I was feeling a bit less stressed because of
earlier artistic triumph.
The sky was ink blue – or so it seemed,
the clouds unusually puffy and light,
giant versions of the cotton balls my sister used to
put between her toes until the nail polish dried.

I was tuning in to my inner vibes and the yard felt
different.
No specific activity sought – calisthenics and the like,
for I was readying for the Big Run in the morn.

While I was still milling about the overcast sky lit up.
My peripheral caught colors that were most assuredly
alien to this hell haven.
Tilting my head back and fixing my eyes on a special
piece of sky, I saw a REAL RAINBOW!

Not the type in magazines or television screens
nor in electronic games or in my childhood school
books
I'm talkin' a REAL RAINBOW.

Majestic purple, ravishing red, brilliant orange, birth-giving green, highlighting yellow and an unmistakable tinge of pink.
Ah pink! Up until now its high point was that it was one of my often-used colors on canvas in an oil painted creation.
Now this understated pale peekin' pigment warmed my chest and set my mind racin' on a menagerie of blissful scenes.

A REAL RAINBOW from nowhere took me everywhere I wanted to be.
It was as if the Goddess of Creativity plucked the colors
from one of my nocturnal paint storms and arched them across the sky.
It was long and illuminating, wider than an interstate...
Imagine hues being lanes.
The forty foot wall seemed very small as I embraced it all.

Today in a place where dulled senses see old time black and white and grey — the color explosion brought a dire burst
that fed my retinas' thirst.

Muti Ajamu-Osagboro
9/15/2000

When I asked Muti how the other prisoners in the yard had responded to the rainbow, he said, "I told them, Look up! Look at that! But they just mumbled Yeah, Yeah, their spirits weary, and kept their eyes down."

As the class progressed, we wrote and talked about everything that impacted on them, from violence, police profiling, gun control, fathers and fathering from prison, women, sexism and racism, politics, health and relationships. They wrote essays, short stories and screenplays.

One night, after talking about yet another study showing how many black youth are caught up in the system, I gave them the five-minute assignment to write about what their experiences were like with the police when they were growing up. I was stunned when I read their stories, for the ones who'd grown up in North Philly all wrote the same thing. As pre-teens, the police would stop and make them get into the police cars and then would drive them to an all-white neighborhood, and, laughing, make them get out and find their way home through dangerous gang territory. They soon learned to run when they saw a police car, and of course who do the cops stop when there's a crime? Whoever is running. . .

I suddenly realized they may have run right by my office at St. Luke's Hospital (now Guiffre Medical Center) in North Philly where I was hired back in the '70's to set up treatment programs for addicts and their families.

While I'd known for years of the racist practices of the police (I'd run training programs for them for two years about addictions and dealing with addicts in a non-violent way), reading their stories was the beginning of my deeper level of understanding of how the criminal justice system conspires, especially against black males.

One of the most beautiful classes was when I led them in a guided meditation to finding a "Safe Place" where they could feel free. Here are a few of their visions:

FINDING A SAFE PACE

I was going along with my meditation, left and right brain hemispheres filled with Earthlight, spouting a cascade of sparkles until Judith spoke about drifting beyond these walls to a place of serenity. At that moment, my spirit stumbled, but gradually I found a way to scale these walls in my mind. I was transported to a seashore in the Caribbean. It was night and I was under a coconut tree with my back resting on the curved tree trunk. I was looking at the sky's orchestra of galaxies. The wind, cool and salty, coming in fresh from the sea, cut a constant rhythm. The waves hummed gently as they caressed the seashore and crept up to lick between my toes.

* * *

A bright, blinding light reflects off a vast pool of brilliant blue. The sand is momentarily covered by a film of milky foam as the water begins to ebb. Knee high waves usher in the next flow of foam. The water seems to continue on forever as I stare from my seated position amongst the skillions of specs of sand. No people. No places to be seen, just the wonderful light and roaring sounds of crashing waves. Time has no place here and I can be everything the world has never allowed me to be. Flying!

* * *

Heaven on earth. A hidden place thought not to exist, where my senses are alive and light flows into me freely, healing the negativity that rains down constantly in this hellhole. The air is filled with the scent of roses, lavender and fragrant gardenias. There is celestial music and a feeling of universal love. I am safe.

* * *

I sit at my mother's kitchen table, just the two of us. We smile as our hearts overflow with the moment. This is something we've both longed for that always seems so far away and beyond the realms of possibility. Oh how long the road leading home has been. After traveling so far and experiencing so much, I embrace the comfort of this place. Here there is shelter, there is love, there is Mother. Snatched away from her and dragged off to a strange and hostile place, a place made of steel bars, concrete walls and evil guards. A place where there is no love, no family, no mother. Everything here is just as I left it. Twenty years have not touched the sacredness and sanctity of my home.

* * *

The rooftop of our building was three stories high and covered with tar. The third floor apartment was abandoned, so it was easy for me to climb out the once-boarded up windows onto the fire escape where I could make my way to the top. This was my private spot. I had a lawn chair in a corner along with some clothes and other things. At night I gazed upon a million stars. This is where I came to be alone in times of trouble. Sometimes I would look down upon civilization and dream of a bright future filled with all the good things of life.

* * *

Sanctuary for me is in the midst of a tropical rain forest just after the monsoon rains have washed over every square inch of this lush, green haven. It is so clean and alive. Soft, natural sounds of life sing pleasantly in my ears. Flashes of brilliant colors streak across the sunny sky as tropical birds. Enjoying their gift of flight, they spread their wings to catch the cool breeze of the wind, living ships that sail gracefully in our haven. In this place, I am happy, safe and at peace in my own Garden of Eden in my mind.

* * *

FINDING BEAUTY
(from another class exercise)

The beast is a huge monster with dimensions that cover 67 acres of land. It is a Leviathan of mega tons. The guts are concrete and steel that if used for a bridge could supply all the material to build another Golden Gate Bridge. Encased within the vast maze are tiny honeycomb caves filled with bee-like creatures that race and scurry about daily. At the extreme end of this beast, I found myself caught in a wonder of nature that shook my senses. I was inside the chapel behind locked doors. A small window was my only view to freedom. The first thing I noticed was snow falling, touching everything and everybody. There were guys in a dog kennel environment attempting to exercise their bodies after long hours of hold time. The snow does not discriminate as man does. As I watched, I saw a side of life that few noticed. I saw two odd shapes moving across the grounds, Canadian geese, just walking like an old, married couple on a morning stroll. My mind was boggled and it reeled at the sight of these beautiful, graceful birds, free to be a thousand miles away. Yet here, today, we are in the same place, a prison. Beauty knows no boundaries or limits. A simple thought and truth stands out for me. It is all a matter of perspective.

NO PRISON CAN HOLD MY MIND!

* * *

As they began to share their stories, the idea for this book was born.

Chapter Two

Innocent but Proven Guilty
Anton Forde/Trevor Mattis
($545,000)

Anton Forde/Trevor Mattis was born in Jamaica and raised in a single-parent household in the poverty-stricken area of Kingston. At seventeen he attended York College in New York on scholarship, graduating cum laude. In June 1987, he went to Philadelphia to seek enrollment into Temple University's School of Dentistry. Months later, Anton witnessed a murder for which he was wrongly accused and for which, despite testimony pointing to another, he was sentenced to life in prison. In 2013, a witness was found in Jamaica who witnessed the crime and wants to testify as to Anton's innocence. All that has to happen is for the court to allow him to present his case, which they may not do.

He was tried, convicted and sentenced on the word of just one man, who later recanted. As Barry Scheck, Peter Neufeld and Jim Dwyer write in Actual Innocence, "Eyewitness error remains the single most important cause of wrongful imprisonment."

When first imprisoned, Anton was severely beaten by guards and required surgery and hospitalization for injuries that are permanent.

In 2001 a Federal Magistrate ordered his release or a new trial. The prosecution appealed on procedural grounds, and the order was reversed. In March 2004, his final appeal to the Supreme Court was not accepted. The only way he'll get into court again is if he can present the new evidence, which he now has.

Tall, athletic, elegant and well-spoken, in the creative writing class Anton always had something intelligent and perceptive to say. When he spontaneously started putting together lists of aphorisms that reflected his impressions of prison life, I told him he should write a book. A year later, *Contemplations of a Convict: Aphorisms for the Heart and Mind* was published. In 2004, he published *Contemplations of a Convict: A Journey To Freedom When Innocence Isn't Enuf* through SageWriters.

Ford/Mattis has since published two novels to literary acclaim: *Yardies* and *Yardies II*.

BEING AN INNOCENT MAN IN PRISON
(A Personal Account)

This is a very emotional topic for me. I have never seriously considered my status because so much pain is attached to it. For that reason, I've have never faced it squarely, I just live with it. Since it might be of some assistance to you in understanding my perspective, I will try my best to finally confront my existence so you may see what I feel.

A little background is in order. I've been incarcerated for twenty-four years and this was essentially my first contact with the justice system. I was wanted for a homicide for a year before I was arrested. I first became aware that I was wanted a few days after the shooting occurred, which I had tried to prevent. A friend informed me after a SWAT team broke down the door of her house looking for me. They left her a fugitive warrant and told her I was wanted for questioning. In the streets, this is a cue, which really means, "We want to lock you up." I thought of turning myself in for questioning, but the reality was then and is now, for a black youth, "If you turn yourself into the police you will be arrested." This was and is my perception of law enforcement authorities. The urban black youth distrusts the police and if you are an urban black male in the underworld, you really distrust the police. I was an urban black youth connected to the underworld, and also a Jamaican immigrant.

I was arrested while having a conversation with three girls on the steps of their house. It was a dramatic arrest with police and detectives surrounding the block and storming the steps. I surrendered without incident. For good measure, the arresting officers planted a bag containing crack cocaine on my person. I was charged with homicide and sent to the county jail awaiting trial. (The only identification I had on me at the time was a fake video rental card with the name Trevor Mattis, so to the criminal justice system, that's my name, not Anton Forde. That's why I write with two names.)

At first I was rather relieved for I knew sooner or later I had to face this obstacle in my life. I was glad to finally get it over with. I was never worried about the outcome since I was innocent. Then I was naïve. I whole-heartedly believed in America justice reigns supreme, so the fact that I was innocent was all I needed. My greatest concern was to survive my immediate violent conditions. I had a strong faith in virtually everything. I had faith in the religious teachings I grew up with. I read my Bible and prayed daily. I had faith in my attorney; he was paid to represent me. I had faith in the system and the society that surely no man could be convicted of a crime he did not commit. Such was my naiveté.

My first months in jail were like living in a very violent day camp for boys. I never allowed the violence surrounding me to deter me from seeking knowledge and improving my mind. The environment pushed me in search of knowledge. This was going to be a temporary stay, I thought. I knew it would take nine months to a year to get to trial and I was certain to be exonerated then.

I was eager to assist my attorney in any way possible. I began a crash course on learning the law, and spent many hours teaching myself in the law library. I asked my attorney to send me a copy of the discovery and he did. I reviewed it carefully, especially the ballistics evidence. I was convinced that this was going to be a very simple case. The ballistics evidence established beyond any doubt only one weapon was used in the shooting. The State's sole witness, the brother of the deceased, concocted a story at the preliminary hearing that he witnessed me and another individual ambush his brother on his left and on his right with guns drawn and fired repeatedly at close range. I knew he (the brother of the deceased) implicated me out of vindictiveness. I wondered to myself how ignorant he must be to think his malicious fabrication could fool the highly esteemed and intelligent judges of the courts.

Aside from the constant violence, I found time to reflect upon my life and introspect. I never wallowed in self-pity, though I did entertain an occasional "why me." Rather, I understood the maliciousness of my accuser. I knew him and his vile nature and was familiar with the Jamaican ghetto mentality with its emphasis on vindictiveness.

The first life-long lesson I learned was that I would never come back to jail after this nightmare was over. Never. This direct introduction into a world of such hatred left me wondering about life and humanity itself. I relied on my Christian faith and began to seek the positives in my (imagined) temporary sojourn. As I studied myself, I began to also study the men, the system, and the environment around me. I also thought it my duty and obligation to help as many of the people around me, who needed fundamental literary assistance, as I could. I used my novice understanding of the law to help my fellow countrymen obtain their freedom. I placed an optimistic spin on my pre-trail months of incarceration. I viewed it as getting rejuvenating rest while vigorously exercising to whip my body into the shape I had always wanted, but lacked both motivation and dedication. Psalm 27 became my mantra: "When the wicked even mine enemies and my foes, came upon me to eat up my flesh, they stumbled and fell." My enemies tried to destroy me by sending me to jail, but I was going to turn the situation into an opportunity to develop my mind, body and soul. This is exactly what I did.

A few weeks before my trial, a friend of mine was convicted of a third degree homicide. We had the same attorney and after he was convicted he cautioned me not to go with a judge-only trial. His conviction alarmed me a bit, but I failed to recognize the portent. I rationalized his case was vastly different from mine. I was innocent and his was self-defense. However, I did express my desire for a jury trial to my attorney. The mention of a jury trial angered him. He pointed out that I did not pay him jury trial money, and that a jury trial would cost me $10,000 more. He stormed out of our meeting. On the day of my trial, my attorney saw me in the courthouse 30 minutes before the trial commenced. He lambasted me about wanting a jury trial and about listening to stupid jailhouse lawyers. He told me how much the people of Philadelphia hated Jamaicans and that he'd made a backdoor deal with the prosecutor not to seek the death penalty if I took a non-jury trial. He stated emphatically that if I took a jury trial I was guaranteed to fry in the electric chair. Then he left. I was shocked at his remarks, but was not given an opportunity to respond. The more I read during my legal research, I discovered that though I had capital offense charges, my case wouldn't qualify for the death penalty. Moments later, I was brought into the courtroom. There my mother approached me with tears in her eyes, pleading with me to follow my attorney's advice, for she feared the death penalty. The sight of my mother so distraught pained my soul. I realized then that my attorney was trying to intimidate me by exploiting her fears and mine. Unwillingly, I relented. I rationalized it was an open and shut case anyway, and there was no need to delay the proceedings. I was in jail nine months already, and I was eager to get out and move on with my life after college.

Right before the trial began, the District Attorney announced that a new eyewitness had just walked into the courtroom. Everyone was surprised. This new witness was brought in from Florida. After a sidebar and some legal wrangling, the trial commenced. The new witness was called first, and to my utter amazement, in a clear, calm and methodical manner, he told the judge he had witnessed me assault and then shoot the deceased repeatedly. As the words flowed out of his mouth, my world stopped turning. I was simply speechless and shocked. A volcanic rage erupted inside me. My head began to throb. My ears were stopped so up I could no longer hear. A whirlwind of emotions disrupted the logical congruency of my brain. I found it impossible to make sense of what was taking place. What I heard had no connection to what I was seeing, no connection to what I saw, and no connection to what happened. When I regained my senses, all I could do was wonder how could he blatantly lie like that. For a second, I thought it was a prank, some wicked joke. What was happening could not possibly be real, but it was. Now I was angry; all I could do was think of taking the stand to testify in my defense against these nefarious fabrications. Up to this point, no legal strategy was ever discussed between my attorney and me. I knew not what to expect nor had any type of preparation. I can't recall my attorney ever asking me what happened on that night. All I'd done was send my attorney what I thought was relevant information from the ballistic and autopsy reports. I'd just left everything in his hands. Immediately, I told him I wanted to take the stand. He ignored me and the trial continued. Next the State's original witness (the deceased's brother) took the stand. To my horror, his testimony changed radically to match the testimony of the unknown twelfth hour witness. His original testimony that two people shot his brother was now changed to my assaulting and then shooting his brother. The incontrovertible ballistic evidence, which I was certain would exonerate me, was now circumvented. I could not put the pieces together; all I wanted to do was get on the stand. The State rested and my attorney advised me not to take the stand. I was incensed. Are you insane? Do you expect me to just sit quietly by and let these people tell all these lies about me? My attorney was not happy; he went to my mother and petitioned her to tell me not to take the stand. I was adamant that I was going to take the stand. When the trial resumed, to my surprise, my attorney addressed the judge. He stated on the record that he was "360 degrees diametrically opposed to my taking the stand to testify on my own behalf." I've never forgotten those words and to this day I don't know what he meant by saying that or why he said it. I took the stand and was convicted of first-degree murder in less than five minutes. I was then sentenced to life imprisonment without the possibility of parole.

The words "I find you guilty" reverberated in my mind for years. The State's two witnesses contradicted themselves in every detail. At one point, each said that the other was not present to see the shooting. One said I had a big, black Tec-9 machine gun; the other said I had a small, chrome 9mm handgun. Yet the verdict was guilty. That moment irrevocably altered me. I went into some type of stupor, in a cocoon of self-denial. There is no way the justice system can convict an innocent person. Society would rather let 100 guilty persons go free than convict an innocent man. That's what I intuitively believed up to that moment. Physically I was here, but mentally a part of me was not. A part of me refused to think for one moment this conviction could stand. I became filled with anger, hatred and distrust.

Once, when I was trying to make a legal phone call, I was beaten so badly by guards that doctors had to reconstruct my face, my vision in one eye is impaired and my arm hurts constantly.

An internal battle raged inside me continuously. My psychological cohesiveness shattered into many aspects of me of unequal size, each a separate and distinct personality contained within one mind. There was the survival me. This part of me was unemotional and rigidly practical. Its only concern was survival at all costs. It functioned on a minute-by-minute basis. To make it to the next day unharmed was my sole goal. Then there was the angry me, once the dormant part of me. Now I was angry at the justice system, the judge, the prosecutor, the lying witnesses and my attorney. This me was like the sun in my internal universe. It shone brilliantly, consuming and driving my other parts.

I was sent upstate to the penitentiary. After three years of facing constant repression in this brutal system, the core of my anger transformed into hatred. Hate was my core and anger my mantle. There was the small part of me that said improve your mind. So I sought knowledge voraciously and there was an ocean of knowledge around me. Most of the knowledge I was gaining became more fuel to my hatred.

It is important for you to understand this hatred. It's the most dangerous and destructive force known to humankind. It feeds on itself, its environment, anything; constantly forming and churning wickedness. It is like a black hole of violence. If left on its own, there's no limit to it. It infects virtually everything and anything around it. It can grow indefinitely and last eternally. I know firsthand what fuels a racist, a terrorist, a Hitler. I could've been any one of them and was all of them. I hated my oppressors. I hated the convicts around me. I hated my environment. I hated the food. I hated the judge, the prosecutor, the police, and the lying witnesses. I wished them harm. I wanted them dead, destroyed, annihilated.

I began to harbor a particular hatred of the original State witness, the brother of the deceased. He deliberately lied. He knew me. He knew I tried to be a peacemaker. He saw me intercede between his brother and the shooter, pleading with his brother, the aggressor in the incident, to calm down. He saw me convince the shooter to peacefully withdraw from the vicinity. After the parties were separated, he knew his headstrong brother was bent on continuing the confrontation outside the residence. He himself tried to physically deter him and failed. This all came out in his various testimonies. He knew he did not witness the shooting, but just lied to implicate me. What never came out at the trial was that after he failed to stop his belligerent brother from rushing out of the house, he ran down to the basement to retrieve a friend in an attempt to have them all leave the premises. As he came back up the basement steps and entered the kitchen at the back of the house, he heard several shots fired outside the front of the residence. In a panic, he and two other people in the house ran back to the basement. He never witnessed the shooting. I knew he fabricated his testimony all along and was able to live with that after I recognized that the scientific ballistics evidence would clearly and convincingly expose his fabrications. I could not foresee the State's skullduggery and I never anticipated his changing from one lie to another at the last minute. (His original story was given to the police minutes after the shooting took place and repeated under oath a year later at the preliminary hearing. It changed at the trial.) One, I never thought it possible; and two, I did not believe duplicity was entertained in the mighty halls of American justice.

Thousands of times I've relived every second of my actions on that fatal night. It remains as fresh in my mind today as the day it happened. Over and over again, I have searched for what else I could have done given the circumstances. First and foremost, the confrontation was spontaneous and not foreseen. (The State came up with a sensational drug turf warfare theory. It was an easy fit into the stereotype of the day about Jamaicans, and the individuals and location concerned. However, it was very far from the truth. The brother of the deceased and I repeatedly denied the State's theory. The only corroboration they had came from their mysterious twelfth hour witness.) Unprovoked, the deceased insulted and then threatened the shooter. (I followed every rational step I could summon to avoid the confrontation between the deceased and the shooter from escalating.) I immediately stepped in between the two parties, risking my life and well-being. All I had to rely on was my judgment. I knew both parties; they didn't know each other.

Though I was completely caught off guard by the deceased's remarks, I did not know him to be violent, but I knew he was temperamental. I did not know the shooter enough to determine how he would react. Though I knew he must've been angry, I didn't believe he would harm me.

I pleaded with the deceased to calm down since there was no need for hostility. The situation was now an ego thing and instinctively I knew I must try and get separation of the parties quickly to defuse the situation. I managed to convince the shooter to withdraw from the immediate vicinity. A deadly "stare down" was in progress, and grudgingly he relented when I suggested going to retrieve the owner of the house who was down the street. This allowed the shooter to withdraw without losing too much face. That this suggestion was accepted was a miracle in and of itself and a great relief. I had accomplished the best any sane person could in those circumstances.

Moments later, all my efforts went for naught as the belligerent deceased left from inside the house to go outside and renew the confrontation. This time I was yards away. I could only look on in shock and horror, as he was shot to death. What was I supposed to do? What on earth could I have done to stop the fateful events at that point? Why am I paying the price of a lifetime of imprisonment?

As for the twelfth hour witness, no words can express my hate towards him. I did not even recognize this individual when I saw him in court. His cruel, calculated coolness on the stand caused me horrific nightmares for years. I would have preferred that both these witnesses put twelve-gauge shotguns in my mouth and blew my brains out rather than lie on me like that. I wanted to strap a bomb on and just blow up the courthouse and everyone in it. I was consumed by my hatred and it was consuming me. The more knowledge I gained, the more my eyes were opened to the evils of the justice system, the evils of this society and the evils of this country. I don't know how it works, but for some reason, in prison most of the information a convict gains is information exposing the evils of western society.

I gained the true knowledge of the history of my people, slavery, Jim Crow, Cointel-Pro, etc. I gained knowledge of the capitalistic exploitations of Third World countries worldwide. I gained knowledge of world history, politics and religion. Everything was filtered through the lens of evil and further fed my hatred. I began hating this society. I lost my faith in religion. I lost my trust in people, family and friends. Virtually nothing was left uncontaminated by this hate. I painted it on with a broad brush in thick coats. I recall these memories with the utmost shame. It's an ignominy I will bear the rest of my life. Of all the things this horrible experience did to me, this is what hurts me the most, the fact it created the conditions that allowed me to plunge to such depths of utter wretchedness. There is something eternally damning once one falls this deep into the abyss of evil. Here one shakes the hands of the Devil. This part of me grew unabated for approximately ten years.

There was also the freedom part of me whose only focus was on obtaining my freedom. For many years, this part of me was unbending in the belief I would be exonerated. It caused me to view myself as not a true prisoner. It made me function as if I was only temporarily suspended in this inhumane environment, with freedom and relief coming with the next appeal. The slow, grinding process of the appellate process kept this part of me alive. This had a mitigating effect on the other parts of me by constantly emphasizing that I'm only a visitor to the penitentiary, and the truth of my innocence will be acknowledged in the next round of appeals.

A small part of me, the essence of me, continued on its path of spiritual development, untarnished and unscathed by the other selves. It knew Love is God. This part of me still amazes me to this day. It's the eternal part of me, like a small star many galaxies away, shining a twinkling point of light in the blackened heavens of my hate. All my life I've been aware of that point of light. It has always been there, unchanging. A pinpoint of serenity and peace, a pinpoint of love and bliss. Regardless of the chaos, confusion, hurt, and hate that raged around me, and in me, it always shone through, a silent, steady shine.

Between the tenth and twelfth years, my inner core of hate cooled and its surrounding anger dissipated. I cannot really explain what happened, how it happened, or exactly when it happened. I don't know if the transformation came about due to my voracious accumulation of knowledge, my constant introspection, my close study of life and my environment, my becoming a writer, or if it burnt itself out. I know not the cause but I live the effect.

The get out of jail, the freedom part of me, had grown strong. A new attorney pointed out one strong issue of merit on which we decided to ride straight to the gates of freedom. Though it was brushed aside in a convoluted specious argument by the State courts, I was now entering the Federal level of appeals. The only legitimate argument the State could find to deny me justice was a technical violation, a procedural default deliberately caused by my inept paid attorney during my first level of appeals. What this attorney did was abandon me in the appeals process by failing to file an appeal after I told him to do so. He did not notify me that he was not going to file the appeal as required by ethical standards, although he gave my mother the impression that he was filing the appeal. He stopped answering my letters and refused all calls. According to the court rules, I had 30 days in which to file this appeal, and because it was not filed within that time frame, my case was procedurally defaulted.

Using this technicality, the State courts dismissed my claim. (The claim was based on evidence I discovered subsequent to the trial that the State's twelfth hour witness, a Federal informant, had told the Federal authorities three weeks before my trial that I did not commit the crime but was only an innocent bystander who witnessed the homicide. This information was known to the State Prosecutor before my trial. However, the evidence was never turned over to the defense.)

The essence of me, that far-away star, gradually began to dominate the heavens of my being. It outshone everything else, and my vision became ever more lucid. Suddenly, I stopped seeing the surface of things and began to see through things. Wherever I turned my attention, I pierced through to its fundamental essence. I turned my attention to my all-consuming hate and anger, and what I saw was, if not forgiveness, at least understanding. I understood justice in America for a poor black man is a game, a charade. I realized that in the courtrooms, justice is not a goal. It's not sought and never was. It's a contest of influence and persuasion and has nothing to do with justice or truth.

I looked at the brother of the deceased and could understand he was hurt and just wanted to get back at somebody for the death of his brother. He did not know the shooter, but he knew me well, and I was an associate of the shooter. His was an understandable human reaction forged by the emotions of hurt, anger, hate and revenge. His last-minute change in testimony at trial, I'm certain, was due to coercion by the District Attorney.

I looked at the twelfth hour witness. He was just a crafty individual under the guidance of the District Attorney who took advantage of an opportunity to save his own skin in a pending Federal indictment. The State used him and he used the State in a mutual exchange of wickedness.

I looked at the prosecutor. He was just being an American, doing the devil's deeds while speaking God's words. He will go on to be governor, judge, senator or president one day.

I looked at the deceased and it was just a tragedy, a senseless loss of life for nothing, just senseless. I would like to meet his mother to tell her with my own mouth that I did not kill her son and that I tried my best to prevent the incident. Though she does not know me and I do not know her, if she's alive, I'd like her to know the truth and share in her grief.

I looked at the world and saw that humankind is full of good people. I saw that a small number of these people do bad things and some evil things, but that's not an indictment of humankind. Good deeds far outnumber and outweigh bad deeds. I saw that most bad deeds are either due to a lack of knowledge, a lack of understanding, or a limited perspective. I saw that these trying times of conflict, confusion, fear, and death are just a transition phase. Humanity is on a slow, inevitable march toward peace, love and harmony; and at the end of each tumultuous transition phase, the world is one step closer to that destined goal.

As for me, I was a fool to believe in anything. I was just a fool and maybe still am. Thirteen years after my conviction, I read the transcripts of my testimony. I could see where I was not clear in the expression of my thoughts. I was overly emotional and in such a rush to blurt my story out that I can see where it diminished the effectiveness of my communication. I kept reverting to my thick Jamaican accent in my excitement to speak and clear my name. I was repeatedly told to slow down, for speaking in my Jamaican dialect at a normal pace made me unintelligible to the unexposed ear, especially to the ears of my judge and jury.

When I looked at the overall presentation of my defense, it was grossly inadequate. I had a paid attorney who made no use of the ballistic evidence and autopsy reports to challenge the State's witnesses' versions of events. A preliminary review of this scientific evidence clearly shows the physical impossibility of their testimonies.

My life is just a distant shadow of who I was meant to be, a mere shadow. I cannot say if I've completely forgiven everyone, but I work towards that goal. I still retain an afterglow of the anger/hate in me, but I hold no rancor towards anyone. I understand life is just a big river, constantly flowing. However you ride down that river makes no difference to Life. It may make a difference to you personally, but life keeps on flowing.

In September 2001, a Federal Magistrate ordered my release or a new trial. He bypassed the technical barrier of a procedural default and reviewed the new-found evidence. Freedom at last! Months later, the State, not liking to be told by the feds what to do, appealed his decision. The order to grant me relief or a new trial was reversed as the Federal courts held that the procedural default barred any court from reviewing the newfound evidence, which proved my innocence. In March 2004, my final appeal to the United States Supreme Court was not accepted. The freedom part of me shrank considerably. For the first time, I viewed prison as the place of my residence.

Now I am no longer a visitor. The only star left in the heavens of my inner being is the once-distant essence of me, my true self. Now it dominates my universe, it dominates me, it is me.

It is love.

I am love.

Postscript

Contemplations of a Convict
A Review by Joan Gauker

The American criminal justice system, in its use of primitive crime prevention tactics, works to destroy the well-being of its charges, to take away their sensitivities and their ability to think for themselves.

However, Anton Forde/Trevor Mattis, the author of this book, denied the system his heart and mind. Instead, he gave his feelings and intellect to his writings by disciplining himself to journal his thoughts before they passed from his mind. The habit became a lifeline for this young black man serving a life sentence for a crime he didn't commit. During more than a decade, Forde/Mattis refined his journaling as he improved his skills at recording what he contemplated, saw, heard, felt and learned.

Even though he is confined in a 6' x 9' cell in a stark, ugly, noisy, large, cinderblock and cement building, he escapes the mundane with his ponderings, which he skillfully crafts into profound understandings for all of society. While he gives us a window into his mind, he also opens windows in our own minds, and gives us new insights into life around us wherever we are. In the best of environments, few can contemplate life as well as Forde/Mattis has observed it in his book. So it is especially compelling when one experiences such profound, insightful writings emanating from a prison's depraved environment.

Contemplations of a Convict is a clear statement from one of the millions of people in America's unredemptive and degrading punishment system that, while the body can be imprisoned, the mind and heart remain free. Forde/Mattis shows us that in his wide range of aphorisms for all people; aphorisms which are sad, happy, angry, sensitive and compassionate, but most of all thoughtful.

Anton Forde/Trevor Mattis

Contemplations of a Convict: Aphorisms for the Heart and Mind:
A Journey to Freedom When Innocence isn't Enuf

"The incredible state of mental breakdown in the nation's prisons is a testament to our efforts to kill not only the bodies but the spirits of our unwanted populations…Even if prison building created no Keynesian stimulus, and there were no private prisons to profit from locking up the poor, and if prison labor were abolished…American capitalism would still have to manage and contain its surplus populations and poorest classes with paramilitary forms of segregation, containment and repression. At the heart of the matter lies this contradiction: capitalism needs the poor and creates poverty, intentionally through policy and organically through crisis. Yet capitalism is directly and indirectly threatened by the poor…Prison and criminal justice are about managing these irreconcilable contradictions."

Christian Parenti
Lockdown America: Police and Prisons in the
Age of Crisis, Verso '99

"When the prison gates slam behind an inmate, he does not lose his human quality; his mind does not become closed to new ideas, his intellect does not cease to feed on a free and open interchange of opinion." Thurgood Marshall

Chapter Three

Preferential Treatment?
Danny Haggard
($860,000)

Danny Haggard's life has been filled with poverty, abandonment, sexual abuse and addiction. Son of a deaf-mute mother who was "forced" by his heroin-addicted father, Danny and his sister are the only ones in their family who are not hearing-impaired. Encouraged by a step-sibling, he began stealing at age six. In addition to getting him money or things he wanted, he soon realized the stealing gave him a "rush." By his teens, he'd discovered drugs and his stealing took on a new urgency to support his habit.

Danny is a handsome man with blond hair and blue eyes, an all-American looking guy. He's a repeat, multiple offender who's spent most of his life in institutions and in trouble with the law. He's stolen and vandalized thousands of dollars worth of property. He has thirteen felony convictions for burglary, one federal conviction and three other felony convictions in other states. At the time of the writing class he was serving an amazingly short sentence of three years. He believes he receives preferential treatment by the criminal justice system because he's white. He has never gone to trial because he's always been caught red-handed.

He's been in many treatment programs, not unusual for addicts, and fears that he may have become "treatment resistant."

Though they write, he hasn't seen his sister for over ten years, and like most prisoners, rarely has visitors. His mother died of cancer three years ago. "I burned my bridges a while ago with my repeated trips to prison and my abuse of drugs. I must deal with the consequences of my actions. In some ways, though visits are pleasant, they can be stressful. I understand the effects my life experiences have had on my psyche, but I don't make excuses for the decisions I've made or who I am, nor will I deny my feelings and desires."

Can he change? Will he continue to be a menace to society?

In the writing class he was excited to discover that he has a vivid imagination and a knack for story telling. He knows he has to straighten up and get his life in order even though he hasn't had much success living on the outside. He hasn't seen his son and daughter in two years, and he wants to improve himself enough to become the father he never had. He's waiting for a place in Graterford's Parenting Program, hoping he can learn to be a good father.

He found the experience of writing his story cathartic.

DANNY

It's been said that time is our most precious commodity, but in prison, it's man's worst enemy. Either you're thinking of sex and the good times of the past, or the future, but never the present. Fortunately I have a future, which is more than can be said for the many thousands in this prison. I know several dozen Lifers, and there isn't a day that goes by that I'm not grateful for the breaks I've been given. The truth is I should be doing more time than three years because I'm a multiple repeat offender, and I wonder if the short sentence has anything to do with the color of my skin. The man in the next cell is in for five years for stealing a case of beer, his first offense. Guess what color his skin is?

There is no doubt in my mind whatsoever that if I was put in front of a sentencing judge today and if my skin was anything but white I'd be spending at least twenty years rotting away in this snakepit. Of course if you are a man of means, your chances for "justice" are dramatically increased in your favor.

It's never completely quiet in prison. It's noisiest during the day, but at night there's always the sound of toilets flushing, pipes creaking, or someone crying out with a nightmare. Even in the early morning hours you can hear the radio, which the guards turn up full blast every night, I'm sure to annoy us. After the final lockdown at night is when I find myself, through reading or writing.

I have a son and daughter who don't really know me. I've been in and out of their lives so many times that I fear I have caused harm. I've decided that I have to prove I can be responsible for myself before I ask to be let into their lives again. I've had no contact for two years because of their mother. I cannot blame her for this even though I feel bitter and sad inside. By the time of my release I'll be 35 years old. I'm long past due for being a responsible person. I have skills that I intend to utilize but my top priority will be completing my parole incident-free, which for me means staying drug free – something that has eluded me to this point.

I was born in 1965 in Milwaukee to a deaf-mute who was a printer by trade. It wasn't easy for her to find work because of her handicap. My older sister, Amy, and I quickly developed sign-language skills so we could communicate with my mother and other family members. Why my sister and I aren't deaf is a small miracle because the majority of the family is, including aunts, uncles and cousins. Amy and I had to be good spellers in order to sign, which I believe gave my education a jump start. Feelings were not expressed, and this probably played a negative role in my emotional development.

By time I was five we were living in an apartment on the South Side of Chicago. Our grandmother lived nearby and we stayed there while my mother worked. In the back of her apartment building was a great maze of wooden steps where we'd play for hours. I still get a warm feeling deep in the pit of my stomach when I recall those stairs.

One of the biggest regrets of my life is never knowing my father. I can't begin to explain the bitterness inside from not having the presence of someone I could look up to in my life. I can't tell you how my father walked and talked, how he smelled, whether he was tall and skinny or short and broad. With the exception of a faded black and white photo of him sitting at a kitchen table, I can barely tell you the shape of his eyes or face. I've had to rely on my mother's version of who he was, and she's been dead now for over three years. Her memories weren't pretty. The few times she'd talk about him she said he was a heroin addict and a no-good drunk who forced himself on her and I was conceived as a result. When I was sixteen and we were living in east Texas, we were contacted by his family in St. Louis and told of his death. There was no money to attend his funeral.

Since early childhood, I've been in trouble with the law. I'm sure if you lined up ten psychologists and asked them what was wrong with me, you'd get ten different answers ranging from I'm a product of my environment to I'm a borderline personality disorder.

What a bunch of crap. I wasn't that different from many other kids. The bottom line is I've always enjoyed living on the edge, and I'm a creature of my desires. I rarely worry about consequences, and despite my many arrests, I've gotten away with a lot of crimes. Fortunately I've only ever harmed myself, though I've come close to doing something that would keep me here forever.

For a short time in my life, when I was about five, I did have a stepfather. Jim was a deaf-mute like my mother. They met through a deaf bowling league. Jim was tall and lanky with a beer belly like a bowling ball. He had two kids of his own, Ronnie, who was a few years older than me; and Jenny, who was a year younger. It was Ronnie who was my mentor in creating my life of crime. Jim worked as a foreman for the *Chicago Tribune*, and for the two short years my mother was married to him, Jim provided us with a comfortable, middle-class lifestyle in the suburbs.

Gary, another deaf-mute, lived in the basement. Deaf-mutes have their own communities just like any other ethnic group. Most deaf-mute households keep boarders who are also deaf-mutes but suffer from additional handicaps like retardation, partial paralysis etc. These boarders perform household duties and provide additional income from social security or menial jobs in the work force.

Gary was slightly retarded and crippled in both hands, which meant he couldn't sign. All the kids loved good-natured Gary, but Jim kept him as a boarder for another reason. Gary was a true hustler and used his handicap to great advantage. Weekday mornings on his way to work, Jim would drop Gary at a designated spot where he panhandled sign-language cards. Even if you didn't know Gary you could tell he was afflicted. Gary made between $200-300 a day, which in the seventies wasn't chump change. Jim got it all, and his bedroom was stacked with hundreds of dollars in rolls of coins.

When Ronnie suggested we steal from Jim, his own father, I'm not sure why I agreed. Jim wasn't a bad man and he'd bought me a ten-speed bike for my sixth birthday. Once I started, I didn't quit. Even at that innocent age, I got a rush from stealing. Jim became suspicious and changed the locks on his door, but nothing stopped us. We always had more money than any of the other kids in the neighborhood.

Each Sunday we were required to go to church, and we'd put in an appearance in our Sunday best and then head for the record store across the street from the church where there were pinball machines and other interesting paraphernalia. We'd spend the time playing games and listening to records. With the exception of Sunday services later during my time at Boy's Harbor, this was the extent of my religious career. I don't believe in a lot of things, but I do believe in man's capacity for evil, and to a lesser degree, good.

By the time I was eight or nine, I couldn't be trusted around anything. My own mother didn't trust me. We moved a lot and were on welfare much of the time. When I was ten, my mother packed us up again, this time for Cedar Bayou, Texas. She had relatives there who would let us live in a trailer they owned. I thought of it as an adventure, though Cedar Bayou and Chicago's South Side were light years apart. Now I was in the land of steers, where football is king and chewing tobacco the nectar of the gods.

My stealing continued until one night I crossed the line and stole my mother's car. When I got into an accident and fled, I denied everything, but people in the other car identified me as the small boy running away. At her wit's end, my mother was convinced that I should be placed in a boys' home. I felt totally rejected by her.

Boys Harbor was by the Bay of Galveston. There were about sixty kids in four cottages according to age. Each cottage had a married couple who were supposed to be substitute parents. Everyone there was either abandoned, a discipline problem or ordered by the courts. For some reason, the two years I was there I kept my stealing to a minimum and I did well in my classes. I was encouraged to do well and for a time I felt accepted. After two years, when I was twelve, I started to rebel and finally my mother was told to come and get me.

Gary was my mother's latest boyfriend. He looked like Grizzly Adams and drove an old Ford Galaxy 500. He could hear and speak, which was unusual for my mother, as in the past she only associated with deaf-mutes. I felt unwelcome. Mom's eyes were full of love for me, but she worried about my future.

Soon I was back to my old tricks and there were nights when I didn't come home at all to sleep on the couch. I had discovered drugs. Cruising the streets, I often ran across other kids like myself. Mom and Gary knew I was high; I didn't even try to hide it. Gary finally told my mother I had to go as I was also stealing from him to buy the drugs. Mom asked my sister if I could stay with her in Baytown, about 45 minutes from Houston. For all the pain and suffering I put my sister through over the years, she never has turned her back on me to this day.

Amy was staying with an older man named Lawrence and his mother. They were poor. They lived in a 28 ft. trailer that was on its last legs, with two tiny bedrooms. My place again was the couch. Though they were barely scraping by, the fact that they took me in had a powerful influence on my life. Lawrence's main source of money was selling weed and hash. He treated me with kindness and always took me along with him no matter where he went, becoming a role model in my eyes. From Lawrence I learned how to deal drugs, how to shoot a gun, and what to watch out for in people who might be cops. We were always high.

I stayed with them for about nine months until I was caught creeping into a lady's house to steal her purse. That earned me a year in juvenile hall, where I soon learned to fight or be walked on. No matter where you are placed in the system, the juvenile detention centers are the worst, because the young and dumb just don't understand the consequences of their actions; and this makes them dangerous. Most of the kids were Mexicans and blacks, and being white was a strike against me, making me an easy target. I always had to prove myself no matter where I went because of my skin color and the automatic assumption that I was a chump.

Two months before my release, my sister came to visit and told me that Lawrence's mother had found him dead in the field behind the trailer. I felt confused. The dreams I had of us being together were gone. To me, he was like the father I never had. He had overdosed, and Amy was hitting the road with some other dude. I wouldn't see her again until 1990, eight years later. Amy once wrote in a letter, "We're not normal people."

Not sure where I should go upon release, the staff had already contacted my mother and Gary. Two weeks before leaving, I received a letter from my Great Uncle Warren telling me that I would be staying with him. It seems Gary didn't want me around. My mother came to visit and explained to me that she wasn't able to afford the things I needed since I was getting ready to start ninth grade. So off I went back to Milwaukee and Great Uncle Warren, the official leader of our so-called family. He communicated with a combination of sign language and verbal skills. Now, with advanced emphysema, he was unable to leave the house. He was a curious-looking man, appearing much older than sixty two, with an indented hole right next to the middle of his forehead from an accident years ago. He was never without oxygen and his bedside table was filled with every medication known to mankind. Warren had money; he had a fabulous gun collection and a coin and stamp collection I was already scheming to steal. From the moment I arrived, I was given everything I needed and much of what I wanted. I was soon to learn a harsh lesson that few things in the world are free.

To this day I still feel twinges of shame when I remember it. My bed, a twin, was in the same room as my uncle's and the first time it happened, I was shocked and confused. One night around 10:00 p.m., I noticed Warren was still awake, which was unusual.

When he asked me to come and lie next to him so we could talk, I felt uncomfortable but not alarmed. He told me how lonely he was and he started fondling me. I just froze up, unable to move. I told him I was tired and wanted to go to sleep, but I was burning with shame and vowed to take this dark secret to my grave. It happened several more times during my stay and I never once said no; I guess I didn't have it in me to reject him. Actually, I had an odd feeling of love toward him.

Another guy and I skipped ninth grade one day and we got an older guy to buy us a bottle of cognac with money I stole from Warren. I also took two matching pearl-handled 38 revolvers. We were going to find a victim to rob. We picked out an older guy just coming from a bank. He ran when he saw us following him and we caught him and wrestled with him in the snow. I remembered the gun when it started to slip from my belt, and I took it out and waved it at the terrified man. The liquor had me feeling mean and uncaring. My finger was on the trigger and I remember thinking what would it be like if I shot this person. You know what saved the man's life? He pissed his pants and when my partner pointed it out, we ended up laughing so hard the man just ran away. We got another bottle and we both got so smashed that my friend passed out on the street and ended up in the hospital with pneumonia.

I never did get my hands on that coin and stamp collection. Soon after the gun scene, my uncle had a major attack and was admitted to the hospital. His son Wally hated my guts and used my uncle's absence to get rid of me. He put me on a Greyhound bus to Houston with no money or food. It took me three days to get there, and another two days to contact my mother, during which I lived in the bus station.

One of the worst places to be in a large city is the bus station, a haven for all types of predators. After three days without food and no money in my pocket, I was an easy target. I kept calling collect the number I had for Gary, but got no answer. I had no choice but to wait at the terminal, and I was desperate. I slept on a bench, and I think it was only my young age and my obvious poor condition that kept them from running me off or arresting me.

By the next evening I contemplated leaving the terminal and taking my chances. An older man with a beer belly who was pulling a dolly of packages asked me if I was okay and I almost broke down and cried. After hearing my story, he explained that he and his son were couriers, delivering packages to the bus station and airport. He offered to let me come with him until I could contact my mother. I accepted his offer, not seeing any other possibilities.

As we got into his van, his son, a man in his early twenties, did not acknowledge my presence. When the man asked me if I was tired and I said yes, he reached into the glove compartment and took out some pills, telling me it was speed and it would help me stay awake. I swallowed one, and an hour later felt a prickly sensation in my scalp. We had dinner at McDonald's before going to his two-bedroom apartment. His son never said a word to me or made eye contact; soon I'd know why.

The man offered me his couch for as long as it took for me to find my mother. The son went into his bedroom and shut the door. I made myself comfortable in front of the television and the man went into his room, I thought to sleep. After half an hour, he came out butt-ass naked, carrying porno magazines. I kept staring at the television when he sat down next to me and asked me if I wanted to look at some magazines with him. I said no, feeling very afraid and not sure what was going to happen. After a few minutes I heard his heavy breathing as he flipped the pages of the magazines. He soon groaned and then sat motionless. I can't describe the feelings and thoughts that went through me as I sat with my eyes fixed on the TV. I only knew I wished I was anyplace else. Without saying anything, the man got up and went back into his room.

Between the speed and the fear, I barely slept. I knew I was out of there the next day no matter what. In the morning, he gave me $10 to run to the store for cereal and milk. On my way out, I peeked through the kitchen door to see him putting his wallet in the sugar jar. My spirits soared because whether or not I was able to contact my mother, I knew I wouldn't be broke. By ten o'clock that morning, Gary answered the phone, surprised to hear my voice. After explaining to him what had happened, he said he and my mother would come and pick me up.

Before they arrived, the man went into the bathroom and I stole his wallet. I justified it by telling myself he was a pervert, but had none of that happened and the old man only showed me kindness,

I still would have taken it. The wallet yielded $80 and some credit cards that I threw out the window.

The first thing Gary told me was that we were moving to a small town called Palestine about three hours away, where he had a job. His parents lived there and he had a two-bedroom cottage where we'd live.

Palestine was a hick town of about 10,000 people, with two movie theaters, a bowling alley, mall and pharmacy where the old-timers gathered to gossip. This is where I met my two best friends, Johnny Salmon and Roger Hilton. We did everything together no matter what it was. It was quickly established that I was the leader because of my vast life experiences and balls of steel. Weekends we'd scrape our money together and get a bottle of Jim Beam and some weed from the projects. Occasionally Johnny would steal some Valium or Dalmane from his mother's stash and we'd pop those for good measure. We'd always end up down at the river, bombed out of our minds, sitting around a huge fire and thinking of ways we could get rich.

I came up with the bright idea of robbing the pharmacy at gunpoint. The next day, after we chased our massive hangovers away with beer and a joint or two, we waited in a field behind the store and staked the place out. In reality, I was trying to work up the nerve when suddenly the door opened and the employees came out. The store was closing. Secretly, we were all relieved.

Deciding instead to break in, we waited until nightfall and, with burglary tools – a crowbar, a pair of bolt cutters and gloves – I volunteered to be the one to climb onto the roof and cut the power to the alarm. Dumb-ass me had no idea how much juice was running through this line, and when I put the cutters around the wire and clamped down, I was thrown off the roof and landed on my side, breaking my leg and fracturing my arm. The head of the cutter was completely melted; the only thing that saved my life that night was the rubber grips.

When Johnny and Roger got me to the hospital, I lied and said I'd fallen from a tree. After eight weeks, things were heating up between me and Gary, for not only was I stealing money from him, but I also took some of the pain medication he took for an earlier shoulder injury. We ended up in a fighting match when he confronted me, and when his gun-toting father intervened and the neighbors called the police, I knew I was in trouble. Gary had the police evict me and my mother, and we had no money or place to live. The police ended up taking us to a woman's house where she took in single mothers and their children. It was one thing for me to be thrown out, but I felt bad about dragging my mother down with me. I believe my mother knew it was going to happen anyway, so she stoically accepted our fate. She was a real trooper.

The woman who owned the house was kind. At fifteen, I was still a virgin, and the woman's daughter, Debbie, started plotting to get me in bed before I realized it. She was 26, had two children, and was married to a big shot lawyer. A real estate manager,

Debbie got me alone one day and started kissing and fondling me, and telling me she wanted me. I was unsure of what to do; I was definitely aroused. She told me nothing would happen until she moved me and my mother into an apartment that she'd set up for us. It was in a three-story art deco building in the middle of Palestine. I have fond memories of the countless hours I spent alone and pondering my life from the rooftop of that building. I had my own bedroom for the first time in my life.

Debbie came over at 5:00 a.m. three or four times a week with a cheap bottle of wine. My mother knew what was going on, but never objected. I was having a good time. I dropped out of school and got a job at the Bonanza Steak House. Roger, Johnny and I started messing with coke and Quaaludes when we could get them. If we didn't have the money we would case a place out and rob it; it was that simple. The cops began snooping around Johnny and Roger's houses asking questions about me, and it looked like Debbie's daughter, who didn't like me, was going to rat to her old man.

I was sixteen years old going on seventeen now and I knew I was going to have to make a move. My mother had accepted a printing job in Houston. I'd heard some old timers talking about the benefits of the military on their own sons and how good the experience was for young men. I was thinking this was my ticket out. I had to wait until I was seventeen and I would still need a note from my mother. Debbie moved me across the hall to an empty apartment and said she'd cover the expenses until I left for the Navy, but we wouldn't be spending any more time with each other. I wasn't surprised.

My mind was on the future and I was on my own. I did well at boot camp and was training to be a yeoman, a glorified secretary. The last weekend of our stay, I dated a woman from New York, Marie, who was sixteen years older than me. This thing with older women was getting to be a habit and this was my pattern for many years to come. At least older women didn't play games.

After my training in Meridian, Mississippi, I was assigned to the Willow Grove Naval Base in Pennsylvania. Every weekend the place was full of reservists from all the service branches; I was one of 300 full-time military personnel that lived and worked on the base.

Philadelphia was about 30 minutes away and this is where I would score my drugs. My first taste of free-basing cocaine came through another active duty person. From the moment I took that first hit I knew that I was going to take a much different approach to everything I did. The intensity of free-basing has no equal. You can never get enough, so you're constantly looking for sources of money. I never had enough money in my pocket for drugs so I started back on my old ways.

I got a job at Christmas in the on-base liquor store, figuring an opportunity would come up for me to make a few extra bucks. I hadn't been able to steal much, just a few cases here and there, but my luck would soon change.

One night, while sitting in my car and waiting for it to warm up, I saw the manager through the plate glass window as he dropped what looked like paper bags into a mail slot that was hidden behind a picture. I knew he was dropping the day's receipts, and I started scheming. I stole a crowbar from maintenance and the next night waited in a bathroom until the building closed. The mail slot emptied into a 600 pound iron safe in a small closet. I didn't have a cutting torch, so I decided to let gravity work for me. If I could get the safe upside down the bags would slip to the bottom and I could reach in and pick them out.

If someone had been watching me trying to wrestle this 600 pound safe they'd still be laughing today. I started rocking the behemoth back and forth until it crashed to the floor. I waited about twenty minutes to see if anyone had heard the crash, but no one came. By 3:00 a.m. I'd gotten all I'd come for and left through a fire exit, which set off an alarm but I was by then safely back in my room before the base police responded.

There was more money than I'd ever seen, $16,000 and several thousands more in checks, which I promptly threw away.

I panicked and decided to go AWOL the next day, which immediately caused suspicion. I took a plane to Houston and my mother; and hooked up again with my old buddy Roger Hilton from East Texas, who was living there with his family. We got an apartment together, and by that time we were full-blown druggies. I sold drugs while he worked and every night was a party. I managed to stay high for six months until my mother warned me that U.S. marshals were asking about me. I was just about out of money since the drug business went bust because Roger and I were our best customers. To save Mom from the trauma, I decided to turn myself in.

When they took me back to Willow Grove, I was immediately questioned about the missing money. I denied it, and since they had no evidence they had to release me. I was given a captain's mast for the AWOL, a lesser form of punishment than a court-martial, but I never made it to the mast because two days later I tried to sneak some stereo equipment off base and the authorities were waiting. I was sent to the brig to wait to be court-martialed. I was by now eighteen, and I knew I was in serious trouble because the military courts were supposedly much harsher than civilian courts. I got the first of many breaks I would get from the system when I made a deal for two years. They could only prove I'd stolen the stereo equipment though they knew I'd also robbed the safe.

The minimum security brig was small by prison standards with only 300 prisoners, and it was run like boot camp. There was also a female barracks, and once or twice a week a girl I worked next to and I would sneak into a storeroom and have sex.

One day I got a visit from Janet, a local girl I'd dated from time to time when she visited the base. She was swollen like a beach ball and I was the father. Our daughter was born while I was still in the brig, but I had no intention of being a father. When I was released, I'd accumulated several thousand dollars in back pay, and planned to go back to Texas. Before I left, I wanted to score some coke, see Janet and the baby, maybe get a piece of ass and then leave. Janet convinced me to stay with her and the baby. In retrospect, I wish I hadn't stayed. Not that it would have changed my ways, because I was still going to do the things I did no matter where I went, but because it would have saved a lot of grief for a woman who practically worshipped me; and it would have saved the children from a lot of pain and confusion.

For the next eighteen months I managed to hold a job as a groundskeeper at a nursing home, but I was still getting high and there were many nights when I didn't come home. I'd spend many nights in North Philly, smoking crack and screwing anything in the vicinity. To date, that year and a half is the longest period I've stayed out of jail.

In 1990, Janet and I had a major blowout and I left for Houston and tractor trailer school. Though I was heavily involved with crack, I managed somehow to complete the ten-week course. I planned to hook up with one of the big carriers and travel. It wasn't to be, for two weeks after completing the course I was caught burglarizing a warehouse and sentenced to a year in the county jail. I began to notice that every jail I'd been in had mostly black prisoners, and when I compared my experiences with theirs, it was obvious that something was very wrong with the system.

During the year Janet and I started writing, and we agreed I'd return to Philly when my time was up. I tried being a family man, but my old habits continued.

There were times when I wouldn't come home for weeks and months, running the streets, staying high, living with whores and committing robberies. For several years, the few times I did show up at home I only brought problems. I was in and out of jail and got my first state sentence after my twelfth burglary and was to serve a two-and-a-half to six year term.

By some miracle, Janet was still hanging on and we had another child, this time a boy. I decided I had to do something about my full-blown addiction and I got into every drug treatment and self-help program I could, hoping to gain insight into who I am. By the time I was paroled, my mother had died of cancer without me at her side, and Janet had found another man and had a third child with him.

For the first time in my life it seemed I was truly alone and had to rely on myself. I got into a drug rehab halfway house; I had great intentions and honestly believed I had changed. It lasted all of 30 days and I was back at it. The attraction of the streets was too strong and I gave in. I'd had a total of 40 days of freedom before I was back in prison with a new felony case for burglary. It was my thirteenth, and it didn't look good for me. I was expecting the worst, that my line had played out. I'm anticipating something in the neighborhood of five to fifteen years, and I was shocked when my public defender got me a deal of two to four. I couldn't believe my ears. By the time we got to court to accept the plea bargain, the attorney had gotten it down to one-and-a half to three years. I was one lucky fellow. Or was it something else?

There are hundreds of men, most of them black, that I see every day, who have committed far less than me, but are serving my sentence three, four and even five times longer. Is it coincidence? I don't think so. I understand that eventually my rope will play out and I'll be thrown away permanently if I don't stop. But why have I received so many chances when the man next to me has received so few?

Here at Graterford, the overall attitude towards prisoners is one of contempt and lack of concern. You must keep yourself in good physical shape, for the medical department here should really be called the horror ward. In 1999, a friend of mine, Woody, who was serving one to three years, died because the medical department didn't treat his asthma properly. The state-employed pathologist, after performing an autopsy, declared that his death was self-imposed because he wasn't taking his medication as prescribed. They are liars. I was there!

In one of my many drug and alcohol treatment programs, the therapist asked what people thought the most powerful motivator out there was. He said it was pain. Although I agree that pain is a powerful force, there is one that is so much stronger, pleasure. A human being will go out of their way to feel good, in many cases risking bodily harm and prolonged misery for a fleeting moment of pleasure.

I can't tell you how many times I've sat in a cell and contemplated my future. The thought of falling prey to my desires is not a pleasant one, but for me it is a very real threat. Don't be quick to judge me because of my history. I have to make some firm decisions in my life, and even though I've grown weary of making plans, I understand the need for support. After experiencing the system for most of my life, I believe the single most important factor in curbing the recidivism rate is meaningful, decent employment. All of the therapy, meetings and good intentions mean absolutely nothing if an ex-convict doesn't remain in MEANINGFUL employment. Even with the support of self-help organizations, friends and families, so important for addicts like myself, I guarantee a return trip for an ex-convict on parole who remains unemployed for a long enough time. I have good, marketable skills I will use upon my release. As far as the rest, I must play it by ear.

I'm not sure where my children will come into the picture if at all. My son is now nine and my daughter fourteen. Neither really knows me and my daughter only has bad memories. I will just work toward picking myself back up and, if the day comes when I can offer something positive to my children, then I will ask to be let back into their lives. There are many things that have happened that I'd like to change, but cannot. But I am not a quitter; giving up just doesn't fit into my life. In a few years I will be freed and given another chance to do something positive with my life. Will it happen? I certainly hope so.

Update for the Second Edition: Danny was released from prison in 2004. Janet took him back, he was reestablishing himself with his children, and he got a job at union wages driving a truck in the town where he lived. We kept in touch by phone and I met him and his family for a few minutes at a writer's conference. Later, after an alcohol-fueled explosive argument with his daughter, he took off for California to see his sister for the first time in twelve years. After a month there, he returned and tried again to make a life in freedom. He was diagnosed with a bipolar disorder and came to realize he desperately needed treatment. I encouraged him to be part of a support group and to keep in touch with his co-authors. He didn't. I didn't hear from him for months and then I got a letter – he was back in jail. He wrote that he realized how much he needed help, but now that he was back in prison, he doubted he'd ever get it.

"No problem can be solved by the same consciousness that caused it."

Albert Einstein

Chapter Four

Not as Guilty as Charged
"Jameel Salahuddin"
($930,000)

Jameel Salahuddin (not his real name) quit school when he was eleven. His teachers had never noticed that he was so bruised and traumatized from the brutality and sexual abuse of his young life that he withdrew into himself. By the time he was eighteen, he was working in a fast food restaurant 60-70 hours a week. He spent his money on fine clothes, even buying tailor-made suits. Living with an older woman who dealt drugs and her eight year old daughter, he found respite in the make-believe family. Wanting to prove his manhood, he agreed to accompany a group of "tough guys" on a supermarket robbery. He says, "I was simply a fool who sought a sense of power and wholeness in the wrong place. Perhaps if there was someone I could have talked to it would have made a difference. But there was no one."

Convicted of the one robbery he participated in and another twelve the cops hadn't been able to solve, he was sentenced to 24-75 years instead of the 1 ½ - 5 years for the crime he actually committed. He was eligible for parole in 2006, when he' was 42 years old. He ended up back in prison for a technical parole violation.

A functional illiterate when arrested, he could barely read and write. When he tried to write a letter to a friend, she could hardly read it. This humiliated him, but also inspired him to improve his skills. While spending much of his first ten years in prison in The Hole, he began reading books and writing letters for the first time in his tortured life. Excited by the worlds that opened to him, he was thrilled at being able to give an articulate voice to his thoughts and feelings. Still resistant to sitting in a classroom, he once stole a G.E.D. preparation textbook and devoured it. Math was his biggest challenge, as he had to teach himself algebra, geometry, percentages and long division, topics totally new to him.

When he scored 261 on the G.E.D., where a passing grade was 225, he was elated. He has completed a ten-credit business management certification program and has an associate's degree in human services from a community college. Over time, encouraged by friends, he took college courses; by the time he is released he'll have completed his bachelor's degree, paid for by his family, from a correspondence course at a local university.

A man who played a pivotal role in Jameel's growth and development was Habib Bilal, an older Sufi man with an ethereal appearance who had been at Graterford for years. Under Bilal's tutelage, the eager student learned about the major religions of the world as well as meditation techniques that enabled him to explore the pain and rage inside him. In Bilal, Jameel finally found a father, a teacher, a brother and a friend. Bilal was transferred to another prison before he had a chance to know of Jameel's academic and spiritual accomplishments. (Inmates in Pennsylvania are not allowed to correspond with each other.)

After counseling some younger inmates recently, Jameel said with pride, "I'm turning into Bilal!"

Optimistic about his future after prison, he dreams of teaching creative writing to at-risk youth back in North Philadelphia. And, he wants to write. He says:

"One day I want to become a great black writer who gives voice to what's going on within the souls of my people. There's so much for me to write about, to let the world know who we are and how we feel. It's time for us to begin defining ourselves. My life experiences, though painful and traumatic, have equipped me not just to fight but to flourish. Recently a guard who's been here as long as I can remember, commented on my change and asked how I was doing. I looked at him and said I'm still in prison, so how well could I be doing? He smiled and reminded me of all the years he had to write me up for not following orders. He said he used to tell his wife about this young, rebellious inmate that was driving him crazy, but whom he respected for his integrity. I smiled, remembering that period of my prison life. Back then I had no idea what integrity was all about, but I knew the value of remaining true to myself. I have changed. Time and struggle have made me wiser. Though in my heart I'm as rebellious as ever, I've learned to channel my energy toward my goals.

I firmly believe that one day I'm going to be all I long to be. I just have to keep holding on. I will."

JAMEEL

I don't know why I agreed to rob the Acme supermarket in suburban Philadelphia that October night in 1981. I was a pretty boy, and ever since I was fifteen, I'd been involved with older women. At eighteen, I guess my need to be part of something caused me to start hanging around with Rick. He was strong, confident and aggressive while I was quiet, naïve and in need of a positive role model in my unhappy life. I was involved with Linda, a beautiful woman with an eight year old daughter. I soon learned Linda was a drug dealer. We had a little make-believe family, picnicking in the country, shopping, and even attending teachers' meetings. I guess I agreed to take part in the robbery as a macho thing to prove I was really a man.

The plan was for another guy and me to go into the market while the others stayed in the getaway car. I barely knew the other two. I was supposed to retrieve the money from the safe while the other man held a gun on the manager. We grabbed a cart and walked down an aisle or two like regular shoppers before we approached the manager's booth. The guy with the gun wrapped in newspaper quietly announced a holdup. The manager, cooperating, unlocked the safe and I quickly emptied the contents into a carryall bag. Then we slowly walked out, trying not to call attention to ourselves.

Just as we stepped outside, a police cruiser entered the parking lot. I later learned the manager had triggered a silent alarm just as we approached the booth. The two guys were nervously waiting in the car 30 yards away. Hoping they wouldn't panic and leave without me, I calmly made my way towards them. I don't think at this point the police suspected me, as I was casually dressed like a college kid.

When I was about ten feet from the car, I looked back and was surprised to see my fellow robber still close to the market, waving his arms at the police and pointing to me. As the police drove towards me, I jumped into the back seat of the getaway car and we sped away, leaving the other guy behind. The driver swerved around the cop and a high-speed chase followed.

In a few minutes it seemed as though the entire police force was chasing us, and we couldn't shake them. The driver pulled over and the three of us leaped out and ran in separate directions. In a flash, I ran behind a large house and jumped a fence at the rear of the yard. In the darkness I didn't realize that the other side of the fence was a forty-foot drop onto concrete.

After being airborne for what seemed like minutes, my body hit the concrete the wind was knocked out of me and pain was shooting through my legs. I lay there hurt and paralyzed, but I had to keep moving, for my pursuers were dead on my trail. I heard many police cars and felt them nearby. Above me, several officers who were chasing me looked down, amazed that I'd made such a jump. They couldn't reach me, and, knowing I had to keep moving, I forced myself to my feet and stumbled into the darkness. Thank God none of them shot me. They could have justified murdering me on the spot.

I ran desperately toward the treeline of the woods, hoping for refuge. Suddenly I was flying headfirst down a steep ravine, falling to what surely was my death. I found myself hanging upside down, clinging to some roots and vines. When I looked down, I was terrified, for I was clinging to a steep slope about 30 feet above a shallow, rocky stream. I couldn't let go or I'd fall head first onto the rocks. I could hear police all around, an army of them, with dogs, floodlights, and the sound of walkie talkies reverberating through the night air. My only option appeared to be staying completely still and praying I wouldn't be discovered.

How had I gotten into this situation? Just that morning, Linda's daughter stayed home from school, excited to spend the day with me and go clothes shopping. Although there were no more than ten years between us, she often called me Daddy. Afterwards we stopped by my mother's and hung out for awhile. On the way home, I picked up some fresh fish for dinner. As Linda prepared the meal, the phone rang and it was Rick, reminding me that I was supposed to meet him half an hour earlier to accompany him and his squad on the robbery. I told him I was chilling and about to eat dinner. Linda, not realizing what was up, suggested I go on and handle my business and she'd keep my food warm until I came back. Like a fool, I left, not knowing I'd never be back.

As I hung there, close to an hour must have passed. As the police searched the area, I was drenched in sweat, my arms and muscles burning from the pain of my injuries and the tension of clinging so tightly to the slope. My heart cried out for God's help and mercy.

After a while, the sounds of pursuit began to fade; the dogs were silent and the lights were turned off. Amazingly, it seemed as if they must have thought I'd gotten away. Then a voice above me called out that he'd found some money on the ground, then some more and next thing I knew the police were following a trail of money leading them closer and closer to where I was hanging. In a moment of greed, while trying to escape the police in the getaway car, I'd stuffed some of the stolen money down the front of my pants. I had no idea that while running through the woods, dollar bills were falling from my pants legs, leading the police directly to me. The last thing I remember after being discovered was letting go and falling through the darkness.

I regained consciousness in the hospital, handcuffed to a stretcher. An examination and x-rays showed that, miraculously, nothing was broken. Besides a concussion and a few stitches here and there, I suffered no major physical damage as a result of my fall.

From the hospital I was taken to the police station and arrested on a host of charges stemming from the robbery. The other guys all got away; I was the only one captured. As the detectives questioned me, I remained silent, my body aching and my head so swollen it felt like it would burst. I sat for hours while they drilled me about the identities of the other men. They even smacked me around. I made no statements. This went on for several days, and they threatened that if I didn't give them the information they wanted, they were going to charge me with so many cases I'd never get out of prison. True to their word, within the week I was charged with twelve different armed robberies, all committed within the past six months. Bail was out of the question, so I sat in prison, overwhelmed at the absurdity of my circumstances, keeping my silence, figuring I could beat those extra charges in court since I was innocent of them.

What I didn't learn until later was that these guys had been committing robberies together for months. When I was arrested, the detectives assumed I was Rick, for we looked alike, except Rick had bad acne.

I was in for a rude awakening.

My first court-appointed attorney showed up and asked the judge to be dismissed because he didn't have time to represent me. The new lawyer appointed by the court never once met with me. All he did was write me a letter asking for a list of alibis accounting for my whereabouts at the times of the other robberies.

A week before trial, the first lawyer contacted my mother and said he'd represent me for $10,000. She somehow scraped the money together, but I didn't see or talk with him until my first day in court. Considered a top gun of criminal lawyers, he wore tailored suits, silk ties and Gucci shoes. When I tried explaining how I came to be charged with thirteen robberies, I could tell by his eyes that he didn't believe a word I was saying about my innocence. I told him over and over I hadn't committed those other robberies. With an expression of contempt on his face, he said, "You might have convinced your mother that you didn't do those things, but I don't believe you."

The courts refused his request for more time to prepare and the trials began. I knew I was doomed.

While I did my best to come up with alibis for the dates and times when the other robberies were committed, I was uncertain. As a teenager who'd dropped out of school at eleven, I had no job and no structured schedule. Of one thing I was certain – I wasn't with Rick and the others when they did those other robberies.

Through several jury trials, I was found not guilty because there simply was no evidence to convict me. Then, in the next few trials, an amazing thing happened. I sat in the courtroom as a witness who'd never laid eyes on me took the stand and identified me as one of the men who'd robbed a supermarket where she worked. Did she think I was Rick? That was something I definitely didn't expect. I lost that trial. But then the same thing happened over and over again in the next few trials. When the smoke cleared, I'd lost three trials in a row involving cases I knew absolutely nothing about. It was clear the cards were stacked against me and my innocence meant nothing. I was witnessing the process by which I was legally lynched.

Before the next trial, the District Attorney approached my lawyer with a deal. If I pleaded guilty to the three remaining robberies, he'd get the judge to run the sentences concurrently and I'd get no more time than I was already going to get. It wasn't a good deal but my back was against the wall. Like a fool, I let them play me right out. I took their deal, a deal with the devil. Later, I stood before the devil as he smiled and sentenced me to 24-72 years in prison.

The irony is that the county where I was initially arrested sentenced me to 1 ½ - 5 years in prison for my part in the one robbery I committed.

The horrible smell of Montgomery County Prison caught me by surprise. The air was filled with the awful, musky scent of caged men. Told to strip naked by guards with blackjacks in their hands, I complied. When I asked why I had to bend over and spread my cheeks, the guard snapped, "Nigger, if you don't turn around I'll split your black, motherfuckin' head!" Another guard explained that exposing my ass enabled them to see whether or not I was attempting to smuggle a weapon or other contraband into the prison. How and why I would stick a weapon up my ass was beyond my imagination, but I turned around and complied with their request.

That single act was one of the most humiliating and dehumanizing experiences of my life.

After showering, I was hosed down with a liquid they said was an insecticide or a delouser, given clothing and locked in a cell with three other men. I just stood there in the dark, unsure about what to do.

In the morning, one of the other guys awkwardly introduced himself and I mumbled my name, too tired and beaten down to socialize. I followed him to the chow hall, where whites sat on one side and blacks on the other. After chow, I got on the phone, first calling Linda.

We'd been living together for about a year, and though she was thirteen years older, I liked her a lot. She had a special way of loving that calmed and soothed my troubled soul. In her arms, I felt peace, for the first time. At fifteen I'd been involved with a woman twice my age. Beautiful older women just turned me on; I preferred dating them to younger women, who were simply too inexperienced for my taste.

My attraction to older women was not one-sided. Linda, who I'd met a couple of other times, showed up one night at the fast food place where I was working, and asked me what time I got off. When midnight came, she was waiting for me in her little car outside the restaurant. As I approached the car, she slid over to let me drive. I felt like a king basking in royal treatment. The neighborhood kids hanging outside smiled and teased me about how I thought I was such a player. When we got to her place, I learned her daughter was away for the week and soon we were naked in her bedroom. This woman did things to my body that had never been done before, and several days later I moved in with her and her little girl. I had a beautiful relationship with her daughter. Though I was a teenager, I quickly adapted to being man of the house and king of the castle.

Being young and totally ignorant of the drug game, I stayed out of Linda's business and asked few questions about the people she dealt with, including several celebrities when they were in town. We got to attend lots of fancy affairs.

Through an acquaintance in the neighborhood, I met Rick and the others who were rumored to be really bad and successful bank robbers. It was these guys I foolishly decided to accompany on their dark deed.

Linda was hysterical when she accepted my collect call. She'd been up all night worrying and wondering what to do. Though I tried to reassure her, she couldn't calm down. I hung up and called my mother just as she was about to leave for work. When I told her I'd been arrested, she had a fit.

My mother and I have always had a great relationship. Besides being the strongest, kindest and most loving person I know, I always knew that as long as I was honest with her, no matter what the problem, I could rely on her to help me sort things out. During the first week of my arrest, as detectives kept charging me with case after case, my mother visited every day, though we had to talk on telephones behind a plexiglass barrier. Through my tears, she encouraged me to be strong.

(Years later, she and I had a confrontation in the visitors' room about her inability to protect me from the sexual abuse. We wept together and our wounds began to heal.)

My father was another story. All my life I've possessed an intense hatred and bitterness toward him, for I had absolutely no respect for him as a man. I never knew him as a child, for my mother left him when I was four. He moved to Detroit, and I didn't see him again until I was about ten. My only early memory of him was a scene where I am standing in the kitchen doorway as my father sat on my mother's chest, repeatedly punching her in the face as she lay screaming.

That single incident made an indelible impression on my young soul.

When I was ten, I asked to be sent to Detroit to live with my father. My mother had remarried, to a white man who physically and sexually abused me. The teachers at school never seemed to notice my bruises and my desperation, and my mother felt she was in no position to risk losing economic support by leaving him.

I thought the move to Michigan would be a good thing, but instead it was like jumping from the frying pan into the fire. I discovered my father wasn't too good at communicating. An extremely quiet man, whenever I acted out to get his attention he responded with violence, beating me with his fists like I was a grown man. After a year and a half, he sent me back to Philly, and I didn't see or hear from him again until I was seventeen.

After losing his legs in an industrial accident, he moved back to live with his sister. I visited him often, but the relationship was awkward and strained. I remember at my grandfather's funeral, with the family gathered in my aunt's living room, my father started talking about the special bond we had. I recall at that moment I thought, "This man ain't got a clue as to who I am." But I just sat there in silence. Shortly after that, I came to prison and didn't see him again. That was more than twenty years ago.

About three years ago, I learned my father was sick and dying in a nursing home. I began to consider the hell that his life had been, and when I placed myself in his shoes, suddenly the hate and bitterness in my heart dissolved. It was replaced with love, forgiveness and compassion toward an old and dying man. For the first time in my life, I realized I loved my father, and I was overcome with a desire to let him know. I called my sister and asked if there was any way I could talk to my father. She investigated, but learned it was out of the question, considering where I was.

I felt like a dark cloud had descended upon my heart. All I wanted was an opportunity to reach out beyond these prison walls to tell my father I loved him before he died. But I couldn't, and it hurt like hell.

That night, I had a wonderful dream. I was free and standing in the midst of a reunion with my entire family present. To my surprise, someone told me that my father was there, pointing across the room. He was standing there, tall, handsome, healthy and strong. As I walked slowly towards him, I noticed how much we looked alike, as if we were mirror images of each other. When I reached him, he smiled and simply opened his arms to embrace me. As we hugged, tears streaming from my eyes, I kept telling him how much I loved him. When I woke up suddenly back in my cell, I felt as if a huge burden had been lifted from my heart. Miraculously, from that moment on, all of the emotional issues regarding my father were reconciled.

This healing was accomplished in a single dream.

The first week of my arrest twenty years ago was difficult, as I was led in chains from one cell to another for over a week, as police questioned and charged me with many other robberies. I knew no one in the county prison and I soon realized how out of my element I was. As a young, skinny teenager, I stood out. Back in the eighties, before drugs ravaged the inner cities, most of the black men in prison were guys who came from poverty-stricken neighborhoods and had resorted to criminal activities as a means of survival. This, combined with the racist attitudes of police officers, the courts and society as a whole, was cause for many blacks to spend their lives in and out of prison.

But I was totally unprepared for prison.

On my first day in the yard, a few guys approached me and asked me if there was anything I needed. I was surprised that they knew my name. It seemed my association with Linda held some weight in such a place. I was embraced almost as a celebrity amidst the subculture of drugs and violence. In no time, I was initiated into their ranks and began smuggling drugs into the prison. Guards met my outside connections and, for cash, would bring in drugs and anything else. On several occasions, they even allowed Linda inside to have sex with me. I was living dangerously in the county jail.

After a fistfight with another inmate, I realized the lifestyle I was involved in went against who and what I was as a man, and I gradually hooked up others to replace me in maintaining the drug connections to the street. My decision to step aside was accepted.

When I heard that the three other men who were with me during the supermarket robbery were arrested and charged with many of the same robberies and had implicated me, I sank into depression. My entire world had caved in and I was slowly being crushed by the weight and pressure of all that had happened.

Perhaps it was their strip searches and false tough guy facades that caused me to hate most prison guards. One in particular, a white sergeant, constantly harassed me. His face would get all twisted and he'd say "How you doing, Mr. Prosperity?" One day, I asked him why he called me that, and he responded, "Cause you think you're somebody when all you is a good for nothin' nigger!" His comment took me over the edge, and I spit at him. In an instant, several guards beat me with blackjacks Rodney King style, and then dragged me and handcuffed me in solitary confinement in "The Hole." Somehow I curled into a fetal position and slept, my body aching from head to toe. In the morning, they strip-searched me, took my clothes, and left me naked.

It was then I began to notice the wretched conditions in the cell. It was filthy, and the sink and toilet in one corner were completely covered with a thick, brown slime. The smell was awful, and to my astonishment, smeared all over the walls was dried human feces. When the guard slid a carton of milk and a small box of cereal into the cell, I asked if I could be transferred. He responded, "This is what happens when you spit on a guard." I began cussing and banging on the door, but they ignored me. Eventually I got quiet. One can only scream for so long.

After 90 days in The Hole, a guard came to the cell and told me to get ready. I was being transferred to Graterford Prison. I was scared to death. Prior to my arrest, guys used to tell me, "Boy, you are too pretty. You better not ever go to prison. They gonna have a ball with you." Rumor had it that Graterford was the roughest prison in Pennsylvania, a place where young guys were constantly raped and taken advantage of. When I arrived there, the guards asked where did I want my body shipped in case of an emergency. When I asked what kind of an emergency, the guard responded, "In case somebody murders your dumb ass!"

Once inside the cell, I hung a sheet over the door, pulled down my pants and shitted out two fifty-dollar bills which I'd placed up my ass earlier to smuggle into prison. After washing the money off, I went in search of a guy someone told me to contact once I arrived at Graterford. When I found him, he gave me a knife in exchange for one of the fifties. Over the weeks, I carried that knife everywhere, intent on murdering the first man fool enough to say anything out of the way to me.

By the time I was released back into the main population, I had decided that there was no room in my life for sanity or anything associated with it. For the next ten years, I lived a predatory lifestyle, surviving and feeding off of the weaker men around me. Whatever hopes and dreams I had about freedom or a better tomorrow, I completely suppressed. To continue dreaming and hoping seemed a complete waste of time.

My violent response to an attempted rape served as an initiation into the ranks of the strong and aggressive within the prison, and with this came a kind of celebrity status amongst other men. Guys I didn't know, who'd heard about what happened, would walk up to me, shake my hand and say something indicating their respect. It felt good to be admired and respected.

Back in the eighties, most of the inmates at Graterford were either Lifers or those serving long sentences. The place was extremely violent, drug-infested and understaffed, with guards ill-equipped to control such a large institution. The guards smuggled in large quantities of drugs in exchange for money. This, coupled with the fact that everyone walked around with a chip on their shoulder and a knife tucked into their waistbands created a hellish environment. The inmates basically ran the prison, with little or no regard for the weak and innocent. There were few counseling or educational opportunities, but even if there had been, I was too busy trying to survive to consider taking advantage of them.

For me, surviving Graterford entailed more than just struggling against the violence, drugs or predatory rapists. There are many negative forces and elements in a prison that slowly eat away at a man's humanity. Hopelessness is one such force. There were times when my vision was clouded and all I could see was the concrete and steel that encaged me. Sitting in my cell, my soul crying out, I discovered that resistance was the only way to ease the pain. So that's what I did, I resisted! Since prior to coming to prison I was a good man, I resisted any and everything that sought to take me away from who and what I am. Often this resistance was expressed in small things, such as refusing to obey the rules and regulations. There was a guard on the cell block who was frustrated because I showed up late every night when it was time to be locked in. When he'd ask why I was so late, I'd say things like "Only a fool would rush to get locked up in a cage." When I'd refuse to close the door, I'd say, "Living inside this cage is bad enough, but I'll be damned if I'm going to close the door on myself!"

He'd write me up and it was back to The Hole.

For years, all I did was go back and forth to The Hole. I simply refused to obey the rules. Actually, to me, The Hole was the only place where I could get away from the noise, chaos and violence. It was also

a place where I did a lot of reflecting and healing.
Inside a tiny cell for a long, long time, denied all
access to other humans, the mind experiences
sensory deprivation, which to me was a state of
consciousness more exciting than any drug I'd known.
There is nothing to hear but yourself, to see but four
walls, to feel but your feelings, to smell but the funk of
your own body. While in it, I had a chance to
challenge and explore all the fears and insecurities
that existed within my mind. At first, they presented
themselves as phantoms who sat guarding the
thresholds of whatever peace I sought. They kept me
from accessing the loftier spaces and places within
myself. But it was there, within the solitude of The
Hole, that I began the painful process of healing.

While in The Hole, I focused on healing. Out of
The Hole, my focus was resisting and rebelling
against the negativity all around me. I refused to
resort to unnecessary violence. Fistfights are common
in prison, because you can't coop men up like animals
without their getting agitated and aggressive. A petty
argument can escalate in seconds into a vicious
stabbing or murder, which I've seen many times. I
only used a knife one time, when my life was in
danger. You never know when this might happen, so
you're in a constant state of dread and defensiveness.

Though I was pretty much a loner, during the first
ten years of my incarceration I became close friends
with four guys, all about my age, all from different
parts of Philly, and all arrested around the same year.
I was the only one without a life sentence. Each was
serving a life sentence for a murder he didn't actually
commit, but each was convicted on charges involving

conspiracy, and mandatory sentencing laws put them in prison for the rest of their lives.

As we struggled together just to survive, we'd sit in my cell and talk about how we came to be in this nightmare, tears flowing as we shared. We struggled to give voice to the pain and horror of what it means to be a black man in America. It was there, sitting in that cell with my friends, that I first embraced the challenge of giving language to what we were all experiencing and feeling inside our souls. I made a promise to each of these men that one day I would find a way to tell their stories, even though at the time I was a functional illiterate. There is no doubt in my mind that one day I will become a writer and do it.

* * *

Jameel's parole has been approved and he waits for space in a halfway house. He plans to continue his bachelor's studies and go on for his master's degree while working as a barber, a skill he learned in prison. He is terrified to be back in the streets after 24 years and is considering living in the suburbs if he can afford to do so while he contemplates his college education.

Right before going to press, I got a letter saying he was being paroled to a halfway house in just three weeks. I enclose the following piece from his daily journal.

"With the recent approval for parole, and the excitement and anxieties associated with my upcoming release, the past few months have been quite stressful, taking a toll on me emotionally. I have even lost fifteen pounds, going from 250 to 235 in a few months.

Last night I laid awake in the dark, unable to sleep. So I meditated in an attempt to identify why I have been feeling so physically and emotionally exhausted lately.

In search of an answer, I began to visualize myself separated from the source of my dilemma. Suddenly in my mind, I saw myself standing in front of a white partition. On the other side of this barrier, concealed from view, was the cause of my troubles. Sensing the presence of something powerful, its energy giving off a radiant glow, I peered over the partition, attempting a glimpse. But I couldn't make out what it was. For an hour I just laid there, struggling for a visual. Giving up, I decided to get some sleep, trusting that what I sought would reveal itself in my dreams.

As I slept, I experienced a powerful dream involving my family and the fear that once free, no one would have me back. When morning dawned, so too did the realization that the fear of struggling alone is what stood on the other side of that partition, its fear slowly eating away at mine."

PART II
Women in Prison

Chapter One

Women's Voices

As horrible as the men's stories are, they sadly pale in comparison to what happens to women in prison. In Pennsylvania, the maximum security prison for women is at Muncy, five hours away from

Philadelphia, home of most of the inmates. While women continue to visit men in prison, only 2% of women who are imprisoned ever receive visitors. A recent study showed that prior to incarceration, the average income of the women was less than $5,000 a year.

I met Bonnie Kerness, co-author of *Torture in U.S. Prisons: Evidence of U.S. Human Rights Violations* and co-director of the American Friends Service Committee Prison Project, when we were both presenting at a conference. The following excerpt from Kerness' presentation portrays the voices of women imprisoned around the country.

WHAT THEY TELL ME
Bonnie Kerness

The relationship between women living in poverty and women being incarcerated is indisputable. There are currently 950,000 women in criminal justice custody in the U.S. with thousands more living under other forms of social control such as parole or probation. Since 1980, the number of women entering U.S. prisons has risen almost 400%, double the rate for men. Women of color are imprisoned at rates between 10 and 35 times greater than rates of white women in 15 states. Nearly a quarter of these women are mentally ill, with untold numbers being infected with AIDS. Forty percent held no jobs prior to imprisonment, two thirds of them are women of color and 60% of them are mothers with an estimated total of 1.3 million minor children. Their average age is 29, and 58% of them haven't finished high school. Without any fanfare, the "war on drugs" has become a war on women and it has clearly contributed to the explosion in the women's prison population.

I'd like to share with you some of the voices of the women in prison that I hear during my day:

From New Jersey: "We are forced to sleep on the floor in the middle of winter with bad backs and aching bodies, cold air still blowing from the vents no matter what the temperature outside. At two o'clock in the morning they wake you up and tell you to clear the room. They go through your personal belongings and then put them in the trash…"

From Texas: "The guard sprayed me with pepper spray because I wouldn't take my clothes off in front of five male guards. Then they carried me to a cell, laid me down on a steel bed and took my clothes off. They left me there in that cell with the pepper spray in my face and nothing to wash it away. They did that to me just because I didn't want to take off my clothes in front of them…"

From Arizona: "…If you want a drink here, you have to drink toilet water…"

From Missouri: "When I refused to move to a double cell, they came and dragged me out and threw me on my back. I was beaten about my face and head. One of the guards deliberately stuck his finger in my eye. I was rolled on my stomach and cuffed and put in leg irons. Then I was put in a device called a "restraint chair" where your hands are cuffed beneath you. They stripped me naked and kept me there nine hours until I fouled myself on my hands which were tucked beneath me through a hole in the chair."

The increasingly disturbing complaints I'm hearing from women in prison describe conditions of torture. They suffer from sexual abuse by staff with one woman saying, "I am tired of being gynecologically examined every time I'm searched." Another prisoner put it, "That was not part of my sentence, to...perform oral sex with officers." In one current New Jersey case, the woman who filed charges of rape has been in solitary confinement since the day she filed her complaint. This incredible woman actually held the semen in her mouth, spitting it into a plastic bag when she returned to her cell. She called me to tell me the guard who forced her to have sex was still working in the prison.

Reports of giving birth while handcuffed and shackled are horrible. One woman's baby was coming at the same time the guard who shackled her was on a break somewhere else in the hospital.

Other abuses include medical care which is often so callous that it is life threatening. Coupled with the increasing use of long-term isolation, lack of treatment for substance abuse, lack of counseling services, concerns about the inappropriate use of psychotropic medications, and inappropriate use of restraints, you have a clear picture of what life is like for our sisters in prison...yet there are far fewer advocates focused on women in prison than men. Part of the reason is that women are used to being the helpers, not the helped.

Each of the practices that the women testified about are in violation of dozens of international treaties and covenants that the U.S. has signed: The United Nations Convention Against Torture, the UN Convention on the Elimination of All Forms of Discrimination Against Women, UN Minimum Rules for the Treatment of Prisoners, the UN Convention on the Rights of the Child and a dozen other international and regional laws and standards.

Presented at "From Cell Blocks to City Blocks: A Movement in Search of Freedom"
SUNY Binghamton
March 16, 2002

* * *

Patricia Allard, associate counsel of criminal justice at the Brennan Center for Justice, presented the composite narrative from which the following excerpt was taken at the 2002 Congressional Black Caucus Legislative Conference in Washington, D.C.

A WOMAN'S JOURNEY THROUGH THE PRISON INDUSTRIAL COMPLEX
Patricia Allard

Imagine that you are a young woman in your first year of college, working as a nurse's aide part-time to help pay your tuition. You meet a young man who is both charming and caring and who works in a factory in town. You fall madly in love with him, get married, and give birth to your first child. Now, based on the stories your mama told you as a child, you know that you will live happily ever after.

During the second year of your marriage the factory closes and relocates overseas. Your husband loses his job. He tries for months to find another job, but has no luck because the economy has gone sour. He starts using and selling drugs. You quit school and go to work full time to pay for the drug treatment your husband needs. He's in treatment, and you think your family is getting back on track.

One night you're awakened by a drug raid, and both you and your husband are arrested for possession of controlled substances. It seems your husband has had a relapse, not uncommon during drug treatment. Ten grams of crack are found in your home. The prosecutor tells you, "I'll cut you a deal if you give me some names." But you can't give him any names because you are not in the drug ring; you've never used drugs. So, you're convicted and sentenced under a mandatory minimum sentencing law to a lengthier sentence than the actual drug dealers your husband knew.

At the time of your conviction, you're expecting your second child. You receive no prenatal care while in prison and give birth shackled to a hospital bed surrounded by prison guards. During your prison term, your mother cares for your daughter but is unable to care for the newborn. So, your brother and sister-in-law agree to care for your baby boy in addition to their four children. Because your sister-in-law has a three-year-old drug conviction, however, she and your brother cannot be foster or adoptive parents, and so your son becomes a ward of the state. After the baby spends 15 consecutive months in the child welfare system, your parental rights to the baby are terminated, and the baby is placed on an adoption list. You may never see your child again.

When you leave prison, you decide to move in with your mother and your daughter, who live in subsidized housing. If you move in, however, everyone can be evicted because of your drug conviction. So you go to a women's shelter. You try to get back your old job as a nurse's aide. Because of your drug conviction, however, you're barred from the field of nursing. You figure you'll go back to college and get another degree. Because of your drug conviction, however, you're denied federal student financial aid.

Your mother falls ill and can no longer care for your daughter. You decide to apply for welfare benefits to provide for you and your daughter until you get back on your feet. Once again, because of your conviction, you're denied access to these benefits. Finally, you figure you'll register to vote so next election you can vote those stinking politicians out of office. Unfortunately you can't register to vote, and now join the ranks of over 1.4 million U.S. citizens who have completed their felony sentence yet face taxation without representation – denied the right to vote. Welcome to the revolving door of the prison-industrial complex.

George W. Bush understands the vicious circle created by these federal laws. During his 2004 State of the Union Address Bush stated "This year, some 600,000 inmates will be released from prison back into society. We know from long experience that if they can't find work, or a home, or help they are much more likely to commit a crime and return to prison." This assertion clearly demonstrates Bush's awareness that current post-conviction penalties, such as occupational licensing bans and the bar on federal financial aid for post-secondary education, are likely to compel people to crime.

Unfortunately, the current commitment to reentry concerns is limited to programs that focus on "fixing" the individuals returning to their community rather than addressing the socioeconomic conditions which led to their contact with the criminal punishment system in the first place, and are likely to lead them right back through its revolving door.

Originally published by the American Friends Service Committee

* * *

While poor people are accustomed to a police presence in their lives, for middle class citizens, the experience can be traumatic. "Marjorie" is a former Philadelphia teacher who sent me her story shortly after her release from a county prison in Missouri. She and her then partner had been traveling across the state to their home in Colorado. They had some marijuana plants in the van when they were stopped in East St. Louis. Now on parole, she says being incarcerated is something she doesn't think she'll ever recover from. Few prison officials acknowledge that most folks coming home from prison are suffering Post-Traumatic Stress Disorder.

Currently there are 700,000 arrests a year for marijuana at a cost of $4 billion. The McClellan Commission studied marijuana back during the Nixon administration, finding that it was not a gateway drug nor was it addictive, and they recommended legalizing it. Instead, Nixon had it classified in the same category as heroin. A growing number of states are voting for the use of medical marijuana, which has been found to ease pain in those with HIV, MS, and other diseases. If it were legalized, the government would save billions per year on enforcement of prohibition, which historically has never worked, as evidenced by the history of alcohol. Federal drug control has spent an estimated $217 billion to date, yet statistics show little change in America's use of marijuana. If legalized, as saner heads suggest, the government would save $7.7 billion per year and would yield tax revenues of $6.2 billion annually if taxed like tobacco.

MARJORIE'S STORY

Tom and I were pulled over at random by a drug task force one Saturday night on an Interstate outside a large Midwestern city. I am a 53-year-old, college-educated, responsible woman, and Tom, my boyfriend of nine years, was driving our van in a manner consistent with his impeccable record. Unfortunately, I had been smoking marijuana, the smell of which constitutes probable cause for a search and seizure. Our experience at the hands of the criminal justice system over the next days and months left me physically, financially and psychologically devastated. Even so, I became acutely aware that the relative advantage of my modest station in life has sustained in me a measure of hope for eventual recovery, beyond what is possible for so many who find themselves behind bars.

On that fateful evening, two hefty officers with crew cuts quickly removed two pounds of pot and ten baby plants from the van. We were then forcefully pulled out, thrown against the side of the van, handcuffed, frisked thoroughly, and asked whether or not we had any "priors." While being pushed into the back seat of the squad car, I overheard one of the cops exclaim, "Hey! There's a German Shepherd!" We were then told we would be lucky to ever see Sage again, and we wondered how she would respond to this highly stressful situation. Would she try to defend us or would she perceive that the alpha beings in this unusual predicament were the big guys and quietly go along with their program for her, whatever it was.   Fortunately, I could see that because she was so obedient and beautiful, they were charmed by her and did not have to be rough with her as they put her in a separate squad car. Tom and I however were kept at the scene for another two hours as the van was thoroughly searched, before being taken to the local station house.

Upon arrival, we were shackled to the wall for eight hours without food or water or my much needed medication. Tom and I were then placed in separate holding cells, where we were kept for five days. These cells, often shared with other people, were four feet wide and six feet long, with a one-foot wide metal shelf for sitting or lying down, and neither a toilet nor a window. The walls were cinder blocks painted brown, the floors unpainted cement. In order to use the single toilet, shared by twenty other *mostly male inmates*, or get a cup of water, you had to yell loudly for the guard's attention. About twenty feet from the cell there was a one-foot square window with bars, the only way I could tell day from night.

This place had no showers or personal washing facilities of any kind. Because I had acute diarrhea from all the shock and related stress, I was allowed to wash out my underwear. I had to beg the female officer on duty during the day for a pill from the colitis medication in my handbag. I was grateful for what she allowed me even though it was only one-third my daily dose. To me it meant that she had at least a fraction of compassion, but she wasn't allowed to give me any of my anti-depression medication. Because of my digestive illness, I drank only the water and chose to not try the packaged donut and bologna sandwich offered at breakfast and lunch. Dinner was a microwaved mystery that made me sick the one time I tried it. There was no way to exercise other than by moving your body around in that small cell space.

With time passing so slowly, the boredom became unbearable. As others from the neighborhood trickled in through the weekend for their various offenses and probation violations, each shared their story. One young black woman, taken from a candlelit and aromatic bath at her home over a probation violation, suddenly found herself locked in the dungeon cell with me. I was glad she smelled so good and was both sweet and knowledgeable as to what living conditions to expect at the next place. There was comic relief whenever the occasional drunk was brought in. One elderly drunk kept calling my cellmate "Sister-girl" and we all bantered back and forth among the three cells for entertainment.

For five days, Tom and I languished in our adjacent cells, unable to communicate with anyone on the outside. We were told we couldn't use a telephone because there were no provisions for collect calls. Local people could make calls but because we were from out of town, this wasn't possible. No cell phones were allowed because "the metal frame of the small building made them impossible to use." Since twenty hours is the legal limit someone can be held in a police station holding cell, we were incredulous to find ourselves being held so much longer. Each day I was led to believe that I, at least, would be transferred to "County" (prison). Tom, however, could be detained longer because he had outstanding warrants for parole violations related to arrests for other pot-growing enterprises long before I knew him. Those in charge simply said we had to keep waiting because of the amount of marijuana we had and the time it was taking to inventory it all!

It was a pleasant surprise when a cellmate of Tom's offered to make a local call to his girlfriend to see if she could collect-call someone for us, to let them know our predicament. Unfortunately this did not work out because no one would accept the charges for a call from a stranger.

Because of the total lack of stimulation or amusement, I fantasized from western movies someone playing blues on a harmonica, or at least a Clint Eastwood type singing the blues. Although all the next residents that came through, male and female, were black and into R&B, I could not persuade anyone to hum, croon or sing anything to make the time go. I begged and pleaded and even threatened them with having to listen to me and I am the worst!

Many of the young men were on or coming off speed or coke or some combination and needed to chill down, but I had been there long enough to be going nuts. Needing anything to take my mind off all the fear and sorrow of what was still ahead of us, I started singing everything I knew any words to. This included nursery rhymes, the first lines to old show tunes, Christmas carols and even the "Star Spangled

Banner." I could go on for hours because I had nothing else to do. Even with all that unpleasant sound coming from my cell, still no one volunteered to accompany or entertain me. Drumming on your thighs was another way to pass the time and again no one else wanted to play.

Speaking of sounds and noise, our hosts, the officers on duty, chose to kill time their own special way. There was always a videotape of something violent and bloody playing on their VCR. Our cells were only a few feet from their office area, so whatever they had on, we heard it all. If they were fighting among themselves, we heard that too. As the days and nights wore on, I found it harder and harder to get any REM sleep. I exercised in my cell on the cement floor so I could get physically tired. I hoped to get one or two hours of sleep with dreams because I'd heard that without dreams a person could go mad. Damage control was all that was left at this point. I knew I had to hold on to whatever mental clarity I had In order to get myself and Tom out of this legal disaster. Often the cement floor was easier to fall asleep on than the metal shelf and I am not sure why. My sneakers and rain jacket were all I had for a pillow and one time I dreamt that I was begging the people in my dream for anything softer to rest my head on.

Because of these difficulties in falling and staying asleep, one night I felt the need to ask if all the noise from the VCR and their very loud conversation was considered part of the punishment of keeping us from getting enough sleep. The shift officer took this a little too personally and became enraged that a prisoner would dare question the way he liked to run his jail.

He must have calmed down later and I found that the noise level was lower the remaining nights of my stay. I was grateful for the improvement and never said another word about it.

I must confess that even though I was working at keeping my sanity, the frustration of not knowing what was going to happen and when was getting to me. We were powerless to make a phone call for any kind of legal assistance or to let anyone know where we were. I figured I would never see our dog again, because the animal control person came by several times to let us know that Sage would be destroyed or given away if we did not get out to claim her in the next day or two. I feared I would not be seeing Tom again once we were finally moved to the next place, and I feared we would have to sell most of what we owned to pay our way out of all this, if it were even possible. Not being allowed my anti-depression medication added to the mounting stress I was beginning to believe I couldn't live through. How could growing and smoking a plant cause me to lose all my civil rights and human dignity? At different times and for different reasons, the other prisoners all agreed it was all too unbelievable.

Sunday turned into Monday and Monday turned into Tuesday. Finally, after midnight on Thursday, Tom's and my side-by-side cells were unlocked and we were brought out to the natural air and put in a wagon with prisoners collected from other local police stations for the trip to "County." We only hoped we'd be able to use the collect pay phones whenever we got there. At this point, we needed all the help we could get.

Spirituality plays a big part in survival logistics. Without some invisible higher power to surrender to, there is no hope or reason left to live. During the days and nights of our isolated dungeon existence, Tom and I worked on every spiritual point of view as to how to comprehend the sorry state of affairs we found ourselves in. Without any normal ways to communicate to the outside world, and all of our civil rights ignored, surrender to a higher power is all any slave or hostage has left. As we were being escorted to our next destination, many other guys came aboard on our trip to the Big House. Upon joining our trip to the next level of Hell's Glory, almost every prisoner was discussing God as he best understood Him or Her and praying for help for his family and loved ones. I felt kinship with all prisoners, hostages, slaves and Holocaust survivors, as we were all powerless to steer our own lives or see what was ahead. Prayer and trusting the compassion of the universe was the only fuel in our tanks to keep us going and we all tried to uplift each others' spirits as best we could.

We did eventually arrive at the "County" and after preliminary health screening, we were placed in the giant intake room. Public phones, toilets and bologna sandwiches were available there for the next hours or even days it would take to get your reservation for your cell on "Upstairs" floors. I noticed immediately the air freshening deodorizers set up all along the interior circular walls, set on timers to go off at different times. These were needed because almost all the newcomers had been held in holding cells for days without any opportunity to wash. Many of the men had to rely on the sandwiches for food and sleep anywhere they could as day turned to night and night turned to day. Sometimes it even took on a party atmosphere as people drifted together based on age, gang affiliation or intelligence level. Young Dead-heads came over to hear our story. Everyone there had a good one and we were no different.

Getting to use the phones made us lose our minds with euphoria and relief. We had the high priority of getting someone to retrieve Sage before it was too late. Hoping to find someone in the area who was a dog lover and a friend or relative on the outside of any of these possibly cool people, we chatted like neighbors at a rock concert. Luckily we found someone who could call his Mom. Our next priority was to get the best lawyers, in a place where we had never been before and therefore knew no one. We were able to get our closest friend on the phone, who clearly knew something was very wrong when he had not heard from us. We directed him to get the best pot lawyer in our East Coast home area and have him look up the best lawyer where we were and call them for us. Although we were not to know for some days, this was the beginning of movement towards our freedom.

To this day, I frequently flashback to this prison when I take a shower, remembering how good it was to feel clean again after spending several days in the holding cell. Because this was a modern, newly built facility, I was hoping for shower heads blending hot and cold water. But we had only a single pipe above our heads, with a single button which when pushed shot out a drizzle of very hot water to rinse under for as long as you could tolerate it. Each push of the button gave you a minute and a half. Still, it felt more like civilization than it had for days.

In my separate female pod, we had a new Commanding Officer who called all of us out of our cells to introduce herself. "I want everyone to take a shower every day and DO your hair, because when you look good, you feel good!" she explained to us. To me looking good to feel good, when all of your freedoms have been stripped away, somehow did not fit together. It was hard to feel good, when sleep was still hard to come by because these accommodations were never meant for actual comfort. Yes, compared to where we had been, we did have beds of sorts, but at my age getting up and down from the top bunk was often challenging. If my cellmate accidentally moved away from the bed the resin chair I used to climb up and down, I was never sure how I was going to get down.

Food consumption was something you did look forward to just to break the boredom. Eating spaghetti with a plastic spoon was how it went. I knew that there was very little real nutrition on these trays and so many of these girls were pregnant. They were given extra milk, canned fruit, and canned vanilla pudding. I asked one lady why there was no chocolate pudding and she said that chocolate gives you a high that is not allowed. Mealtime was limited to 15 minutes so the next part of the pod could get their turn. That included standing in line.

Frequently, all inmates ask themselves, "Why the hell do I have to be in here?" I know I did. How to make the time go is everyone's common activity. Life is so hard on the outside, but it is so empty and deadening on this "inside." Occasionally you may come across an intelligent and spiritual person to talk to, and yet it still does not ease the sensory deprivation and the deep despair that fills you despite all you thought you knew.

Wrapping this story up, I was eventually seen by a young lawyer half my age from the town's best law firm, located just a quarter block from the prison. She said she would try to get me out on bail and get my dog back by using whatever charge card and checkbook balances I had left. Because the trauma from all that I had recently been through had taken its toll, I found it hard to believe that she was real and that what she was saying made any sense.

Things were actually moving along, regardless of how powerless I was feeling. The sense of survival had to come back strong to pull the rest of this nightmare together enough to get to freedom. When she really did get me released on $60,000 bail, it was *Friday at 4:30 p.m.* She then instructed me to use my remaining credit card balance to rent a car to get back home and use my cell phone to call the dog handler to see where I could pick up Sage. The van itself was to be impounded along with all the personal belongings inside.

A month later I did get to pick my van up at an inner city auto yard, but it was so torn apart I wasn't sure it was even drivable. All our belongings were gone and I had to pay over $1,000 in accrued storage fees, because it took so long for my lawyer to get the prosecutor's office to agree to release the van to me.

As for my dog, thankfully the district's animal handler was a caring person and was considering keeping her for himself if we never could get back to him. Using my cell phone, we were able to hook up at an intersection on the Interstate and transfer the dog into my newly rented car. After thanking him with a hug and hugging my dog, I was actually free to take her and go home.

These experiences are truly etched in my mind as I now have the heart to write about them a year or so later. I most certainly know that there are people who need to be removed from society at large for violent and destructive behavior. In the prison system they rise to the top, with the power to harm other inmates and control whatever they can, but citizens who allegedly commit victimless crimes do not deserve and do not need to be punished in all the same ways. My sensitivity is much more sharpened to the unnecessary suffering and losses that the poorest people are currently forced to endure.

As I drove the rental car I was lucky enough to afford, I was feeling severely traumatized, like a tormented hostage finally released. Daylight was difficult to adjust to and it hurt my eyes. When night fell, the headlights of other cars were also hard to take. Using what was left to use on my credit, I checked into a motel so that I would be driving safer and better after a bath and some sleep. As the water ran in the tub, I had the TV on with CNN's discussion about Rush Limbaugh and his illegal possession of and addiction to the strongest painkillers. I wasn't sure I was hearing this right, but they continued for the next hour covering the details.

a year later, he enjoys having his career ınd is free to speak his opinions on the ıadıo and the internet. I, on the other hand, had to go *even* deeper in debt for lawyer fees, court costs, fines, travel expenses and the continuing probation fees each month. We had to sell everything we could sell and liquidate my retirement account. The loss of all the material things was actually easier than the emotional toll. At first I felt dead inside and couldn't even feel affection for my dog. Coming out of so much fear and stress and needing to continue to survive requires an enormous amount of strength and courage. The sweet understanding and compassion of dear friends and relatives can go a long way to help the healing begin. But if you are not focused on the need to heal, you will just spiral down to the lowest despair possible.

Months later I was watching TV when the story about Abu-Graib was leaking out. I began reliving my experiences back in the ghetto dungeon and in "County." As this story took on greater and greater worldwide attention, I learned that many of the guards that committed these atrocities were never trained by the CIA or the military to behave this way, but were prison guards from the U.S. penal system. This is where this type of inhuman cruel behavior is commonplace and always condoned as self-defense. Once an American citizen has been taken into custody, officers and guards can have a field day at the prisoner's expense. Studies have shown that given so much latitude and so much power, the average person in society will frequently succumb to the temptation of abusing other human beings!

Knowing that now, I can only accept this as a reality and no longer take whatever I went through personally. All over the world human beings in wars and in prisons show the greatest of human endurance. Maybe if we were not created with emotions and sensitivity to physical suffering, it would not be so unbearable to face this about our system but the level of punishment rarely fits the so-called crime. Civilization as a whole loses big time from not ever evolving to the next step. Stopping the endless opportunity for the average people working in these "Corrections" careers to indulge in their various levels of sadism is essential to bring on a more balanced approach to our so-called justice system. This rarely gets discussed unless it becomes a worldwide embarrassment.

Who knows what's ahead for us. We can only hope and pray that we and those we love and care about don't have to suffer unjustly as Tom and I did.

* * *

"What you deny to others will be denied to you, for the plain reason that you are always legislating for yourself; all your words and actions define the world you want to live in."

Thaddeus Golas

Chapter Two

Society's Castaways
LaChae Singletary

LaChae Singletary is an inmate at Muncy who wrote to me after reading the first edition of this book.

I was pleased and honored when Ms. Trustone asked me to participate in the second edition of *Celling America's Soul.* I didn't feel confident at first that I was the right person to represent the voices of the women here at Muncy. As I was trying to come up with a better excuse why I shouldn't participate, I remembered that in the first edition, only one person, Donetta Hill, spoke on behalf of the women at Muncy and Cambridge (the state's two prisons for females), and she was on Death Row. Although what she said was accurate, imagine what she's prevented from seeing by being isolated from the main population. And since there are now a lot more incarcerated women in the general population than there are on Death Row, I decided to write despite my insecurities about my abilities.

We women in prison are often stigmatized as prostitutes, drug addicts, and sex-crazed lesbians. Yet we share inside ourselves a greater stigma than these stereotypes, one we've so commonly come to ignore, disregarding its effects on our lives.

One out of every three females has suffered some form of childhood sexual molestation, including rape. (It's one in seven for males). It happened to me, and until two years ago I blocked the experiences out of my life. I was molested as a child and raped as an adult. I'm sure it would have stayed buried in the back of my mind forever if I hadn't been sexually assaulted by a prison doctor while he was performing an unauthorized physical examination. The first time it happened I was able to persuade myself that I must have been imagining his unwanted touches, but the second time there was no denying what happened. I felt five years old again, and this time I was unable to control the memories that woke me out of my sleep. I signed into "The House of Hope," a program that helps women in our prison deal with abuse issues. When I entered the program, I discovered that more than 80% of the women who come to prison and suffer from drug addiction or psychological disorders have been affected by childhood abuse.

It's difficult for me to explain who I was before prison without mentioning this trauma because in all actuality, that is who I still am today, 27 years later: a sexual abuse survivor. Some survivors turn their abuse into miracle stories full of extreme accomplishments, proving to themselves and to the world that they will not wear the title of victim. Then there are some who turn the anger and confusion of being violated inward on themselves, becoming their worst enemy. I guess that would be me.

On the surface I had a fairly good childhood and a loving family. When I exclude the molestation that I suffered at age five by two cousins while living in Georgia with my mother, I'd swear to you up and down that I had the ideal family and childhood. Later, I was told that my aunt knew about it, and it had been since I was one year old. (My mother wasn't at the house at the time and was unaware of what was going on until I told her about the "games" I'd played with my two cousins; games that had lasted off and on for several years until they were exposed.)

When I was five, I moved to Philadelphia to live with my grandmother, who was my surrogate mother, and her two daughters, who were more like sisters than aunts. My mother stayed in Georgia, where my grandmother originally came from. I didn't grow up in the traditional two-parent home, yet I knew that my grandmom and aunts cared for me a great deal. In my mother's absence they provided me with the basics and then some. I attended dance and etiquette schools, went to the best public schools in the city, and was exposed to all sorts of cultural activities.

We lived in a section of Philadelphia called Mt. Airy. Although not technically a suburb, it drew its prestige from its location next to Montgomery County, one of the richest counties in the country; and from nearby Chestnut Hill, an affluent neighborhood where Philadelphia's social elite resided. I lived on a block with big old trees on each side that connected in the middle, forming a canopy over our street. The neighbors took pride in their well-kept, manicured lawns and perennial rose bushes, and they made sure our block stayed clean and litter-free.

For a while I kept up a good front and was a normal child. But seemingly out of nowhere I began to rebel. I never related my rebellion to my childhood abuse until recently. When those close to me questioned my lack of motivation for school, my excessive drug use, or my obsession with the streets and criminal behavior, I had no answer. How could I form sentences out of the thousands of emotions I was feeling?

I didn't understand why people had so many high expectations of me. I had already accepted the fact that I would be a failure at anything I tried. It wasn't long before my actions were viewed as spoiled and ungrateful. But that was the furthest thing from my mind, or intent. I did love my family back then, but as I matured and began to understand more clearly the abuse I had suffered as a child, I became angry at them for not standing up for me. I wondered if the only reason they bought me nice things and treated me nicely was because of their guilt. Then, just as quickly my anger towards them turned into my own guilt; after all, they took me in when my mom couldn't take care of me. I should be grateful, I thought. The more I volleyed back and forth these conflicting feelings and thoughts, the more vivid the images of my assault would get. Not knowing how to deal with what I was going through, I ran fast and far away from those who reminded me of my past. My children were no exceptions.

My life from the age of 13 to 22 is a blur. All that really stands out is how I discovered the benefits of escaping through strangers. They were safe because they had no real connection to my past. This combined with the fast pace of the streets, and soon my obsession with material possessions blossomed. There wasn't anything that I wouldn't do to feed my exterior self, especially since this made it easy for me to be accepted by people I considered my friends. Among these distractions I found plenty of room to lose myself. No one cared enough to ask personal questions, and that was just fine with me. In the midst of all this I was able to create the image and identity of someone who had never been abused or unprotected. But if you scratched the surface of my made-up image, you would have found layers of insecurity, denial, and self-doubt.

Basically, before prison I spent a great deal of my life running away from the past instead of dealing with it. I could write in more detail about my crime, which was burglary, but that fact is a small matter in the bigger scheme of why I ended up here. Now that I've sat down long enough not to run and am forced to confront these deep issues, my eyes are open to how many more eyes are shut both inside and outside the prison.

What's prison been like for me? When I look through my kaleidoscope frames, I can see this prison from many different angles. I see a lot of hate, carefully orchestrated manipulation of authority, sorrow, pain, happiness (despite this environment), friendship, and love. I'll start off with the worst parts.

Most of us here are mothers and those who aren't still had some sort of responsibility for our families and loved ones on the outside. It is very shameful for us to be in a situation that exposes the lack of maternal instincts and responsibility as women that got us here. Once stripped of the circumstances that led us to commit the crimes that brought us to prison, reality slaps us in the face and we are forced to see our own errors in a humiliating way. Most of the guards and other prison officials, with just a few exceptions, use this information against us as a source of control. The most common technique is to abuse their authority to document petty misconducts, knowing full well that such infractions are held against us when we go up for parole, pre-release or commutation. Most of the guards, administrators, health care staff and maintenance workers are either related to each other, neighbors, or long-time friends; consequently, if an inmate has a problem with one person, she could very well have just offended everyone that person knows without realizing it.

As I read stories about what male prisoners go through and how cohesively they stick together when confronted with issues that affect male prisoners as a whole, it magnifies how passive and submissive we women are. Not necessarily because we choose to be. The administration dangles, like carrots, the few privileges we still have, daring us to utter a word of complaint. This keeps us cowering like scared dogs, leaving no room whatsoever for suggestions of change.

This happens even when it violates us as women. For example, after three male prisoners escaped from SCI Pittsburgh in 1998, a whole list of new security rules was issued for all state prisons. Here at Muncy, they took away the shades on our windows that shielded us as we got dressed or washed up. Without them we were now exposed to the male guards and other male staff who walk the interior perimeter of the campus. When we tried to get them back, the administration's response to our complaints was that we should just turn our lights out.

Before I venture into further observations and personal experiences with guards, I'd like to give credit to those officers who're called "inmate lovers" behind their backs. I wouldn't call them that. To me they are professional people who come to do a job. In the process, they see past our stereotypes and treat us not as second-class human beings, but simply as fellow human beings, period. Some of them will take the time to ask how we're doing after discovering someone in our family has passed on, or during the holidays when they know we're missing and being missed by our children. Sometimes they'll just give an encouraging smile when they notice that we seem down. They're the ones who won't write a bogus report to support a lie by a fellow guard. Or if they see that someone is sick and needs medical attention, they won't just disregard their pain and tell them to "Sign up for sick call tomorrow!" Unfortunately, these guards, along with counselors and administration staff peppered here and there, are a minority at Muncy. This shouldn't surprise anyone when you think about where this prison is located. For the majority of the staff, we're the only black and Latino people they see or have contact with except on television or in passing.

A lot of the correction officers make it obvious that they don't care for us by the derogatory remarks they make about us being women in prison. They will pick the rowdiest, most troublesome, ignorant, black or Latino inmate to compare us all to in order to validate their already negative and prejudiced views about us. They're spiteful, judgmental, and hold grudges for the slightest thing whether it's our fault or not. The behavior you would expect from an inmate is often the same behavior that they portray.

Just recently a female c/o (corrections officer) was caught having an affair with an inmate. When the guard was given a choice of being fired or retiring, she opted for the latter. It was evident that this guard bought what her hand called for by taking the same risk a lot of us took that landed us in prison. We had to pay, and so did she, but the buddies she left behind don't see it that way. They have made it their personal mission to make the entire unit where she worked pay for her mistake. They feel, in their warped minds, as though the whole unit is responsible for her getting caught. Now what sense does that make?

In contrast to the male facilities, the guards at our prison don't have any cause to be on heightened alert concerning possible violent attacks by us. You might think this would reduce the tension among them towards us. Yet it's evident that they would much rather spend their eight-hour shifts complaining about how good we have it in prison and implement the treatment *they* think we should endure. It's not enough that we're already in a position where we don't have any choice but to dwell on the mistakes that landed us here, or the fact that we're already taken away from our children and loved ones. No, we have it too good because our families send us money for commissary and TV's. We're lazy when we opt to go to school and better ourselves rather than work in one of their legalized slave jobs for 19 cents an hour. And we dare not compare the treatment of black and Hispanic inmates to white ones or we're seen as guilty of playing the race card and taking the focus off ourselves.

The prejudice is so subtle and so hard to prove that if by chance one was given the opportunity to prove her point, she's the one who would come out looking crazy and race-sensitive. It's not enough that these guards have health and retirement benefits, 401(k) plans, sick and vacation days and paid overtime, and make ten times the amount of what their G.E.D.'s and high school diplomas would have fetched them in any other position. No, they're ungrateful for the opportunity they gain for themselves and their families.

When we do file grievances against these officers and their behavior, our responses are often returned with an explanation that our accusations were frivolous and without merit. Yet, when they write us up, the hearing examiner always believes them and responds with the usual cliché response denying the lies the guards made up and saying that, "All inmate are liars and manipulators!" We get this regardless of what our past behavioral record. Some guards are honest and will admit that working at Muncy is the sweetest job in the world. These are the guards I referred to earlier who may not always like us as individuals but treat us like human beings and don't think their grey uniforms are an extension of our sentencing judges' robes.

I want to touch on one program in particular, called "Wings Of Life," an inpatient drug and alcohol treatment program. If you manage to survive it you are almost guaranteed a good recommendation for parole or pre-release, but failure to complete the program's 9-12 months of extreme rules and criteria makes it even harder to get out. Even if it's been years since you last used drugs and sometimes even if you never tried them, your name is put on its year-long waiting list. Not surprisingly, W.O.L. is highly feared. Despite evidence that supports its reputation of killing our chances to go home, the administration does nothing to alleviate the strain, probably because the state receives a grant for each inmate who enters the program. Here are a few examples of why people have been kicked out of W.O.L. If an inmate passes food that she doesn't want off her tray to another table, takes sugar off her tray out of the dining hall, refuses to tell on another inmate, or associates with inmates deemed inappropriate for her, she is in violation of their rules, which is grounds for immediate dismissal from the program.

As for the food here at Muncy, let's just say that the men are just recently getting acquainted with the Healthy Heart Program; we've been eating this way for years. This would probably explain why the Corrections Food Service Manager here at Muncy has won, for many consecutive years, an award for spending the least amount of money allotted to him each year for our food, as well as a personal incentive bonus check. He downplays this honor when confronted about the slop he serves us. If you think slop is an exaggeration, then what would you call:

spaghetti and fish sauce, last week's mixed veggies mixed with last week's broth, and last week's over-cooked noodles, i.e., this week's soup? Or the sausage patties that expired in 2002, yet are served in 2004? Then there are the turkey and beef loaves stretched with stale bread that, according to them, are always well-done despite their pinkish centers. These are just a few examples. Kitchen workers may be threatened with misconducts when they refuse to serve food that is spoiled and tainted. The only time we receive hot and half-decent meals is the week of inspections.

Several inmates approached the inspector this year and told him about all of the horrific food conditions, taking a personal risk since these inspectors are chaperoned by an administrative official who "knows all and sees all." They found out later from inmate kitchen workers that this same inspector was seen standing around lolly-gagging with the food supervisor, while only a few feet away pounds of uncovered roast beef intended for our dinner swarmed with flies, while piled on a gurney that doubles as the trash pulley.

I could go on about the medical conditions and how so many inmates die. One died just a year ago because she didn't have access to her asthma pump, which we aren't allowed to have anymore. Or about how they restrict medical treatment to long-timers and lifers because that would be wasting money since they're old and will eventually die in prison anyway. A few months ago, a doctor who had been terminating peoples' medicine left and right was escorted off the grounds after the discovery that her license had expired.

I could tell you about the "hush-hush" attitude toward sexual assaults by the male guards. Such assaults go uninvestigated until the problem is too out of hand and exposed to ignore. Then it's the female inmates who are left to defend themselves from retaliation by his peers.

There is a female Lieutenant who has been twice married to former correctional officers here at Muncy. Both of these officers had affairs with female inmates while married to her. Not only did she attack one of these women once she found out, but she was also allowed to keep her job, and has since been promoted several times. She has made no attempts to hide her dislikes for us inmates, and I am sure that her bias stems from the affairs that ended not one, but two of her marriages. It's funny how when their wrongs are publicized it's most of the time swept under the rug and we're supposed to turn a blind eye. Yet when we make a mistake, it's the biggest deal ever. Personally, and there are plenty more who agree, I think her being here is a conflict of interest. But it's obvious that the D.O.C. feels differently.

I wonder what their retaliation will be for me after they find out about this. Spiritually I believe God (Jesus) has and always will protect me and is giving me the courage to step up. Yet, realistically I am aware that this could affect my future parole/pre-release recommendations. I am really looking forward to starting my life over again and spending quality time with my sons. Yet, I feel so strongly about these conditions here at Muncy. I'm in a Catch-22 situation: speak out and possibly get treated like shit or don't speak out and possibly still get treated like shit. So I figure I might as well give them a reason.

This system is so full of contradictions that it depresses me to dwell on these subjects any longer. I can admit that I put myself here but what about those who didn't? What about the lifers who have been here since their teens, paying with the rest of their lives for a mistake they can no longer remember, and have already paid the price a thousand times over? Or what about those who would have had a better chance and a lighter sentence if they'd gotten adequate counsel? These women are not the same people they were 20 and 30 years ago! Why is it nobody else realizes this?

I've seen some things that to my conditioned mind aren't all that surprising anymore, and that scares me. People on the outside don't believe us, or don't want to, and the powers that be try their best to manipulate their power and control to magnify our wrongs and all but ignore theirs. It's very sad, and unless you build up your resistance to support yourself through these times, then you're liable to lose hope in yourself just as those who govern us have done.

I've spent more of the last eight years in jail than out. When you add the years before that when the streets were my second home, you might understand why I'm now closest with the women I've met here at Muncy. Here I have women who represent every facet of a normal family on the outside. I won't go so far as to say we get along peachy keen, because we argue, don't speak for a while, get all up in each others' business when we're not welcome, but just like all families, if we need help we know it's not too far away.

Through these women I've had the opportunity to see the fast-forward version of what my life surely will become if I continue to allow my past to dictate my future. No, not through the prison's on-paper philosophy of their mission statement, or their pseudo-reconstructive therapeutic groups. No, I've found beauty in the castaways of society, my peers. A self-made family that consists of mostly lifers and long-timers, and other women just like me who've spent their entire life fuckin' it up, yet desiring a better way of living. There are a couple of motherly types who get on my last nerve, drive me crazy and everything, yet I know their best intent is always at the root of their nagging. I have several grandmas who keep us all in check, and they are never without the time or patience to share the wisdom of what their eyes have seen, and precautions, precautions, precautions! There's plenty of aunt and sister types to go around, just like in any huge family.

Through these women, I have learned a lot about self-acceptance, gratitude, and the advantages of being able to start over, even through my rowdy, out-of-control sisters. They help me to see my own growth by watching how they go through the changes when they challenge authority, jump into unhealthy relationships and welcome negative popularity. All they're really trying to do is fill the void that can only be filled through self-acceptance. There is a message behind their actions that I can relate to; it speaks louder than their self-destructive behavior, if anyone took the time to listen. But because they are adults, they're written off as sociopaths, social riff-raff, and unredeemable. Maybe it's just unresolved hurt that's been oppressed so long that it comes out the only way it knows how.

Before my rebellious stage, I blocked out my sexual abuse with books. From *Curious George* to Judy Bloom, I would dive into these characters' lives, becoming so much a part of them that I felt I'd lost a friend when the book would come to an end. Through my fascination with books I gained a vivid and colorful imagination. Sometimes I wonder what would have happened to me if the little girl I used to be hadn't been raped of her innocence. Would I have become a famous writer or would I still have ended up in jail? I am looking forward to my second chance at freedom, though I have to say, and it may sound corny, but I'm starting to experience that kind of freedom that's not limited to one's surroundings. It gives me a lot of hope to finally come to the tip of that turning point. I have a long way to go yet, though.

I wonder if it's too late to nurture my two boys after breaking their trust so many times. Will I be able to help mold their imagination now that they're 12 and 10 years old? Or to inspire them to read, dream and make good choices, to respect women, to build their self-esteem on the knowledge of God, and to know that they are predestined for greatness despite what anyone might tell them? I pray so, and I hope I'm not too late. My oldest son has not adjusted to me not being there for him. As I write, he is sitting in a group home for violating his probation just days after receiving it. His crime, like mine, was burglary.

So I sit here in prison, my second violation, wondering if I have what it takes to break this cycle in my personal and family life. Yes, this system is unfair; they belittle us at every turn, have inhumane medical care, feed us garbage and make us work for pennies while expecting us to be responsible for our needs and pay for fines and costs? Puh-leese! This place has more contradictions than I can count, but where do I fit in this, is the question. How do I improve myself so that I can one day reach back and help my sisters left behind, mend my broken family, as well as myself? I really don't know all the answers but I do know this: It damn well won't be with the DOC's help!

Untitled
Pencil on paper   **Inez Nathaniel Walker**

Inez Nathaniel Walker was imprisoned at the Bedford Hills, NY, Correctional Facility in the early 1970's for killing a man who most likely abused her. Elizabeth Bayley, a teacher at the prison, found several of Walker's drawings on a chair in her classroom. There were 56 in all, drawn on the backs of prison newsletters and other scrap paper.

Her drawings were mostly of other inmates whom she called "The Bad Girls." Mrs. Bayley showed the drawings to a local folk art dealer who purchased many of them for exhibition. Walker had her first show in 1972; her paintings are currently in many galleries including the Smithsonian. She died in 1990 after her release from prison.

PART III
Innocence

"You must make the injustice visible."

Ghandi

Chapter One

A Portrait of Innocence
Muti Ajamu-Osagboroe
($825,000)

At 50, Muti Ajamu-Osagboro could pass for twenty. Tall, slim and athletic, with dreadlocks framing fiercely intelligent eyes that flash with humor, Muti had his life stolen from him when he was seventeen. Sentenced to life in prison for a crime he not only did not commit but attempted to dissuade the perpetrators from committing, he has faced the daily challenges of remaining a decent human in prison with compassion, discipline and integrity.

With an incompetent attorney and a Philadelphia assistant district attorney, Richard Michaelson, who was later found to be a cocaine addict and dealer, the teenager didn't have a chance at justice, especially when one of the real criminals implicated him to obtain a shorter sentence, less than 24 months, for himself. All four perpetrators have either pled guilty or confessed to the crime, exonerating Muit.

Muti has not only survived but flourished, transforming himself, despite tremendous odds, into an accomplished writer, and an award-winning artist and poet. Outspoken and honest in his quest for rights, he suffers continual harassment by guards and prison officials for speaking out.

MUTI

"I was shocked at the number of inmates who had not received adequate counsel."

Ernie Preate
Former Pennsylvania Attorney General

"I am disturbed by the sentence. It seems unfair when another youth who cooperated in the investigation was allowed to plead guilty to third degree murder and faced only a possible 10 to 20 years in prison. You were not the actual shooter," said Judge Charles L. Durham as I stood before him at age 17 and was sentenced to mandatory life in prison for second degree murder. I was accused of being a lookout in a robbery that resulted in the accidental shooting of Korean grocer Sook Ja Yu in North Philadelphia.

That feeling was the most awful I'd ever experienced in my young life. Not only had I tried unsuccessfully to dissuade the others from their deeds when I realized they were serious, I had left the store and was walking fast more than half a block away when the fatal shot was fired. At the time of my trial, I had no idea that the man who prosecuted me, ADA Richard Michaelson, would soon resign after it was learned that he was a cocaine addict and dealer with underworld ties. The DA's office has never re-investigated his cases, for to do so would no doubt leave them vulnerable to the massive civil litigation that would certainly ensue.

Because of this, I am a political prisoner.

Unlike most of my peers, I had no record, didn't do drugs and had big plans for my life. Despite growing up in the infamous Richard Allen Homes in North Philadelphia, I didn't know that as a young black male from the projects, I wasn't supposed to dream. I saw no limitations on my aspirations, no small feat in an environment notorious for crushing the goals and spirits of young people. I wanted to be part of the U.S. fencing team at the Olympics (I had already competed in the Junior Olympics). I had visions of being a professional magician (I was so serious I'd had business cards printed up).

My backup plan was to eventually take over my brother-in-law's heating oil company, Brown and Waller. He said I was gifted when it came to advertising. My sister, who ran her own successful business, told me what a good salesman I was, so I wanted to go to college to major in business with a minor in architecture, as designing buildings also fascinated me.

Unfortunately, I rarely applied myself at school because the curriculum, for the most part, was neither challenging nor relevant to the harsh realities I faced daily. I spent a lot of time making my classmates (and faculty) laugh because I always found humor in everyday dramas (though after almost twenty years in this pit of pain, my sense of humor is wearing thin). Many teachers told me I was going to be the next Richard Pryor. I loved the school atmosphere. While everyone around me rode the trolley, I was the only one in my neighborhood with a silver and blue moped. I loved the feeling of freedom. The world was mine.

Friends nicknamed me "Professor Rich Boy" because they said I was bright. Curious about a lot of things, I explored knowledge for its own sake. The "Rich Boy" part was because I would often feed them from our well-stocked refrigerator, which was a sharp contrast to their chronically empty ones. I actually believed my family was indeed rich, for the poverty I witnessed at the houses of others was brutal; the fundamental things people need to grow as human beings were missing in most of their homes.

When my mother, a divine woman, learned of my nickname, she laughed, a long, belly achin' laugh, and said, "Rich, huh? I'm going to take you to work with me so you can see money doesn't grow on trees."

At 3:00 a.m. the next morning we were standing in the dark and cold, waiting for the trolley to take us to her job as a food server at the Youth Study Center (YSC). Once we were behind the steel doors and metal gates of the juvenile detention facility, she said, "I want you to look real good at their (young detainees') faces, because if you don't listen to me, this is what you will look like and where you will wind up."

I believed her.

My mother worked hard to provide creature comforts for my eight siblings and me. My father, in and out of our lives, did what he could when he was around. With a loving family, lots of books and magazines, and always plenty to eat, the abundant life inside my home was in stark contrast to the turmoil right outside the door. Our lives were surrounded by drugs and violence. The fact that my mother was able to maintain her sanity against this backdrop makes me both appreciate and marvel at her success even more.

As I got older, I was ripe for the encouragement of a dynamic community activist, Sister Nadirah Williams, co-organizer of the Million Women March. She convinced me that not only could I help my community, I was duty-bound to give assistance wherever needed.

We organized pickets and effective demonstrations against the neglect of Richard Allen Homes by the city. Under Sister Nadirah's tutelage, I counseled children, fed them breakfast and lunch, and supervised them in arts and crafts. We went to film festivals, nature walks in Fairmount Park, trips to the zoo, the Art Museum, the Academy of Natural Sciences, and local swimming pools. We cleaned up graffiti, painted walls, put out trash cans, swept up broken glass, and planted flowers and vegetables. Our rewards were block parties with bands and cookouts and certificates of service, all of which instilled community pride.

Sister Nadirah taught me the importance of fighting for freedom and getting in touch with my African roots and identity. I legally changed my name to constantly remind me of my life mission to build a

foundation for growth centered in African culture.
Muti Ajamu-Osagboro means he who protects from harm, makes his meanings clear and who fights for what he wants. This gives my very intelligent son, who was almost two when I went to prison, a strong, positive cultural identity.

Daily pain, terror and unrelenting suffering were not supposed to be my life.

Here's what really happened that fateful day.

It was a balmy, late afternoon on January 2, 1981. I stepped into the crisp sunshine for the first time that day and went to see a friend, Pierre, who also lived in the projects. Pierre wanted to stay in, so I left, looking for the inevitable party. While I was talking to an acquaintance named Buttons, four dudes walked by that I knew from the neighborhood: Elliot, Goldie, Robinson and Thomas. Elliot was loud and talked fast, one of my competitors in school for class clown. Goldie was shy and quiet. He used to live in the apartment below us, but had moved out of the projects months before and I hadn't seen him for a while. Robinson and I were just associates. Thomas was known in the neighborhood as a hobo sort, with dirty clothes, droopy body posture and a hair full of lint. He was thought to be retarded, and it was rumored he didn't know how to read or write. His older brother had been a member of one of the biggest gangs in the area and had served time at the YSC.

Although dead on her feet from work, my mother always took time when she arrived home to share the experiences of some of the juveniles, which proved why it was important for me to stay away from drugs. She'd tell me all about dudes like Thomas' oldest brother and how I was to be careful around them because they could cause trouble in a blink of the eye.

That day, as the four walked quickly by, I called after them, asking where they were going. Thomas and Robinson ignored me, but Elliot said, "Come on, man." They were on their way to Robinson's house in another part of the projects so I went along, having nothing better to do.

Once there, Thomas pulled out some marijuana and some stuff in a brown bottle called "locker room" and they all got high. Even though everyone knew I didn't do drugs, he kept offering them to me despite my repeatedly saying no. They began to laugh and Thomas remarked that he wanted to buy my moped when they came back. Then Robinson pulled a gun out from under his pillow and gave it to Goldie. Seeing the gun was no big thing as they were common in the neighborhood. Thomas blurted out something about how they were going to get the Koreans, as if they had an inside joke. I took their words and behavior to be a mixture of drug-induced ramblings and neighborhood braggadocio. In the projects, it's called "frontin'" and you can hear similar chatter in any men's gymnasium or locker room.

I asked, "Which Koreans are you talking about and what are you going to do?" Thomas chimed in, "Just you wait and see." I thought nothing of it because Goldie not only worked for Koreans but was also good friends with some of them. Then someone said, "What time is it?" Robinson replied that it was almost 6 o'clock and time to leave.

We walked for about three blocks, and the whole time they were laughing wildly and acting very paranoid. Again, nothing unusual. At the corner of 12th and Mt. Vernon, a couple in a car near the corner called Robinson over. While they were talking, I went into the corner store for something to eat. Inside, I had to wait in line. Mr. and Mrs. Yu, the owners, were at the front of the store. They were both nice people.

While I waited, Thomas, Elliot and Goldie came into the store. One suddenly had a hood on and another had his collar turned up. The three were crouching as if trying to disguise themselves. Like a lightning bolt it hit me that the Koreans Thomas had referred to earlier were these particular people and the time was now! More shocked than scared, I immediately let them know that what they were about to do was wrong. They stared ahead blankly and didn't even acknowledge me. I told them I was leaving and wanted nothing to do with them or their robbery.

Outside, Robinson was still talking to the girl in the car. I turned back toward the projects and started walking fast, wanting to get as far away from them as I possibly could. When I was about half a block away, I heard what sounded like a gunshot, and I started to run, totally shaken. Once I got home at around 6:15 p.m., I stayed in for the rest of the night. I discussed what had happened with no one.

A couple of days later, Goldie came to my house, scared and shaking. Surprised, I asked him what had happened. He said the Korean woman was dead, which was the first I'd heard that someone had died. When I asked him if he'd shot her, he replied that she had hit the handle of the gun and it had accidentally gone off. He asked me what he should do and I told him he had to decide. About a week later, I saw his picture in the Philadelphia Daily News. Accompanied by his mother, he had surrendered to Daily News columnist Chuck Stone and another reporter, Linn Washington (frequently a guest columnist for the Philadelphia Tribune). Goldie had confessed his crime to both reporters. Nothing in the police report mentioned any involvement by me. (Robinson just recently confessed from prison to a reporter as well.)

On May 5, 1981, detectives called my house and told my mother they wanted to question me in the shooting death of Mrs. Sook Ja Yu. When my mother, two sisters and I arrived at the Police Administration Building (the Roundhouse) so I could be questioned, my mother told the police they couldn't question me without an attorney present. They immediately arrested me and charged me with conspiracy and homicide robbery. In my mother's (and my) worst nightmare, I was sent to the Youth Study Center. Robinson and Goldie had already been there for four months. I was arraigned, given a preliminary hearing and sent to trial. Thomas had implicated me in the crime as a lookout man.

My "trial" was a travesty. Prosecutor Michaelson not only broke several laws but he also violated my constitutional rights in order to get a conviction.

"Assistant District Attorney Richard Michaelson has been suspended without pay from the D.A.'s office pending an investigation by the U.S. Attorney's Office and the F.B.I. into allegation of possible wrongdoing...Sources said that federal officials are investigating Michaelson's involvement in a narcotics case and possibly in drug trafficking."

Philadelphia Daily News, May 27, 1982

"(mob) Drug dealer turned F.B.I. informant Ronald Raiton has told federal investigators that he sold a large quantity of cocaine to Assistant District Attorney, Richard Michaelson, on a Caribbean island...Michaelson resigned Thursday. The Daily News has learned the DA's office conducted an internal investigation of Michaelson in 1979, after he appeared at least twice as a spectator at the Municipal Court trial for (Joseph N.) Disantis, Jr. (mobster) and was seen talking to him."

Philadelphia Daily News, May 29, 1982

Michaelson got Thomas to give false testimony against me to the trial judge Charles L. Durham (now deceased). Thomas testified that the DA's office never promised him anything in exchange for his testimony against me. Actually Michaelson promised and delivered to Thomas: employment, time served, release on bail, warrants from a previous conviction lifted, no penalty for previous violations of probation and suppression of his previous criminal record. He was told he would be home by Christmas if he didn't mention the deal to the judge. In exchange for his false testimony that caused me to be sent away for life without any possibility of parole, the reward he got from Michaelson was less than 24 months for a homicide-robbery he admitted he'd planned.

Judge Durham never learned about the criminal actions of the prosecutor. Had he known, his growing suspicion of the relationship between Thomas and the prosecutor would have compelled him to drop all charges against me. To make matters worse, the prosecutor allowed Thomas to give false testimony about the planning of the robbery, telling the judge the plan was hatched at Goldie's house in Richard Allen on the same day as the crime. Michaelson knew the conspiratorial conversation never took place as Goldie had moved out of that house at least six months earlier. According to the law, by creating my involvement in a conspiracy where none existed, this made me subject to everything that happened after the fact, the robbery-homicide.

My court-appointed attorney, Arlan Mintz Kardon, was grossly incompetent and inexperienced in homicide criminal defense law. She allowed the prosecutor to trample any constitutional rights I had. She coerced me to take the stand in my own defense, and the prosecutor, with deceitful and knowingly false questions, got me confused and I incriminated myself before I knew what was happening. He drew inferences where none existed. My seventeen-year-old naiveté was no match for the raw and well-seasoned misconduct of the prosecutor.

Unbelievably, Ms. Mintz didn't perform basic legal procedures such as researching, investigating and interviewing known witnesses who would have totally refuted Thomas' testimony and the entire basis of the Commonwealth's case. In spite of my lawyer's incompetence and Thomas' perjury, it was the unchecked power by prosecutor Michaelson that put me, an innocent man, in prison for life, and gave Thomas, the real criminal, his freedom after 24 months.

To see how prosecutors in Philadelphia routinely circumvent and break the law, consider former Assistant District Attorney Jack McMahon's instructions to new prosecutors about how to select a jury in a training tape entitled, "Prosecutorial Instructional Training Tape." McMahon, now in private practice, after making several racist remarks about black people and how to keep them from sitting on juries in homicide cases says, "Let's face it, there's blacks from low-income areas...you don't want those people on juries; in selecting blacks, you don't want the real educated ones..." He concludes, "The law says the object of getting a jury is to get a competent, fair and impartial jury. Well, that's ridiculous. You're not trying to get that. You are there to win...the only way you're going to do your best is to get jurors that are unfair and more likely to convict than anybody else in that room."

If prosecutors would break the law to deny the constitutional rights of black, tax-paying, educated citizens who've not been accused of any crime, how many laws will they break to deny the rights of black defendants waiting to be tried? The answer is, they will break as many laws as necessary to get a conviction . . . justice be damned!

Judge Durham, in a non-jury trial, after hearing only part of the evidence, found me guilty of conspiracy, robbery and second degree murder and then sentenced me to LIFE. He said, "I want the record to reflect that if I had any discretion in this case as far as the sentencing, it would not be one that the statute provides for. I want that on the record because I think his part in the conspiracy doesn't warrant the type of sentence the law says is mandatory."

After my sentencing, my world shrank to a 13 ½' by 5' by 8' cage, which is smaller than most bathrooms. I couldn't have gotten through those early days without the continuous support of my family, especially my beloved sister, Rosalyn, whose visits both comforted and strengthened me.

I began to study law, completed my G.E.D., studied electronics and learned how to tutor the illiterate. I developed an Afrikan-centered curriculum for the literacy program to make it more relevant to the students. I earned an associates degree in business administration and accounting and additional college credits. (A lot of these educational opportunities have been discontinued so politicians can prove they're tough on crime.) As chairman of the Graterford branch of the NAACP's Press and Publicity Committee, I learned how the media does not seem interested in listening to the voices of the suffering.

Muti's beloved sister, Rosalyn Payne

My quest to undo the damage done by my attorney and the District Attorney turned me inward. I began a spiritual journey to learn who I was and what my life's mission could be under these circumstances. My independent studies enabled me to tap into my spirituality, which gave focus to my strength and allowed me to better comprehend why and how this was happening.

New vistas opened to me as I began to connect with new possibilities. Beautiful things began to awaken and pour out of me, parts of me I thought had been killed in that courtroom. I became a teacher and started helping prisoners learn the law, to read (a problem for more than half of the imprisoned), to get a job in order to make parole, etc. I discovered a talent for writing and have created songs, plays, essays, books and poetry. When I started drawing and painting, the creative process was cathartic. I was amazed when I entered my work in several art exhibits and people from all walks of life responded enthusiastically. My work was part of four exhibits in Philadelphia, one at the infamous Eastern State Penitentiary in Philadelphia, now a historical site where horror movies are made. One of my art instructors was Philadelphia's nationally-recognized treasure, Lily Yeh. Another is Kevin O'Neill of the Painted Bride Art Center.

As I devoted my energies to my studies and to helping others, I began to mend the emotional wounds of being imprisoned for something I did not do. It requires strong vigilance to remove the daily, psychological shrapnel that the prison constantly hurls at me; I'm convinced I have Divine protection.

While I was doing my best to blossom without sunshine or spring rain, my sister Rosalyn hired a series of attorneys who were glad to take her hard-earned money without filing a single petition on my behalf. None of them had the courage or integrity to challenge the District Attorney's office.

Acting as my own attorney, I filed a Post Conviction Relief Act (PCRA) petition after receiving a package from a federal investigator with proof of my innocence. My petition was "dismissed pending appeal" in February, 2001. I also have two additional petitions pending in the PA State Superior Court. Proof of my innocence is in the cumbersome wheels of justice. I'd feel more confident if I could afford a lawyer I could trust to oversee my petition's progress through the courts.

I see myself becoming free, very soon. Once people learn what is really going on in courtrooms, my unjust sentence cannot stand up under fair, legal scrutiny. When I was first imprisoned, I promised myself I would keep four things: my desire to learn and grow, my sanity, my manhood, and my love for my people. Because of the support I've received these four qualities are not only intact but have grown in ways I could never have imagined.

Once I'm free, the first thing I want to do is visit my father's and mother's graves. They've both died since I've been in this house of horrors, and the PA Department of Corrections would not permit me to go to either of their funerals.

I look forward to simple things, like going to the refrigerator when I want a snack, swimming and biking. I want to take long, luxurious baths. I want to explore landscape painting, and work on my books. I want to do what I can to help my community, especially the young people, who are so confused. I want to smell freshly-cut grass as I picnic in the park or go hiking in the woods.

Most of all, I want to be free to enjoy life like a man is supposed to.

(In 2007, Muti continues to fight for his freedom from Houtzdale, a rural Pennsylvania prison many miles from his family and supporters, where he was recently put in the Hole for 45 days for using his legal name.)

"It is one of the most beautiful compensations of life that no man can sincerely try to help another without helping himself."

Ralph Waldo Emerson

"Defacto criminalization of black manhood under the guise of a tough-on-crime pose, means we have built the foundation of a world without African-American men. We've become used to throwing away these men's lives without making even the first effort

at redemption. We've come to see it as normal, part of black men's reality."

Leonard Pitts

Chapter Two

Will DNA Testing Set Him Free?
Robert "Muhkam" Hagood
($1,175,000)

"A thing of beauty may be consciously realized as a result of distinguishing one's self from the perceived ugly within the environment of one's captivity and isolation."

Robert "Muhkam" Hagood

Robert "Muhkam" Hagood was convicted of a crime for which he claimed innocence, saying he never had any physical contact with the victim, who was a stranger to him. As with Muti and Anton, who were sentenced to life based on the word of just one person, It was only the testimony of a prostitute – who may have been the real murderer – that put him in prison for life. His case was explored and then denied by the Innocence Project. He passed into Spirit several years ago, ill and his spirit broken.

In his more than forty years behind bars he became a poet, considered by some one of the best poets in Pennsylvania. A quiet, deeply religious man, he had little contact with the outside world since his beloved wife died five years ago.

His is a love story, a tale of deprivation and the power of love to transform.

Papering his cell walls with photographs of flowers and nature, he said he had "the most beautiful garden at Graterford." With help from Muti, he was waiting for the Pennsylvania legislature to pass a law paying for DNA testing. Then he'd file a petition to secure the test which could prove his innocence – if the evidence is still available. According to the New York-based Innocence Project, by 2003 DNA testing had proven 115 people were sent to prison for crimes they did not commit. In almost half of the exonerations, local prosecutors refused to release crime evidence for DNA testing until litigation was threatened or filed. For an innocent person like Muhkam, the hope of getting access to the evidence for testing was a crap shoot, dependent on the whims of the state, the county, the judge or a clerk.

In our class exercise to find beauty behind prison walls, Muhkam wrote about a picture of school children in Ghana he'd been given by Queen Nana Ama Akoffo, co-founder of the Pan African Studies Community Education Program at Temple University in Philadelphia and one of two elderly women who are now his only visitors.

Beauty

There were fifty ivory smiles
One hundred sparkling brown eyes,
Faces not unlike any I've seen before,
In fact, quite alike.
There was nothing unlike the starched white shirts
And navy blue trousers of any parochial school in the
states.
Perhaps it was all imagery, imagination, illusion or
delusion.
Still, I found the photo Queen Nana sent me
Of her adopted children of Akyim Hemang village
In Ghana, West Africa, to be the most beautiful…
Beautiful African boys and girls thirsting for
knowledge.
Beautiful Children of the Future…
Precious jewels of my eyes.

He wrote to me the following week:

After you typed it, I looked it over in my cell and decided that with some light touches it was worthwhile. I sent a copy to Queen Nana and, to my surprise, a joyous thing happened. At the time, the chief of her tribe, Dr. Apori, was in Philadelphia, participating in the Pan African Studies Community Education Project at Temple University. She read him my poem and he loved it so much he asked to take it back to Africa to be read to the children that were in the picture that had reminded me of beauty.

* * *

MUHKAM

I remember as if it was yesterday the judge, saying, "I sentence you to a state correctional institution for the rest of your life." In that moment back in April 1973, I remember thinking, this is unreal. I can't believe someone is taking my life away for something I didn't do. I knew that I hadn't killed anyone, but no one else seemed to realize it. I had come up on the streets and had been involved with a lot of petty criminal activity. Still, I was naïve enough to believe that when it came down to a life sentence, if you didn't do it, you wouldn't be convicted. I felt that this couldn't be happening.

I grew up in Passaic, New Jersey. My earliest childhood memory is that darn table that I was always trying to get away from. Mom tells me that I can't remember that far back, but I do. Mom considered me to be a wanderer. She had a little harness that she placed around me that connected to the leg of the kitchen table. She'd hook me up whenever she had work to do. I seemed to be in a constant struggle with that table, trying to get away from the weight. Looking back, that seemed to be some kind of a sign that as I struggled through life, I was going to have to carry a lot of weight on my back.

There's not a lot I can tell you about Pop, Lemmie John Haygood. He was in and out of our lives until Mom made her final decision that enough is enough!

My father was an orphan from Barbados who had been adopted by an American woman who wanted a companion for her son. Mom and Pop met at a dance when he was working for the Civilian Conservation Corps. When I was in third grade, I convinced everyone in the family to drop the "y" from our name because I thought it looked better. I remember Pop looking across the table at me with his large, very dark face. His teeth were as white as the keys on a new piano. He parted his wavy hair in the center and he was clean-shaven except for a thin moustache. Short and wide, he had the muscles and forearms of a bodybuilder, and his stomach was flat even after he was 50.

As I waited for his reaction to my wanting the name change, he suddenly smiled and looked over at my mother and said, "You teach my son to read and write before he can wipe his ass, and now he thinks he's a genius." He used to brag to his friends about how well I could read and write, and sometimes in the morning his friends would come by and I'd read the help wanted ads for them, marking places that needed their skills. As a child, I thought they did this for luck, but years later I realized that Pop and his "no good friends," as Mom called them, hadn't learned to read.

Once a promising student, my teachers wouldn't tolerate my errant behavior, and until I finished my education at Graterford, I was almost as ignorant as my father and his friends.

Looking back, I see he was never abusive to me and my sisters, but he and Mom just couldn't get along. I don't know why. Pop died on New Year's Eve in 1974. He'd slipped on ice and was injured, and he later had a stroke. I was already incarcerated when this occurred; I got the message from the chaplain. I was not allowed to attend his funeral. I recall sitting in my cell just saying over and over, "Damn, Pop, Damn!"

As an adult, I lived in Harlem. I was traveling through Pennsylvania when I was arrested. I'm still trying to get through Pennsylvania…

In reflecting on my life, I feel shame for the man I was then.

I was the oldest of five children of a single mother who was hard-working and would do any honest work with dignity and pride, encouraging her children to do the same. Still, I had no dreams or aspirations other than what could satisfy my immediate selfish desires. I had no bonds with anyone, male or female, that were not connected to my needs or personal gain. I took advice from no one and only punishment deterred me. I had no goals. I remember in grade school, teachers would ask the class what we wanted to be when we grew up. I didn't think I was going to be anything. I had no vision of anything good coming out of my environment or my life, so I never had any plans or false dreams.

Some of the children would say they wanted to be firemen, or doctors, or cops. I just wanted to be. If I existed today and survived, then maybe I'll exist tomorrow. Every day was survival time. No one put me on TV, but I was a survivor and that was it.

I couldn't point to a single person as a role model and I didn't want to. My environment suggested that if I wanted to survive, I had to be a certain way despite evidence around me that people were doing a lot more than surviving. Because of the limitations I'd placed on myself by not daring to have a dream beyond that microcosmic world, I became what I was.

I was a criminal in my mind and in my deeds. I felt that any action (other than hard work) that led to my survival or enjoyment showed my courage and intelligence, and that made me worthy of respect. The fact is that I had never experienced love or respect until I met and married Doris Dean Hagood, my first and only love, the woman I married sixteen years after my arrest and conviction. I'll talk about that in a minute.

The reason I could be accused and convicted of a crime I did not commit was because of my criminal mentality and actions. Because of my brutish behavior, my academic and social ignorance, it was not unlikely that someone could eventually be killed by me. It wasn't beyond me, and most people on the street considered me quite capable of just that. But I have never killed; I never wanted to kill anyone. Yet I've been falsely accused and literally lynched for the murder of a white man I'd never known.

I've been in prison now more than 30 years, costing the state more than $1 million. I spent the first ten years bouncing my head off the concrete wall, thinking my rebelliousness was going to alter my situation. I thought that by striking out, kicking, screaming, growling and putting myself in more unwholesome situations, things would change.

My cries of innocence fell on deaf ears, my countless attempts at appeals failed, and for years I wallowed in disappointment and self-pity.

During the years of my imprisonment certain events that occurred or facts that were made evident at my trial have come to mind. Some of these occurrences may seem unbelievable to those outside of my experience; however, one truth should be evident, and that is, I am innocent and the activities of all involved denied me the right to a fair trial.

THE KNIFE:

During the trial, the detective told the court that the alleged murder weapon was given to him by his captain. Also, that the captain told him that a forensic check was not necessary because the weapon had been handled too much. Question: BY WHOM? Unanswered.

The detective continued to say that the captain told him that he had been directed to the weapon by an anonymous caller.

:

Questions

(A) Why did the captain go alone to a secluded area to pick up this weapon that he was directed to by the anonymous caller?

(B) Who else did the captain know had handled the weapon besides himself and perpetrator?

(C) Why were there not photographers and a forensic team present when the captain retrieved this weapon that he believed was the cause of a homicide?

(D) Who was the anonymous caller?

(E) Was there a caller at all? If there was not an anonymous caller, did I receive a fair trial? Linda Lane, an admitted prostitute and drug addict, and the state's star witness, testified that she pulled the knife out of the victim's body and threw the weapon into an abandoned building. Also, that she did not recall which building. She denied making the anonymous call or that she had told anyone where she had thrown the knife. However, Linda Lane identified the knife as the murder weapon for the state.

The captain was never called to the court by the prosecutor or trial counsel to explain his behavior, unusual in a homicide case. The trial judge, the prosecutor and trial attorney each acted in a concerted manner to deny me a fair trial. By not forcing the captain to take the witness stand, my conviction was the result of conjecture rather than one proven by evidence.

Since others have been found innocent based upon DNA evidence that did not exist at the time of their trial, and both the state and the state's star witness alleged that I was in an altercation (physical fight) with the victim and stabbed him with a knife, that testimony is at least suspect if not tainted. I know that DNA evidence from the clothing and person of the victim as well as DNA evidence from myself will prove that I am innocent of the crime for which the trial judge, prosecutor and trial attorney have caused me to spend thirty years of my life in prison.

I need people to help raise funds and to represent me in the courts and to demand that I be given an opportunity to prove my innocence through DNA testing.

In and out of The Hole, I was fortunate enough one day to sit down and for the first time begin to reflect on my situation.

The process of change started then. I decided the way I was wasn't working for me, and I started thinking seriously about my wasted life and why I thought that was the only way to be. As I pondered God and Satan, life and death, good and evil, heaven and hell, I decided to change. I'd rather serve in heaven than rule in hell. That is still my choice today.

Sometimes a seed of transformation has been planted in the soil of the mind that you're not aware of until it manifests in the future. In December 1984, after spending a year in The Hole at Huntingdon for "leading a protest" against the beatings and horrible food, I was transferred to Graterford and attended a Kwanza celebration. The program concluded with men and women guests greeting each other. I was still a little paranoid about crowds of people, so when I saw the crowd of large men standing like trees around a small, cute brown woman, I watched from a chair while my heart tried to leap out of my chest. She had a pleasant smile for all who greeted her and an occasional dimple would appear on soft cheeks. As I watched her slowly walk out the door, I promised myself that the next year I was going to meet this wonderful lady.

By the next year, as a result of my involvement with cultural activities in the institution, I was the host for the Kwanza program. I also read with drama one of my poems about the 1985 Move tragedy in Philadelphia. The inmates and outside visitors roared their approval.

I sat behind the podium after introducing the next performer and heard this sweet voice sing into my ears, "That was a beautiful poem, brother." I responded, "But not as beautiful as the lady in my presence." It was Doris, the woman of my dreams. We smiled and chatted easily, and I was taken aback when she declined my invitation to write, something she'd already said to others with the same proposal. As we walked down the corridor after the celebration, her hand brushed mine and, without a word, we walked with our hands linked, unaware of the stares of visitors and prisoners. When we reached the security bubble, she turned and told me she was going to give me a chance to write to her. "I'll write tonight, pretty lady." And I did.

I don't remember what I wrote, but I remember vowing that I would never lie to her about who I'd been or what I'd done. I answered her questions with an honesty of which I didn't know I was capable. She came to visit often, arriving at 9 am and not leaving until the mandatory 3 pm. When I told her about my case, she trembled in my arms and tears streamed down her face. My heart quickened and I stopped talking and just held her gently, her cheek on my chest. This was during the time when men and women could still embrace each other in the visitors' room; now there is no touching or the guards can terminate the visit. Doris looked up at me, told me she believed in my innocence that she would do whatever she could to help me. I didn't know a happier day except for the day she told me she loved me and would be pleased to be my wife.

We were married in the visitors' room in 1990 in the presence of her son, two of her three daughters, her granddaughter and her two closest friends, Annie Hyman and Queen Nana, co-founders of the Pan African Studies Community Education Project. Both of these wonderful women have remained close friends to me even though Doris died of a brain aneurysm on June 28, 1997. Because of their age, they don't visit often, but were it not for these occasional visits I would probably have none at all.

My mother is also elderly, residing in Shelby, NC. I'll never forget the wonderful surprise that Doris and my mother gave me back in the summer of '93.

My mother flew alone for the first time from NC and spent a week with Doris. We're only allowed four visits a month, so Mom visited me three days in a row and saved the last visit so Doris and I could have time alone. When I went to the visitors' room that morning and saw the two women I loved with all my heart and soul walking down those steps, I released all the energies of love, joy and excitement that could flow from what my wife called my "romantic soul." No, I never loved a woman with the depth of integrity, with the commitment, trust and caring that I reserved for Doris.

After our marriage, it seemed that my attitudes, my way of thinking and my behavior changed. I became much more tolerant of others and I was suddenly participating in every possible program in the prison. I got my associates degree and helped others learn.

I've never known a greater love than that which flowed so freely and abundantly from the heart of this magnificent lady, the wonderful woman and my wife, Doris Bridges Dean Hagood.

I haven't seen my mother since then.

I've transformed myself from a 34-year-old man with an eighth grade education capable of doing only third grade math to one who got a "C" in Algebra from Northampton Community College. I have 86 college credits and an associates degree in business management. I have more than five years experience teaching or tutoring other prisoners wanting to pass their G.E.D. tests. I've been President of the

Pennsylvania Lifers Association at Huntingdon Prison, the first President of the Board of the Graterford branch of the NAACP, the founder of a group called "Students of Cultural Arts," chairman of the Lifers Cultural Affairs Committee, a team leader with the "End Violence" program, and a facilitator for the People Against Recidivism program (PAR), which helps young prisoners stay out of prison once they're released. As a poet and artist, I've been involved with making a documentary in conjunction with Kevin O'Neill and the Painted Bride Arts Center in Philadelphia. Presently I'm a peer assistant for the Institution's Community Orientation/Reintegration Program (COR) where I teach resumé writing, cover letters, etc. for prisoners going out on parole.

Equally important is that I have become a man of faith. I think a lot about what it means to be human on this planet. My faith is a major factor in my daily life. While I've forgiven myself for being the man I was, I pray seriously to be forgiven by any people I've harmed, hoping that if they are in a state of prayer, they will forgive me.

There are trillions of incidents and accidents that occur in life that you don't have anything to do with, but they impact on your life nonetheless. I may be in my cell maybe eight or nine hours, studying the Qu'ran or trying to work out the rhythm of a poem. If I decide I want to go down the block to talk with a friend, I'm awakened to another reality because maybe my cell is double-locked. The block of 500 men is shut down, maybe the whole prison. Something has happened that has impacted on me that I had nothing to do with.

This can happen at any time, day or night. In this environment by the time you walk out of your cell to shower you will meet at least 50 dudes who will get you more time, any time, whether you like it or not. Because these incidents have a way of forcing themselves on you, there are limited alternatives: you deal with it or you run away from it. Running away can have greater disadvantages in a prison situation; whoever you run from, you will eventually have to face them. If you're a man like me, struggling to be free, you must deal with what's in front of you, like it or not. Even though you've changed as a human being, your guilt or innocence doesn't matter. What matters is surviving what is right in your face. Because someone has gone crazy and is on a mission to destroy themselves, they bring their misery into my life and I'm compelled to restrain them. Meanwhile guards are watching to see how I deal with whatever I'm faced with. This can happen at any time. I pray every day that I can avoid this kind of situation. I don't want to test that!

Aside from my writing and reciting my poems, when I'm free I envision myself telling people about the disparities in the criminal justice system and what can occur when police officers and prosecutors abuse their offices in order to gain political power. I want to talk about how cultural biases and prejudices of both judges and juries impact on verdicts despite evidence or lack of evidence. Close to my heart is the vision of speaking to children in the poorest neighborhoods and public schools about not only the importance of education, but the greater importance of not allowing the violence and corruption in their environment to become entrapped their minds and hearts. Also, I'd tell them that as they struggle against crime, violence and corruption with their minds and hearts, they will be empowered to rise above it and create a better life for themselves.

The Circle of Oppression

The circle of oppression is wide and we are all inside being screwed in the same vise.

Lest anyone misunderstand.

I am unaware of the Arab marauders and the European pirate exploiters who kidnapped and murdered millions of African men, women, and children and distorted the pure beauty of Kemetic civilization while they pillaged and occupied the land...

Still, if the issue was as non-complex as skins being black or white, Mother Earth would have long ago cleared and freed herself of the pale savage blight.

The circle of oppression is wide and we are all inside... The injustice that touches me touches you...

The injustice that touches you... touches me!

Through a video lens, the "beast" observes the shanty towns of the downtrodden.

Their night-crawling prostitutes, drug abusers, street sleepers; alley creepers and long lines of unemployed standing in front of overcrowded prison houses...

He sees what he alludes to be "The white man's burden." A sarcasm! A lie that he imagines to be subtlety.

The injustice that touches me touches you...

The injustice that touches you... touches me!

In the catacombs of society, prisons house captives made wise by the experience of being gnawed in the crunching iron jaws of the beast, and who has seen with minds of crystal light, the beast's giant claws dripping, dripping, with the blood of the slaughtered oppressed who cry out their admonishment with pleas for solidarity -- their voices unheard -- in the blowing of the wind.

The circle of oppression is wide and we are all inside... The injustice that touches me touches you...

The injustice that touches you... touches me!

Within the circle of oppression, minds attracted to the glare of computer windows believe that their new house in town has made them separate, different from those who stare at conveyor belt where they twist one and tap twice, but we are all being screwed in the same vise.

The circle of oppression is wide and we are all inside...

Robert "Muhkam" Hagood

Postscript

DNA Evidence Exposes System's Flaws

William DiMascio
Former Executive Director, Pennsylvania Prison Society

Prosecutors' quests to win disregard the damage done to innocent individuals. New evidence by DNA testing has fueled a watershed development in forensic science. Its certainty in identifying people makes fingerprinting look like guesswork. The odds against DNA mismatches are said to be in the realm of a quadrillion to one.

In recognition of this powerful tool, Pennsylvania is one of many states to pass laws regulating its use in the criminal justice system. Despite some early squabbles, the law that was finally passed has been roundly applauded by defense attorneys and people they represent, as well as prosecutors and tough-on-crime politicians.

Ironically, however, the most profound benefit of DNA technology may have less to do with making sure the "right" people get convicted and more to do with highlighting the substantial flaws in our current system.

Police and prosecutorial misconduct are among the most frequent factors in wrongful convictions, according to the Innocence Project, which has championed the use of DNA evidence. These acts – not accidents or errors of judgment – include suppression and destruction of evidence that might be helpful to defendants, fabrication of evidence, coercion of witnesses and confessions, and other deliberate misdeeds.

The quest of courtroom "wins" has cut a putrid path littered with 115 wrongful convictions that have been overturned by DNA evidence so far. Each of these incidents represented a tremendous waste of public funds, as well as the far more costly erosion of human lives. Prosecutors and others are fond of currying favor among the masses by bold talk of making criminals take responsibility for their actions. Who now will take responsibility for the loss of years suffered by the 115 we know about?

These wrongfully convicted individuals served an average of more than ten years for each of them. (Cost to taxpayers: approximately $40,250,000.)

Former Montgomery County's (PA) District Attorney, Bruce Castor, did his best to deny DNA testing for inmate Bruce Godschalk, who served 15 years on a double-rape conviction. (Cost to taxpayers: $525,000.) His attorneys had to get a federal court order before Castor would provide access to DNA evidence. After two independent comparisons of the evidence, Godschalk was released. Castor was still unwilling to accept the facts and only grudgingly conceded to the news media that he didn't believe Godschalk was innocent, just that he couldn't be proved guilty.

"Prosecutors don't want to admit to any mistakes – past, present or future," said Ray Krone, who spent three years on Death Row, then seven more under a life sentence in Arizona ($350,000) before DNA analysis showed he was innocent of the murder, kidnapping and sexual assault of which he was convicted.

"DNA is going to be the undoing of them if they don't start doing a better job in the courtroom. It's a good sign that some prosecutors are willing to act in good faith."

In a way, DNA is laying bare the sins of a system that is often too adversarial, with reckless disregard for the damage done to innocent individuals. Now it is time for an informed citizenry to demand a higher level of accountability from the people who are paid to see that true justice is being served.

"There is nothing training cannot do. Nothing is above its reach. It can turn bad morals to good; it can destroy bad principles and recreate good ones; it can lift men to angelship."

Mark Twain

Chapter Three

Did He Ever Have a Chance?
Tony Harper
($965,000)

Tony Harper was born with his feet on backwards. His early life was one surgery after another. Like several of the other prisoners, he's been in prison for over 30 years for a crime he did not commit. Tony dropped out of high school at sixteen because he was so far behind due to illness. Most of his childhood and early teenage years were spent in hospitals and rehab centers for a disease that "made his bones soft." As a young child, he was once in a body cast for four months.

When he was interrogated by the police for a robbery-homicide possibly committed by his almost identical-looking brother, Tony was beaten so badly that his injuries put him in the hospital for three weeks. His brother was later killed in a drive-by shooting.

One of the beginning writers in the class, Tony, who could only write his name when he was first sentenced, shows promise. He is intelligent, has an excellent eye for detail and is a curious and sensitive soul. Once, while waiting to be escorted out by guards after class, I noticed him sitting alone in a corner. When I sat down on the floor next to him to discuss his work, he seemed surprised. And pleased.

We made a strong connection.

His work was confiscated by guards during one of my interrogations that led to my resignation, and he became afraid to write, saying in a letter:

"I was disappointed to learn you resigned as our writing teacher, though as I looked at the situation and the way the guards treated you, I can understand why you had to step away from this place. The people who run this place are not nice. You are awesome because you came into these conditions to spread some much-needed light. I congratulate you for staying as long as you've done without doing emotional harm to yourself. I do understand.

Since this happened to us, I have not written a word. I felt violated to the point of being scared. I just wanted to thank you for the encouragement. You have allowed me to shine."

A year later, after steady correspondence, his spirit was again strong as he wrote,

"The only thing I have left in this life is my voice, and I won't allow anybody to stop it no matter what. The state only has my body; my mind is my own. The way things stand, I may never get out of prison. Do you really think I will let them take any more than they already have from me? I fight for whatever rights I have based on my values, not theirs."

Tony suffers from Hepatitis C, diabetes, a weakness in his bones and a strange lung disease that interferes with his breathing. He is harassed by guards when his feet swell so badly he can't put on shoes and instead wears sandals, which they claim is against regulations.

During a recent trip outside for medical treatment, his first time outside prison walls in 25 years, Tony was so sick he slept most of the trip there and back, barely noticing all of the changes.

Tony's aging father, a World War II hero, and his family are his constant supporters. His father, 88, says he knows his son is not guilty because the police know who did the killing. "My son is innocent and I'll spend my whole life trying to get him free!"

* * *

"The mind, once enlightened, cannot again become dark."

Thomas Paine

TONY

I was born Tony Ricardo Harper on October 31, 1958. My parents had ten children, four girls and six boys. Most of them have passed away since I've been incarcerated, the biggest blows of my life. My grief was low-key, for people in here who can't keep their emotions in check aren't looked at kindly. My younger years were full of nothing but turmoil. For me, every sight and sound was a source of wonder, and I had a thirst for learning what this world was about, even its underbelly.

I'll never forget a church trip to Canada when I was thirteen, my first exposure to people of all colors. I recall being amazed at the streets uncluttered with trash and the way the people related to each other. I promised myself I'd one day revisit this land. My father, who'd seen the world during WWII, wanted his children to see and experience the true beauty of different places and different people.

When my sister, Jerry, died during childbirth, it seemed to do something to my parents. It was like something dark was hanging over the house; it was so bad I went to live with my sister.

I remember once coming home from middle school and finding my mother with her head down, sobbing, at the kitchen table. Unhappiness filled her daily. When I asked her what was wrong, she told me I knew about my father having a relationship with another woman and I owed it to her to tell her who it was. I told her I knew nothing, that the trips we went on were to collect rents from some of my father's tenants or to attend sporting events. She hollered at me that I knew what was going on and she'd fix me along with him. From out of the blue, she slapped me in the face because I wouldn't tell her who the woman was. I told her to talk with my father.

That evening, she tried to end her life by taking an overdose of pills. She'd been badly abused in her first marriage, which my father knew. A few months later, when my mother got out of the hospital, she told us she'd be moving in with my brother-in-law to help take care of the motherless baby. She abandoned her own children to look after her grandchild and the family broke up without resolving any of their issues.

In retrospect, I think if my mother had stayed around to raise us, we would have turned out better. I've never held her abandonment against her, because only she knew what she was dealing with. I keep in touch with her once or twice a month, but she never visits me.

I left school at sixteen and was working when I was arrested.

On September 12, 1975, I had the day off from my job at a Philadelphia hospital and I slept until about 9:00 am. After making myself breakfast, I rode my bike around to 71st Street and stopped to talk with some friends. It was around 10 am. My brother Robin came up and asked me if he could borrow my bike; I gave it to him and told him I'd be waiting on the corner. Frances Wilson lived in an apartment on the corner, and she asked me to come up and see her, and I told her I'd be by later.

After a while, Robin came back with the bike and I rode it to Frank's gas station where I talked with Frank and my father for about half an hour. A police car pulled in and the cop told Frank there had been a homicide a few blocks away. We stood and talked for awhile, then the cop drove off. My brother, Marcel, asked that I wait at his house for his son to be dropped off by his mother.

I left the bike in front of his door when I got to his house. I was there for about twenty minutes when Robin and another guy, Gator, knocked at the door and asked me if I wanted to get high. I was using drugs, all kinds of drugs, every day. We went up to my brother's bedroom and got high. Later, when my brother came home, he asked me if I wanted to ride with him to see my mother. We went downstairs and played with his son while he took a bath, saying we'd go about 6 pm.

Marcel hollered at me that the police were outside and to dump the drugs. I thought he was joking. I was at the top of the stairs when the police, who'd forced their way in (though they later claimed the door was open), were at the bottom of the stairs and told me to come down with my hands behind my head. The cop slammed me against the wall, hitting my face. I thought it had to do with drugs, but I soon learned this was not the case.

They asked me if I had a grey sweatshirt. I asked why? They searched the house and all three of us were taken to the Roundhouse, the police administration building. Robin, Gator and I were taken to separate interrogation rooms. I was handcuffed to a stool and left alone for an hour. Two detectives came into the room and asked me my name. I said I wanted a lawyer. He said the guy I shot didn't ask for a lawyer and the other detective punched me in the neck. I had trouble breathing for awhile and they walked out. Two more detectives came into the room and I again asked for a lawyer, saying that I didn't understand what was going on. One of them kept punching me in the ribs and the other kept saying I'd robbed and killed a man at the corner store. After an hour of beating and questioning, they walked out. Another officer came to the doorway and stood there with a police dog, which I thought for sure he was going to command to attack me. He just stared at me, then walked away and closed the door.

With blood pouring out of my nose, I was alone in the room for about half an hour.

Another guy came in and asked me if I needed anything and I told him I needed a doctor and a lawyer. He said they'd make sure I saw a doctor after I answered the detectives' questions. I told him I wanted a lawyer, that I knew my rights. He responded, "You have no rights."

The two detectives came into the room, one holding a thick phone book, and said Robin said I did the crime. An old guy came into the room and sat at a desk, writing something. While one of the cops kept saying I'd done this crime, the other kept hitting me with the phone book, over and over until I almost passed out. The old guy got up and asked if I had anything to say. I again asked for a doctor. He hit me on the side of my face and told me to sign a paper. I told him I wasn't signing anything. He finally left the room where I stayed alone for two or three hours. During the beatings the detectives used all kinds of racist statements, saying several times, "We could kill you and you would not be missed, nigger."

The two detectives returned, cuffed me and as we walked out of the room, a woman and her children looked at me and one of them said, "They beat him up!"

I was pushed past them real fast.

When I was placed in a cell, I told the sergeant I needed a doctor and he sent me across the street to the police hospital. The doctor looked at my eye, felt my side and gave me a painkiller, telling me to see my family doctor the next day. I was returned to my cell. After many complaints, I was taken to the prison hospital for observation. From there I went to an outside hospital where I spent three weeks healing from internal injuries.

Once back in jail I was placed in a unit with people with drug problems and I was told I'd have to continue taking a drug that would "put my system back to normal."

A few months later I was taken to a hearing to see if I could stand trial for the homicide. My court-appointed lawyer, Ralph Swartz, said he'd take care of the fact that I'd asked for a lawyer during my interrogation and had been denied. He never did anything about it or many other miscarriages of justice.

After the hearing, I was transferred to Holmesburg Prison, where I was placed in some kind of a mental unit and given drugs. I stayed medicated all through my hearings and at my trial. I realized this is what those racist crackers wanted, for me to be doped up. Before this happened, I did not use words like racist crackers towards white people. But what happened to me has taught me to hate, and I do it with passion. I was wronged by those detectives and the whole system. So I started taking the drugs every other day until I was eased off them. I asked my lawyer to postpone things until I could get off the mind-numbing drugs, but he said to just relax. I couldn't formulate my thoughts and everything came out jumbled.

My attorney didn't object to an all-white jury, for some reason. The court found me guilty. I really had no idea what was going on through my arrest and trial; the judge acted like I wasn't even in the room. I was sentenced to life without the possibility of parole. The judge was Paul J. Silverstein.

When first in prison, I was unable to deal with what had happened. Behind these walls we are subjected to the harsh realities of what one man with the keys does to another when no one is looking. My jailers inflict pain with so much ease, hurting us in the name of some perverted justice. They think they can do whatever they want to us in the name of whatever they perceive to be the wrongs we've inflicted on society.

I became cold emotionally. When I fell into the old pattern of getting high, the warden did me a great service by shipping me to another jail. That's when I started to get myself together, enrolling in a G.E.D. program. I owe all that I am to God and having my family stand by me.

Over the years I've been involved in many groups, programs and therapy classes. I became willing to change and offer the community my efforts and talents. All this has contributed to my growth.

Once I was found guilty of murder, I called my girlfriend Marge and tried to break things off with her. I didn't think she had the staying power. She claimed she'd be there for me as long as I needed her. She lasted two years. I knew in the back of my mind that not many people on the outside could endure the pain and suffering heaped on the people who care about those of us behind these walls.

My family and their love and support helped me change my life without becoming bitter with the conditions of prison. My oldest brother, James, is one of my greatest fans. He learned at my father's feet that we are indeed our brothers' keepers. The whole family suffers from my incarceration.

I've acknowledged my drug problem. That first night at Graterford, I tried to overdose.

While spending a few months in the mental health unit, I found a copy of the Bible. Trying my best to read it despite my inability to read, I was inspired to enroll in basic education classes, and my hunger to learn continues to this day. Though my case is now in federal court, I have to not let myself hope that I might someday be freed from this house of insanity.

At this time I am going through something horrible. It all started when the prison painted my cell. When I moved back in, I smelled shit, like someone had taken a dump in my cell. So I went about cleaning the cell again. But the smell still prevailed so I chalked it up to bad paint. Then I discovered that someone had taken the light fixture casing off and stuffed shit up into the holes of the light, and it started to fall down on the casing.

I came in from work a few weeks ago, and learned that someone had thrown pee on my cell door. This has been going on for a while. One day, during count, I went to get my insulin from the medical department. When I came back to my cell, someone had thrown water on my floor. Each time something happens, I get the impression that a few of the guards are allowing these abuses. I have every emotion running through my body from rage to pure anger about this indecency to my life. I even thought that this young boy in the cell next to me had something to do with it, but could never prove anything. So I have started to limit the number of people I have around me. As they say, "what doesn't kill me will make me stronger."

If I was freed, the first thing I'd do is get out of this backward state. I have a sense of who I am, and what I've learned is that parole officers send people back to prison for the flimsiest of reasons. I'm not sure I want to risk it.

But my father is getting older and I know he needs someone to be there for him. Some of the things my Dad taught me about love and loyalty to family have stayed with me in spite of the pain and suffering that prison heaps on me daily. My love has grown even stronger. My father wiped my butt when I could not do so out of his love for me. When age becomes too great for my father, I want to be there to insure him that what he taught was not lost on me.

Of course I'll need a job, and I know whatever society states they will not be kind to an ex-convict. I'll have to keep in mind the most important thing I'd have to deal with is the parole people.

My family needs me, and as I've had the strength to survive the prison experience, I can do anything I want to as long as I stay focused.

I've always yearned for the love of a woman, which I've only had a taste of. But I have become a more aware person and because I have medical concerns (Hepatitis C and diabetes), I don't want to harm anyone else. I will most likely stay single so I won't infect anyone else.

Life has thrown me a fastball with these illnesses, but I will learn to find other things which I can devote myself to.

I will look after my father when he needs me, and will find interests to keep me strong.

I might even start the vending business which I spent a lot of time preparing for in prison.

Who knows what the future holds. Right now I'm struggling just to breathe. All I hope is that whatever comes my way will bring beauty to this man who yearns to be free.

(Tony continues to fight for his freedom and struggles daily with the challenges of his medical condition.)

* * *

"There is no birthright in the white skin that it shall say that wherever it goes, to any nation, amongst any people, there the people of the country shall give way before it and those to whom the land belongs shall bow down and become its servants."

Annie Wood Besant (1874-1933)

21st Century's Dawn's Early Light

My country tis of thee
this is about your reality.
By the 21st Century's dawn's early light
there ain't no justice for you here
if you ain't white.
Sweet land of liberty
bitter was the taste of your slavery
and that putrid taste remains strong
in all of our mouths
as we now see you lynching us
downtown in your courthouse.
The whole world watched
you beat down Rodney King
then we saw white jurors
who couldn't see what we were seeing.
With open eyes their closed minds
saw that the police were right

You know there ain't no justice for you here
if you ain't white.

Today's lynchings are performed
via police state-style trials
perpetuating this injustice American style
highlighting the unstated semantic reality
that lynchings don't require bodies
hanging from trees.
Oh say can you see
strange fruit no longer hangs.
Now in the land of the free
and home of the brave
prisons conceal the lynched children
of America's slaves.

Remember Martin told us
to let freedom ring
so my country tis of thee
that I sing
Now in the land of the free
and home of the brave
prisons conceal the lynched children
of America's slaves.

Leonard C. Jefferson CL-4135

* * *

This poem has been the most controversial part of the first edition of the book, causing it to be banned as "racist" at several U.S. prisons.

Chapter Four

Some Thoughts about Guards
Lee D. Landau

I'll bet this information is not given by those who recruit new prison guards in high schools. They wouldn't dare to mention this fact, because it cannot be denied. If they told the truth it would tarnish the luster they portray about the prison system to potential recruits.

Take what I've written home to your loved ones and let them be the judge of your moral goodness. Afraid you might lose their respect?

There are a few guards who treat us decently. However, they are still ENABLERS! Enablers assist the politicians with their nefarious plans to continue the very lucrative expansion of prisons, the fastest growing industry in the country. With enough money, you too could have your very own McPrison, now that the system can be privatized. All at the expense of people's lives! Innocent people's lives stolen to make jobs for others. So even though they treat us decently, they too bear the mark "I HELP TO IMPRISON INNOCENT PEOPLE."

Adding to the injuries we suffer, you LIE about this being a freedom-loving democracy. You LIE!

What? You're angry with me for telling the truth? Well, go ahead and retaliate; you probably will.

But first chew on this: There has never been any prisoner in the world who has victimized 190 innocent people, 365 days a year, year after year. I guess that makes the Department of Correction and all its enablers the biggest criminals in the history of the world!

* * *

"A white correctional officer was asked at a party, 'What type of work do you do?' He answered, 'I keep niggers in check.'

A Black correctional officer was asked 'And what type of work do you do?'

'I keep niggers in check too,' he quipped."

Anton Forde/Trevor Mattis

Chapter Four

Framed for Murder by Officers of the Law
PF "Free" Lazor
($2,450,000)

The stories of long-term victims of the American criminal justice system can be difficult to read, each in their own way, because all of the victims display a degree of bitterness and very strong emotions in regard to their treatment. Often, the victims were caught in the system before they had a chance to escape the environment of poverty, family dysfunction, inadequate schools and neighborhood violence that already rendered them vulnerable.

As the following story illustrates, even those who have already overcome such disadvantages can suffer the same fate when their challenges expose blatant lies and injustice in their trial and incarceration, and then these challenges lead to retaliation by the guards and other prison personnel. This extensive account of one man's experience of justice denied and abuse in prison may be unusual in its degree of detail, but it describes events that are frequently experienced by the millions of inmates in U.S. prisons.

At the time of his incarceration in his late twenties, Mr. Lazor was a patents-holding inventor, well-known recording artist, stage performer who had acted in minor and major motion picture films, and a composer with hundreds of songs and other musical pieces to his credit. He had founded and operated several small businesses and helped others start theirs, individually and through offering training seminars. He held licenses and special awards in piloting, skydiving, real estate, and insurance. He was a finalist candidate to be the first private person (non-government sponsored) in history to enter outer space as an astronaut, for "Project Private Enterprise" founded by a retired NASA engineer. He learned sign language to help the deaf and also helped and visited the elderly.

P.F.

The courts and prison systems across the U.S. are jointly being misused to kidnap and imprison innocent American citizens. I have been imprisoned in that manner for 21 years. When much of a person's youth was carefully invested in future aspirations, as was mine, those years have also been stolen.

I have never been involved with any form of violent or non-violent crime. More than 200 sworn declarations from outstanding people who've known me personally have been submitted to the courts, noting my non-violent nature and my life-long commitment to my own betterment and that of my community. (These references can be made available on request.)

INCIDENT SYNOPSIS

I was in my home alone one afternoon when a crazed man, who had been stalking me with escalating threats and violence for ten weeks, broke in. He managed to open my locked front door and then kicked and body-slammed my locked bedroom door some fifteen to twenty times, all the while yelling threats to kill me. When the door finally crashed open, he swung a meat cleaver at me, just missing my head, and came at me with a handgun. The gun turned out to be a high-powered BB-pellet pistol, but it looked like a real semi-automatic firearm.

I had a legal, loaded handgun and I fired it to save my life. Even though in dire panic, losing conscious perception and judgment, I stopped firing when he went down, leaving unfired bullets in my gun. When he stood back up on his feet, unarmed, I immediately called the police and ambulance to save him.

He lived three or four hours (depending which police report you read, as there are even discrepancies in listing exact time of death) and he would not have died, had there not been delays, caused by the police, in getting him the necessary medical care. He was on his feet when the police arrived and they admitted that he was hard to restrain, despite his wounds. Nonetheless, I was charged with premeditated first-degree murder.

I was acquitted of that charge, but the same jury convicted me of second-degree murder, with a parole date of 1992. Twelve years after my parole date, I am still in prison. The crimes in this case were committed by the attacker and the police / prosecution agents, to deliberately frame me for murder.

The fact that I had slight contact with the attacker previously, and all the other surrounding events, simply have no relevance to innocence or guilt, as my action was caused **solely** by the violent attempted, imminently fatal attack on me. Even so, the following information will encapsulate the precipitating events.

CASE BACKGROUND AND SURROUNDING EVENTS

On Thanksgiving Day, 1981, I began renting and renovating a house as my residence in Los Gatos, California. New owners planned to demolish the house and build high-rise condominiums on the property. Paul Garnier, representing the new property owners, was so happy with my renovation of the premises that we reached an agreement whereby I would maintain the property in exchange for continued residence and the right to sublet extra rooms to offset my renovation costs.

By July 1982, I'd purchased the house structure outright, with the option to move it to another lot within 30 days after the owners obtained financing for the planned demolition (which never came through). At this point, I was required to pay a rental fee **for the land** on which my house sat, as long as I, and the house, remained there. As a licensed realtor, I'd done similar transactions in the past with no problems, and I faithfully paid the rent at all times, as agreed.

In September of that year, Garnier introduced me to his nephew, John Allred, a man from far out of town, newly arrived in Los Gatos. To help a fellow man in need, I gave in to their pleas to let Allred rent a room for three weeks. He moved out thereafter, as agreed, but left a roomful of belongings, for which they had agreed to pay me storage rent.

It was a scam, but I wouldn't know that until after Allred's death. In my businesses, I often worked away from home, on the road, doing sound recordings and night music-stage performances. Therefore Allred and I never had more than fifteen minutes' contact from the day we met until he died. Most of the contact came during his stalking and violence against me. The jury was misled to believe that when the shooting took place, Allred lived in the house and I didn't, when in fact, it was the other way around and it was rightfully my house!

Allred manipulated two other unsavory tenants, friends of Garnier's family, to carry on a secret campaign of slanderous complaints behind my back to induce Garnier to breach our tenancy contract. It was later determined that Allred was enraged because my purchase of the house had prevented him from inheriting it.

Three months later, Allred's schemes succeeded. On December 20, Garnier suddenly demanded that I vacate the property immediately, notwithstanding the fact that I owned the house that sat on this land. He even admitted that he never gave a 30-day notice to quit tenancy as required by California law. Allred sealed this breach of contract in a public restaurant. He dove over a table, lunging at my throat. Garnier had to pull him off.

Bending over backwards to keep peace and provide safety for my possessions, I began moving my things from the house, in increments, over the next few weeks, while contacting civil attorneys and tenancy agencies for a civil resolution and restraining order. But Allred cut that short with his attack.

Less than 30 days after the illegal demand to vacate, I was packing the last of my most valuable items in my car to store elsewhere. I was even preparing to let the house go, as it wasn't worth the trouble, in light of other life successes that I'd invested thirteen years to achieve. So that it wouldn't be sitting in my car, my legally registered handgun, loaded as advised by the gun dealer, was to be among the last items I'd remove from my room. The bedroom door was the type that automatically locks when closed.

I'd be packed and gone within the next fifteen minutes.

Except, fate tragically intervened.

During my last call before leaving, while I was on the phone with a tenancy agency, the door-bashing suddenly began. When Allred crashed it open, I was panicked to the point of semi-consciousness. Without my glasses on, I could hardly see as he swung a meat cleaver at me, with great force. The bashed-in door smashed into my already previously injured knee, putting me in great pain! This physical pain surge probably contributed to my near unconscious state of panic as I fired the gun sporadically. I thought I shot maybe two rapid-fire shots, after one wild shot went off into the air.

The same Los Gatos police officers who had treated me with hostility over the previous two months when I called them for their intervention against Allred's stalking, threats and battery on me, were assigned to handle the shooting "crime" and serve as prosecution witnesses in the murder trial. These very same officers are especially notorious for corrupt police activities. Now, 22 years later, evidence indicating a very intimate romantic relationship between one of them and Allred remains suppressed by the prosecution team, with the aid of my duplicitous defense attorney.

PRISON: THE NIGHTMARE HAD NOT YET BEGUN

Twenty one years of torture later, still in prison; twelve years after parole date has passed.

I have never been legally sentenced to prison – for twenty one years. The judge refused to let me complete my motion for a new trial before pronouncing judgment. California statutory law (Penal Code §1202) says that makes my judgment and sentence void; it doesn't legally exist, but the courts have no regard for what the law says in this case. Even if I had been actually guilty and my commitment to prison had been legal, my parole date was nonetheless March 1992.

I've suffered from a form of MCS (Multiple Chemical Sensitivities) since birth. When I entered CDC (California Department of Corrections) in the early 1980's most doctors didn't recognize it as a real physical and medical disability. My complaints of illness led to my being charged with "manipulation of staff" which, within CDC, is worse than any other crime. Thus began a terror campaign with thousands of malicious, false reports, and self-perpetuating special punishments. (It is self-perpetuating because "labels" are designed to re-enact the punishment.)

My imprisonment has become a unique nightmare that may have no end short of death by actual prison-torture. My adverse reactions to halogens (including fluoride and chlorine in public and prison drinking water and many foods), means that I cannot drink water that's not specifically filtered or distilled without becoming toxically ill and dehydrated. The same applies to many foods. (Fluoride, incidentally, is the ingredient used in D-con rat poison to bring about their agonizing death, which involves a dehydration process.)

Sparked by the labeling of my MCS condition as "staff manipulation" (the highest form of "troublemaker" and "danger to the public"), over 1,500 named CDC employees would eventually jump on this bandwagon of sadistic hatred in a literal war of terrorism against one man, while I behaved consistently as a model prisoner. They simply concocted a profile of the most extreme opposite, and affixed it to my name and prison number. More is regularly added in secret. This profile has kept me in the most violent, oppressive prisons in the state for most of my imprisonment, and exposed me to torture methods that prisoners of war are not supposed to be allowed to be subjected to.

Here are a few highlights these tax-paid "officers of the law" have achieved in this insanely sadistic war of terror, because in trying to get minimal, reasonable accommodations for my disability, I inadvertently exposed their vicious cruelties and demented criminality:

- I've been violently brutalized by guards. One almost murdered me, holding me over a high balcony headfirst to throw me off, and was restrained at the last moment by another guard. In another incident, a guard lifted me off the floor by my chin, then dropped me back to the floor, tearing out much of my beard by the roots, then dribbled out these hairs a few at a time, while laughing hysterically (1984-1995);

- I've been persistently set up by guards, "counselors" and administrators to have other prisoners brutalize and murder me, giving the most violent, homicidal inmate "shotcallers" the "green light" to have me viciously "hit" (1992-2003);

- They've destroyed my previously perfect hearing, one ear virtually deaf, and the other damaged with a rare hyperacousis condition, where certain pitches of normal sound strike my brain and nervous system so traumatically that it's akin to being hit in the head with a baseball bat and shocked in the heart with high voltage (1986-present, with continuous confiscation/destruction of my hearing aids);

- My vision has been severely damaged by years of forced toxic ingestion, repeated head trauma and other abuses, almost certainly permanently damaged (1983-present, continuously);

- I have permanent spinal, pelvic and elbow damage from a car accident, when horseplaying guards smashed their "chase" car into the other car I was in. At the time, I was being transported to a hospital after almost having my arm amputated from an infection deliberately inflicted by guards and medical staff, whose prolonged denial of intervention exacerbated the condition to this degree (1994);

- Eleven times I have been starved, dehydrated and emaciated by cachexia to the point where it was doubtful my life could be saved. On hundreds of other occasions and generally for 21 years, I've been kept in a state of chronic dehydration-torture as a daily norm (1983-present);

- They've tortured me with bromine poisoning, used as a chemical nerve-toxin, pumped in our cell vents (they admit that they have done this, supposedly to kill air duct bacteria). I've been laughed at while screaming in pain day and night in a locked cell for days on end, as they tried to force me to commit suicide, as I nearly did, to end the pain. This pain is greater than all pains experienced in my life all combined, with one exception (2001-2003);

- I've been shot twice (1998, 1999), while set up by CDC employees to be stabbed to death by inmates (these were block guns, but the old style that shot compact blocks that would split the meat of the body open, blind and kill);

- I suffer extreme toxic reactions daily from chemical sensitivity to cleaners, deodorants, tobacco smoke, chemical food and water additives, which I'm forced to breathe and ingest continuously day and night, unnecessarily. These conditions affect me severely, because of my MCS condition (1983-2004);

- In 2001 the guards set me up to be kicked and stomped in the head repeatedly by other inmates, from which I have permanent brain damage, affecting my balance, memory and other intellectual and artistic processes. The inmates were not punished, whereas I was sent to The Hole. Three years later, I'm still trying to get a medical examination, which was ordered specifically as an aftermath of this attack. Only part of one test (of two tests ordered) was done; it was aborted before completion. *(Editor's note: We suspect that the results of these tests prove a physical handicap as a direct result of this incident.)*

- I've had toxic boils repeatedly surgically excised, after which CDC agents have repeatedly falsified the official medical documents to cover up this senseless horror (1980's, 1990's);

- CDC agents have robbed me of my property over 75 times (usually grand theft) sometimes to the tune of thousands of dollars worth of irreplaceable items, such as my music compositions, other art, and legal evidence proving my innocence (1983-2003);

- I've experienced over 30 retaliatory transfers all across the state, to continuously sabotage my court actions and destroy my relationship with my family;

- I've been denied any canteen/commissary for 20 years continuously (with one exception) as a penalty (punishment), for litigating against the CDC while literally starving due to food allergies, and denied needed medications for years, available only via canteen. (This is unheard of as to any other prisoner in California prison history);

- These rogue agents (all members of the CCPOA guards' union that has owned the past few California governors), have sabotaged and blocked my court access for the past 21 years, destroying every court case I ever filed, and, consequently, I am procedurally barred from using the courts due to the state of indigence which CDC keeps me in;

- I presently suffer under a crushing "Central File" (my "profile") of over 8000 pages. I have been illegally denied a full review of it since 1987. Because of the massive amount of paperwork in my file, neither the parole board nor anyone else can ever even find the dozens of laudatory reports submitted by the few courageous, honest guards and administrators who have stuck their necks out to tell the truth about my continuing model prisoner conduct;

- Similarly, my honest, favorable psych reports are now buried beneath a deluge of malicious, scurrilous ones, dishonestly penned in retaliation, resulting in my parole perpetually being denied. This, along with drugging prisoners senseless with violence-inciting dope, has now become the CDC psych department's primary function and purpose.

All of these shocking crimes have been committed (and continue to be) by a literal street gang of terrorists, a private army carrying on a personal war of horrors in their secret cities on American soil. This is at the cost of millions of dollars, for the sick, sadistic sport of twisted, depraved sociopaths imprudently deputized and trusted with badges, guns and misplaced authority, to carry on a personal war; in this instance, against one man.

What I have described is only a ripple in the skin of the tip of the iceberg of this worst form of death ever devised by demonically driven men: Death by Imprisonment, USA style. Contemporary language has no words to define or describe what is going on in these places.

My great desire is to expose these injustices and to make the general public aware of what is going on in this country. I hope that I have somewhat achieved it in this brief exposé. To everyone who reads this and is touched by it, your involvement to stop this sickness and insane terror is necessary and urgent not only for me, but for us all, for what is left of our country. For anyone who would be interested in writing to me, who could perhaps offer some form of outreach, I welcome your correspondence, at:

PF-Lazor C-73842
c/o Gayle Travis
P.O. Box 2994
San Ramon, CA 94583 (USA)

Tele: 925.277

Your support in whatever way possible would be appreciated and welcomed. This could have been you. More than ever now, it still could be.

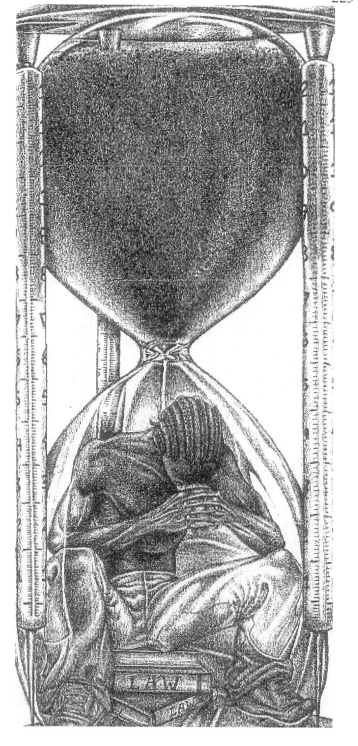

PART IV
Abuse

Chapter One

Rapes, Murders and Abuses

According to prisoners, but routinely denied by authorities, there is rape in every prison by either inmates or guards on a regular basis. Over 2.6 million Americans live every waking and sleeping moment under the threat of rape or assault. The California-based advocacy group, Stop Prisoner Rape, estimates there are almost 400,000 rapes each year in U.S. prisons. Many feel the estimate is way too low.

Sadly, these rapes are material for many comedians and cop shows. As a culture, we accept the possibility of violent sodomy as part of incarceration as we chuckle and snicker at "Vaseline" jokes. Last year an inmate at Graterford died of a "heart attack" after a confrontation with guards when he demanded overdue medication. The word among prisoners is he was stomped to death. One writes,

"The guy who died in here a few months ago is coming back to bite this jail in the rear end. From what I learned, his family has filed a formal complaint against the guards who attacked him. They said he died from heart failure, but the family learned he had a crushed windpipe. I hope those guards get jail time for what they did."

This chapter was the hardest for the men to write, and not all were able to participate, as if these horrors were just too much to dig up and revisit. One said, "Please don't ask me about that!"

For obvious reasons, the identities of most of the writers in this chapter will not be revealed.

* * *

It never ceases to amaze me about the absurdity of power-crazy people. I give you the following as a prime example.

I am informed that, when those on Death Row are scheduled for execution (legalized murder) they are asked to insert a butt plug. The reason for this is, You (the murdered) don't want to soil yourself do you? As though they really care about your welfare. How absurd can you be? The person is facing imminent death, and they assume he/she is concerned about soiling him/herself.

The real reason is, and it isn't hard to figure out, the butcher who is going to do the autopsy doesn't want to put up with the mess! Well, I say screw you, butcher, if you are going to be part of a system that murders me, you can damn well put up with the shit! By the way, about the autopsy: explain to me why you have to further desecrate the body of your victim, when you already know what was the cause of death? What kind of perverse thrill do you get out of further desecration of the victim? You are, in my book, a Ghoul!

* * *

I was in a cell with a 16-year old and an older mentally ill man about thirty. Twice a day, a prison nurse, accompanied by a guard, came to give the older guy medication that kept him like a zombie. All he did was eat, pass gas, sleep and use the toilet. He never washed or showered and his smell was awful. We were confined to that cell 23 hours a day.

The young guy and I became pretty tight. He was from the suburbs and had a family that visited him regularly. Though he wasn't from the inner city like me, we had a lot in common and spent time talking and playing cards, writing letters and basically just trying to keep our sanity while living like caged animals. The stress of such intense confinement was extremely hard to handle and we did the best we could. After awhile, we grew to really appreciate each other, even meeting each other's families in the visitors' room. Because I was a little older (18) I took on the responsibility of looking out for this young guy and making sure no one took advantage of him.

One day, after the mentally ill man was transferred, the guards moved a state prisoner into the cell with us. Right away, I sensed something wasn't right. He'd served 12 years of a life sentence, and had been brought to this prison after stabbing another prisoner. You could tell he was a predator and that he had his sights set on the young guy. I knew he wouldn't try anything while I was there.

Then I went to trial and was gone for a month. When I came back to the same cell, the young guy was alone; he seemed withdrawn and tense. The other guy had been taken upstate.

He told me that one night the older guy made sexual advances towards him and when he resisted, they started fighting. Though he fought as hard as he could, the older, stronger guy beat him up and raped him. He told me there was absolutely nothing he could do about it as the tears streamed down his face. I could feel the depth of the pain and humiliation that some madman had forced upon him. There were no words to ease his suffering.

About a year later a guy stepped into my cell when I was alone, closed the door behind him, pulled out a knife and announced his intention of raping me. I rushed him, catching him by surprise and getting the knife out of his hand. Ignoring his screams, I repeatedly slashed and stabbed at his face, and by the time I stopped there was blood everywhere. Guards arrived and began beating me with blackjacks. I was handcuffed and dragged off to The Hole. The other guy was rushed to the hospital and I was charged with aggravated assault and attempted murder. One week later, the guy showed up at my hearing, his face all bandaged, and testified I'd called him into my cell and started stabbing him for no reason. I was convicted and received a two-and-a-half to five-year sentence. On top of that I was held accountable for the guy's hospital expenses and locked up in The Hole for almost a year.

* * *

Personally I'm subjected to what I call low-intensity abuse every day in prison. The fact that I'm doing time for a crime I did not commit is the quintessence of abuse itself. In addition to that, I'm tall, black, muscular, intelligent, sport dreadlocks and maintain my dignity. This makes me a very serious threat to the system, so I'm a favorite target for harassment by many of the correctional officers, especially those with racist tendencies. Their goal is to break me before I infect the already broken, a moot cause, for after you've broken a man's spirit, all the king's horses and all the king's men can never put it back together again.

* * *

Prison is designed to dissolve a man's humanity as well as his sense of individuality. From the moment I entered, I was stripped naked and forced to conform to a system designed to render me powerless. My name was replaced with a number. My clothing was taken and I was issued a uniform. Separated from everything and everyone I loved, I was forced like an animal to live in a steel and concrete cage. And though no one is capable of totally resisting the many negative influences of the prison, those who try to find it difficult to maintain such resistance for a long period of time, for there is a constant bombardment of madness on all sides. To resist in one area often means succumbing in another. Total resistance is impossible.

Just the other day I was walking in the yard and talking to a younger prisoner, he said, "Someone told me you'd been in here for twenty years." When I said that was true, a pained look came over his face as he said, "But you don't look like you've been in here that long!" I asked him how is a man who's been here that long supposed to act? He thought for a minute and then responded, "He's supposed to act crazy!" This young guy, like many people, was judging me by what he imagined the impact on his mind would be after twenty years. I don't claim to be the sanest man on the planet, but I am far from crazy. The level of sanity I've been able to maintain is a direct result of my ability to resist those forces that seek to diminish me. I am a human being! Not an animal!

* * *

Racism in its blatant and more subtle forms is a daily experience for incarcerated black men at Graterford. Remember when blacks had to ride in the back of the bus until Rosa Parks stood up against it? That same cold-hearted attitude of privilege in white employees favors white inmates with better treatment than blacks or Hispanics. The most treacherous form of subtle racism experienced by black prisoners is the superior, self-righteous air of dominance most whites hold toward blacks. Add to that all of the negative stereotypes they carry about blacks and you have pre-existing psychological conditions that support the systematic abuse of black and Hispanic inmates.

Of the 29 state prisons in Pennsylvania, holding approximately 60,000 citizens, some are considered better than others. In the language of inmates you have "black jails" and "white jails." The difference is like comparing the treatment inner-city children receive in the public school system to that received by white children in suburban schools. From this perspective, considering Graterford a "black" prison, it becomes a term synonymous with abuse. The reality is that the prison experience of blacks and Hispanics is based on a foundation of systematic, institutionalized racism.

These differences are so routine that no serious challenges are ever made against them. Yet these racial slights are like a weight over the lives of black and Hispanic prisoners, affecting our freedom through parole, medical care and equal educational and employment opportunities.

What makes it subtle racism? It is the fact that although these practices occur consistently, they are not so glaring as to rise to the level of mass protest and rebellion.

* * *

Let me tell you about the Camp Hill prison riots in 1989. The prison population was very high at the time, with double-celling in every block. Half the population had no jobs as they were all filled, and showers were regimented to a total of ten minutes. The abuse of prisoners was so high that The Hole was so full they were double-celling there too. There were many occasions when prisoners were tossed down a flight of stairs for just talking back to a guard. HIV/AIDS was epidemic and the staff housed the sick and suffering with the general population. This caused a lot more tension, and the riot started with two guards who didn't know how to do their jobs.

After the first day of rioting, the guards came into the cell blocks along with the state police to help them lock us down. The guards knew the housing units couldn't be locked down because the panels to the locks were open. They knew before they left that they could not be locked down. So a few hours later, the blocks were opened and all the prisoners were back out of their cells. The state police told us to come out with our hands up. We were handcuffed with our arms behind our backs, and then were taken to the big yard where for four days and nights we were forced to sleep in our own urine. The nights were so cold many people became ill. What amazed me was that the guards said we'd destroyed our own property, which was a lie, and the press consumed their lies like they were cotton candy.

After the fourth day in the yard, we were escorted, still in handcuffs, back to our cells where we were forced to strip naked in front of men and women to see if we had any illegal items on us. Then groups of eight of us were placed in 12' x 6' cells, where we remained for another week. Some cells had ten prisoners in them. When the guards wanted to beat someone, we were forced to face the wall so we couldn't see what was happening. I was taken to the prison hospital with an eye injury from a guard beating me while I was handcuffed. I let the guard know my anger, and the next day I was transferred to another prison where I spent two years of my life in The Hole.

My life behind these walls was forever changed to the point where trust comes hard for me. The abuse that's allowed to happen in prisons is well beyond my understanding, because human beings are not supposed to subject other humans to this kind of abuse. But they get away with all the illegal stuff they do to us prisoners.

* * *

I worked in the library with this guy Billy. He was about thirteen or fourteen years old. We got along well together because I'd come to prison when I was only a couple of years older than him. I always wondered why this state would allow its young offenders to be housed with the adult population. It was as if prison officials knew that something would happen to Billy.

I learned after Billy didn't come to work for a week that he'd been raped by four guys on the block.

From what I could piece together, they lured Billy into an empty cell at the back of the block and all five proceeded to get stoned. They gave him all kinds of drugs while they pretended to be his friends. Once Billy was beyond understanding what was going on, the four guys took turns penetrating him in the butt until he passed out. When the officials found Billy later in his cell, bleeding from the four guys' handiwork, he was taken to the hospital where he stayed for a long time.

Yes, there are some people in these environments who take advantage of the young whenever they get a chance. I blame prison officials for what happened to Billy. They knew what would happen to someone Billy's age if left alone for some time.

One good thing came out of it for Billy – he was released from prison a few years later and allowed to renew his life, what was left of it after he experienced such horrible brutality.

* * *

I recently filed a complaint against a guard who wrote me up for violating a dress code. I have several severe medical problems, one of which, diabetes, causes my feet to swell, which makes walking difficult. Not able to get shoes on my feet, I am forced at times to wear open-toed shoes with socks. He said I was wearing shower shoes to the mess hall, which was not true.

When I went to his superior, they acted like I was wrong without even hearing my case. The officer has used policy to subject others to mistreatment. They sometimes just think up rules to justify their behavior. I've seen this officer standing out front of the control office just waiting to stalk whoever comes by. It may be something as simple as a button being undone, yet he blows it all out of context. This attitude is expressed daily, and for some of us, it is what we have to cope with for the rest of our lives, with no signs of relief.

* * *

Iron Thunderhorse, Grand Sachem of the Quinnipiac Nation, is a prolific writer, syndicated columnist and artist who has published over 100 books, articles and columns. He is a Vietnam vet who was convicted in Texas in the late 70's for a series of crimes by a man who resembled him physically. He is the senior mentor of SageWriters.

When I first arrived in the Texas Department of Criminal Justice (TDCJ), at about 1978, there was a massive work stoppage that began at Ellis Unit and spread to eleven other units. I was there, and TDCJ was still segregated at the time. This is how TDCJ handled it: Convicts were herded into the gym at the end of the building. They were then forced to strip naked or be tear-gassed. Then they were nudged with cattle prods through the door, and all along the hallway corridor men lined both sides. Some were TDCJ staff, others were infamous building tenders. They each had an axe handle, or baseball bat, or a length of rubber hose. The men had to run the TDCJ gauntlet and were beaten to a bloody pulp.

To me this was comical. I WAS IN MY 30s then and still in TOP SHAPE. I had competed in kick boxing matches in the 70s. My "cellie" and I would also do a thousand pushups every day before going to work out in the fields. Staying in shape was our way of surviving. In Vietnam, many of us trained for stick fighting competition, a very popular sport then. To train for this, we would take pieces of bamboo and beat each other on the upper body and thighs until we were hard as rocks. The actual sticks, held one in each hand, were about 3 feet long and wrapped with burlap on both ends.

SO, when I ran the gauntlet, TDCJ could not understand why I went back a second and third time and grinned like a wildman when struck. They were certain I had gone "mad-dog crazy," but this was psychological warfare to show them NOTHING they could throw at me would break my spirit. Breaking the psychological bonds of prison enslavement is what set me free. I hardened my body, and I sent my soul free, the dream soul, over the fences back home to the Dawnland, where it belonged, and in my mind, I began revitalizing my Nation's language, religious practices, arts and crafts etc. I literally turned the stigma of bondage into a positive and productive experience reversing the intended effect of erasing my tribal heritage. This, like my martial arts training, is known as "conditioning," and it stemmed from a vital lesson I learned in Vietnam.

(Despite his physical condition and years of torture, Iron is still reaching out to help others. Using two magnifying glasses, he still does legal work and communicates with supporters around the world, inspiring all with his determination, strength, and creativity. Though I've spoken several times with Ruth, Iron and I have never met. Iron's biography is *In the Footsteps of a Stone Giant* by Ruth Thunderhorse, Infinity, 2007)

The Visit

I expect a visit full of anticipation
My number's called full of elation
As I draw close full of expectation
Bend `n spread `em, pure humiliation.

I have the kind of sorrow that never shows,
the kind where all seems well and no-one ever knows.
I have the kind of sorrow that grows and grows,
the kind of sorrow that comes from soft and tender blows.

Strange bonds develop between men in peril.
Attachments form against your will,
while the threat lasts, it doesn't matter
whether they be friend, foe, or some other.

Years living with men in close proximity,
the same space shared intimately,

stripped naked of all privacy,
yet still I don't know them and they don't know me.

Two men, strangers not friends,
in an area four by ten,
sixteen hours a day, seven days a week.

I can hear his heart beat and smell his feet.

Anton Forde/Trevor Mattis

* * *

"My religion is very simple. My religion is kindness."

The Dalai Lama

Postscript

State's Meanness Shameful
Joan Gauker

To encourage family visits for prisoners in England, the government reimburses family members for transportation costs between their home and the prison – usually within a 25-mile radius of the offender's home. Keep prisoners close to home in our country? Encourage family visits? We don't think so!

And there's more! Prisoners in England can buy phone cards – they don't do collect calls. In visiting rooms, there are snack bars manned by volunteers where prisoners and visitors may buy food. Those in minimum-security prisons may have four visits a week, go home on weekends, have their own dishes, bedding (pillows, blankets) and clothing from home – even their own stereo. Women prisoners are treated with respect. When a pregnant woman delivers her baby in prison, she and the baby stay in a Mother & Baby Unit for six months.

Other civilized Western nations recognize separation from society itself as the punishment and don't try to make that time even more miserable. They see imprisonment as the perfect time to encourage such noble undertakings as continuing education, getting job training, honing social skills or strengthening family ties. But not us.

For us, prison time is "mean time" for prisoners and their families. We in the U.S. would never think of having volunteer-manned snack bars in prison visiting rooms, allowing minimum security prisoners to go home for the weekend and have their own bedding – for heaven's sake! Instead, we feel we must belittle, demean and punish our prisoners – and their families – at every turn – even in little ways.

For instance, the mail. Mail sent by Pennsylvania prisoners is unnecessarily demeaning and embarrassing for family and friends who receive it. Across the front of the envelope is stamped: "**INMATE MAIL, PA DEPARTMENT OF CORRECTIONS**."

Other states — oppressive for prisoners — don't embarrass their citizens on the outside in such a way. Prisoners' mail from Florida, Georgia, Texas and Utah, to name a few states, arrives with no indication on the envelope front that the mail is from a prison. Texas mailroom people drop a small note into the envelope before it is sealed saying it is from a prisoner, some other states mark the back of the envelope, and others do nothing. Cannot Pennsylvania, at least, put its offensive stamp on the back of envelopes — if they must be stamped?

And there are the drab or striped uniforms, expensive phone calls, restricted visits, lost family days, reduced education support, diminished commutation opportunities, etc. Is it just plain meanness?

Consider the rules for Pennsylvania capital cases and their visitors. For some Draconian reason, our officials believe these people must be isolated — from each other and from family and friends. Pennsylvania confines death-row prisoners to their cells 23 hours a day and allows them outside (weather permitting) for one hour in a dog-run-type yard, and then only at a time when no one is in either run next to them. While prisoners who have killed are in the general population, those who have killed and received a death sentence must be isolated from human touch. What is the logic?

We learned of more state meanness from a member of an anti-death-penalty organization in England who recently visited a Graterford Death Row prisoner. She also had visited in Texas and Georgia, and was surprised by Graterford's crude visiting arrangements.

For instance, in Texas, where no prisoner receives contact visits, Death Row prisoners share the same glass-divided visiting room as the general population. But, even with 35 booths, the acoustics are good for conversation. The visitor-side of the booths is large enough for two people and has two phones to speak in normal tones with the prisoner. There are vending machines and microwaves on the visitors' side and toilet facilities on both sides of the glass. Visitors may bring food, and have it delivered by an officer to the prisoner.

At Graterford, the small death-row visiting room is far from conducive to a relaxed visit. The booths are tiny and the narrow room lacks acoustical amenities. There is a small grate in the dividing glass to which folks are supposed to put their lips and ears to speak and listen to each other while leaning uncomfortably forward. Still, they struggle to hear above the noise of other visitors' voices or correctional officers lurking nearby talking on their cell phones or walkie talkies or to each other with little regard for the visitors' efforts to have a meaningful visit. Nothing may be taken into the securely divided area by the visitor or prisoner – no food, no pictures, nothing of their worlds to share through the separating window partition. No vending machines or toilets are available for either party. If one party must leave to use the toilet, the visit is ended.

Georgia Death Row prisoners have six-hour contact visits. They may hug family members, play with children, share photos, have their picture taken with visitors, and leave gifts, to be given visitors upon leaving. The state gives its death-row prisoners a TV, permits arts and crafts materials, group recreation outside two hours a day, and gathering in a dayroom from 6-9 p.m. to play cards or board games. Often, it's little things that show a mean streak – like not letting capital cases play cards together, or stamping prisoner's mail with the equivalent of a scarlet letter. These things denote a state or nation's humanity.

Our English visitor told us the prisons in her country are more concerned with the process of preparing the prisoners to return to their families and society. "We treat prisoners like human beings," she mused. Should we do less?

Graterfriends, November 2001

Chapter Two

Abu Ghraib, USA
Anne-Marie Cusac

Anne-Marie Cusac is an award-winning investigative reporter at The Progressive magazine. Reprinted with permission.

When I first saw the photo, taken at the Abu Ghraib prison, of a hooded and robed figure strung with electrical wiring, I thought of the Sacramento, California, city jail.

When I heard that dogs had been used to intimidate and bite at least one detainee at Abu Ghraib, I thought of the training video shown at the Brazoria County Detention Center in Texas.

When I learned that the male inmates at Abu Ghraib were forced to wear women's underwear, I thought of the Maricopa County jails in Phoenix, Arizona.

And when I saw the photos of the naked bodies restrained in grotesque and clearly uncomfortable positions, I thought of the Utah prison system.

Donald Rumsfeld said of the abuse when he visited Abu Ghraib on May 13, "It doesn't represent American values."

But the images from Iraq looked all too American to me.

I've been reporting on abuse and mistreatment in our nation's jails and prisons for the last eight years. What I have found is widespread disregard for human rights. Sadism, in some locations, is casual and almost routine.

Reporters and commentators keep asking, how could this happen? My question is: why are we surprised when many of these same practices are occurring at home?

For one thing, the photos of prison abuse in the United States have not received nearly the attention that the Abu Ghraib photos did. And maybe we have so dehumanized U.S. prisoners that we have become as distant from them as we are from foreign captives in faraway lands.

In February 1999, the Sacramento Sheriff's Department settled a class-action lawsuit alleging numerous acts of torture, including mock executions, where guards strapped inmates into a restraint chair, covered their faces with masks, and told the inmates they were about to be electrocuted.

When I read a report in *The Guardian* of London of May 14 that it had "learned of ordinary soldiers who . . . were taught to perform mock executions," I couldn't help but remember the jail.

Then there's the training video used at the Brazoria County Detention Center in Texas. In addition to footage of beatings and stun gun use, the videotape included scenes of guards encouraging dogs to bite inmates.

The jail system in Maricopa County is well known for its practice of requiring inmates to wear pink underwear, and it is notorious for using stun guns and restraint chairs. In 1996, jail staff placed Scott Norberg in a restraint chair, shocked him twenty-one times with stun guns, and gagged him until he turned blue, according to news reports. Norberg died. His family filed a wrongful lawsuit against the jails and subsequently received an $8 million settlement, one of the largest in Arizona history. However, the settlement included no admission of wrongdoing on the part of the jail.

The Red Cross also says that inmates at the Abu Ghraib jail suffer "prolonged exposure while hooded to the sun over several hours, including during the hottest time of the day when temperatures could reach 50 degrees Celsius (122 degrees Fahrenheit) or higher." Many of the Maricopa County Jail system inmates live outdoors in tent cities, even on days that reach 120 degrees in the shade. During last year's heat wave, the Associated Press reported that temperatures inside the jail tents reached 138 degrees.

Two of the guards at Abu Ghraib, Ivan L. (Chip) Frederick II and Charles Graner, had careers back home as corrections officers. Graner, whom *The New York Times* has described as one of "the most feared and loathed of the American guards" at Abu Ghraib, worked at Greene County Prison in Pennsylvania.

According to a 1998 article in the *Pittsburgh Post-Gazette*, guards at the Greene facility behaved in ways that eerily anticipate the allegations from Abu Ghraib.

At Abu Ghraib, according to the investigation Major General Antonio M. Taguba carried out on behalf of the U.S. Army, there was "credible" evidence that one inmate suffered forced sodomy "with a chemical light and perhaps a broom handle." The Taguba report says U.S. soldiers were involved in "forcibly arranging detainees in various sexually explicit positions for photographing" and "forcing groups of male detainees to masturbate themselves while being photographed and videotaped." Guards beat inmates and wrote insulting epithets on their bodies.

The *Post-Gazette* reported that guards at the Greene County prison beat inmates, sodomized inmates with nightsticks, and conducted "nude searches in which every body orifice is examined in full view of other guards and prisoners." An inmate claimed that guards had used his blood to write "KKK" on the floor.

Although twelve guards eventually lost their jobs, Graner was, according to *The New York Times*, "not involved in that scandal." A lawsuit by an inmate who had been held at Greene accused Graner of beatings and other mistreatment, though the lawsuit ended up being dismissed.

Guy Womack, attorney for Graner, told CNN, "And, of course, in Abu Ghraib what he did--which was bad enough--is he was following orders. So he did nothing that was wrong. He was following lawful orders." Womack failed to return several telephone calls from *The Progressive* requesting comment.

At the very least, Graner moved from one prison where abuse was commonplace to another. Abu Ghraib was a familiar environment.

In a Utah prison, Michael Valent, a mentally ill prisoner, died after spending sixteen hours nude in a restraint chair in March 1997. As it turns out, Valent's death has a connection to Abu Ghraib. Lane McCotter was serving as the director of the Utah State Prison system on the day that Valent was put in a restraint chair. After Valent died, McCotter resigned. Six years later, McCotter was in charge of reconstructing Abu Ghraib, though he has denied involvement in the abuses.

The point is not whether McCotter or Graner are personally responsible for Abu Ghraib. They are part of a well-established system.

In another incident reported by Amnesty International that happened during McCotter's watch, an inmate at the Utah State Prison "was shackled to a steel board on a cell floor in four-point metal restraints for twelve weeks in 1995. He was removed from the board on average four times a week to shower. At other times he was left to defecate while on the board. He was released from the board only following a court order."

A preliminary injunction banning the restraint chair in Ventura County, California, found that jail policy "allows deputies to require restrained arrestees to either urinate or defecate on themselves and be forced to sit in their own feces or 'hold it.' "

The practice of forcing prisoners to soil themselves allegedly occurred in Iraq, as well. On May 6, *The Washington Post* published a description of the abuses Hasham Mohsen Lazim said he had endured at Abu Ghraib. After guards beat, hooded, and stripped him, Lazim said, "Graner handcuffed him to the corner of his bed," where he remained for days. "We couldn't sleep or stand," Lazim told the paper. "Even to urinate, we had to do so where we sat."

A few days later, the *Post* reported similar allegations from Umm Qasr, where Satae Qusay, a chef, said he was forced to "urinate on himself when he was prohibited from using bathrooms."

One Iraqi prisoner says he was force-fed a baseball and claims also to have been urinated on.

While most of the allegations from Abu Ghraib describe the torture and mistreatment of men, Iraqi women have also been subjected to rape behind bars, according to *The Guardian*. "Senior U.S. military officers who escorted journalists around Abu Ghraib . . . admitted that rape had taken place in the cellblock where nineteen 'high-value' male detainees are also being held," the paper reported in May.

Here, too, there is a resemblance between the reports coming out of Iraq and incidents at prisons and jails in the United States. In 1999, Amnesty International reported, "Many women in prisons and jails in the USA are victims of sexual abuse by staff, including sexually offensive language; male staff touching inmates' breasts and genitals when conducting searches; male staff watching inmates while they are naked; and rape."

"That was not part of my sentence, to . . . perform oral sex with the officers," Tanya Ross, who was jailed in Florida, told *Dateline NBC* in 1998.

Amnesty International has reports of "prolonged forced standing and kneeling" in Iraqi military prisons, as well as allegations of "the excessive and cruel use of shackles and handcuffs" at Guantánamo. Again, the Iraqi allegations seem almost to be extracted from earlier Amnesty International writings on human rights in the United States.

In a 1998 report on the treatment of women in U.S. prisons, Amnesty International noted, "International standards restrict the use of restraints to situations where they are necessary to prevent escape or to prevent prisoners from injuring themselves or others or from damaging property. In the USA, restraints are used as a matter of course. A woman who is in labor or seriously ill, even dying, may be taken to a hospital in handcuffs and chained by her leg to the bed."

In an earlier report on the United States, Amnesty observed, "In Alabama, prisoners have sometimes been tied to a restraint pole (known as the 'hitching rail') as punishment, sometimes for hours in the sweltering heat or freezing conditions. At Julie Tutweiler Prison for Women in Alabama, inmates have been handcuffed to the rail for up to a day."

In a deposition from the case *Rivera vs. Sheahan, et al.*, the Cook County Jail acknowledged that it would shackle a hospitalized inmate who was in a coma, reports Amnesty.

Abuses of restraints in the United States sometimes involve different technologies from those apparently in use among some soldiers in Iraq these days. According to a 1996 U.S. Department of Justice lawsuit filed against Iberia Parish Jail in Louisiana, one inmate allegedly spent eight days in a restraint chair. A pretrial settlement led the parish to stop using the chair.

In Iraq, the Red Cross evaluated people who had been subjected to solitary confinement, and the organization discovered indications of psychological damage. The group's medical delegate said Iraqi prisoners were "presenting signs of concentration difficulties, memory problems, verbal expression difficulties, incoherent speech, acute anxiety reactions, abnormal behavior, and suicidal tendencies. These symptoms appeared to have been caused by the methods and duration of interrogation."

In one case, an Iraqi prisoner who had been "held in isolation" proved to be "unresponsive to verbal and painful stimuli. His heart rate was 120 beats per minute and his respiratory rate eighteen per minute. He was diagnosed as suffering from somatoform (mental) disorder, specifically a conversion disorder, most likely due to the ill-treatment he was subjected to during interrogation."

Long-term use of solitary confinement happens in U.S. prisons all too often. Supermaxes are the most avid users of the technique. Prisoners at these ultra-high-security facilities often remain in isolation cells for nearly twenty-four hours a day. American prisoners also find long-term isolation psychologically traumatizing.

The *San Francisco Chronicle* reported in 2000 on a woman who had spent nearly four years in the The Hole at the secure housing unit of California's Valley State Prison for Women. She claimed to have had no human contact except for food trays that came through a door slot and threats from the guards outside her cell. She also said that the guards often denied her sanitary pads and toilet paper.

In 2001, a class action lawsuit filed by inmates of the Supermax prison of Boscobel, Wisconsin, called the facility an "incubator of psychosis" and alleged that mental illness was "endemic" at the prison. A judge ordered the removal of all mentally ill inmates, which Ed Garvey, a court-appointed attorney in the case, says amounted to "about one-third of the prisoners." Some of the inmates at the Boscobel prison, including those who had the most severe reactions to their isolation, were juveniles.

"It was interesting that the International Red Cross was upset that prisoners were held more than thirty days in isolation and for twenty-three out of twenty-four hours," says Garvey. "In Boscobel, that's the case every day. In the standards of the International Red Cross," the prison at Boscobel is "out of compliance with the Geneva Convention, which doesn't apply as such, but it gives you a measuring stick."

The Red Cross mentioned deaths in prison in Iraq, and the Pentagon is now looking at the deaths of at least thirty-three detainees in Iraq and Afghanistan. Two of these deaths have already been ruled homicides.

Inmates have died in U.S. prisons and jails under suspicious circumstances as well. U.S. deaths that occurred in connection with the use of restraint chairs alone numbered at least fifteen by 2002, according to Amnesty International. The Bureau of Justice Statistics is currently compiling information on the cause of death in custody in U.S. prisons and jails. Prisons and jails around the country are self-reporting the data as part of the bureau's new Death in Custody Data Collection Program. In U.S. prisons, in 2001 through 2002, there were eight homicides against inmates in custody that were not committed by other inmates. In U.S. jails, from 2000 through 2002, the number was thirty. The homicide numbers do not include deaths that result from such factors as poor medical treatment.

How could such things happen in the United States?

For one thing, since the early 1990s, American prisons have acquired a distinctly military cast. This influence is evident in boot-camp-style punishment, in prison technology, and also in prison and law enforcement conferences like the one I attended in 1996. That conference included long discussions on the ways military knowledge could help police and corrections to control crime. The sponsor of the conference, the American Defense Preparedness Association, was at the time sponsoring other conferences with such names as "Enhancing the Individual Warrior," "Undersea Warfare," and "Bomb and Warhead."

There is something else going on. Particularly in the last couple of decades, with the rise of ever-harsher criminal justice laws, Americans have become hardened to the people we put in detention or behind bars. We have acquired a set of unexamined beliefs: 1) people who land in jail deserve to be there; 2) criminals are bad people--almost subhuman--who can't be rehabilitated; 3) therefore, punishment can be as harsh as possible; and 4) we don't need or want to know the details.

These beliefs are constantly reaffirmed--in the mouths of pundits, in our news media, in our TV shows and movies, even in video games. They may help to explain why revelations of prison and jail abuse in the United States, which have been numerous in the past two decades, can fall on deaf ears in this country even as they prompt protest abroad. The revelations at Abu Ghraib shock us because our soldiers abroad seem to have acted out behaviors that we condone, yet don't face up to, at home.

In conversations over the past few weeks, I have heard outrage and anger over the abuse at Abu Ghraib. I have rarely heard such reactions in connection with abuse of prisoners in the United States.

When we tolerate abuse in U.S. prisons and jails, it should not surprise us to find U.S. soldiers using similar methods in Iraq.

George Bush said he was exporting democracy to Iraq, but he seems to have exported a much uglier aspect of American public policy--some of the most sadistic practices employed in the U.S. prison system.

* * *

The Taguba report is available on the World Wide Web at http://www.msnbc.msn.com.

The Amnesty International reports cited here are all available at www.Amnesty.org.

The leaked Red Cross report is available at http://image.guardian.co.uk/sys-files/Guardian/documents/2004/05/11/ICRCreport.pdf.

Anne-Marie Cusac's articles on the U.S. prison system can be found at www.progressive.org:

"Stunning Technologies"

"Shock Value: U.S. stun devices pose human-rights risk" "The Devil's Chair"
"The Judge Gave Me Ten Years. He Didn't Sentence Me to Death."
"Arrest My Kid: He Needs Mental Health Care"
"You're in the The Hole"
"Ill-Treatment on Our Shores"

Chapter Three

But What about Pedophiles?
Bobbie Harvey

Often when I speak in public the question comes up: "But what about child molesters?" When Bobbie Harvey, a writer friend, told me she was working on a book based on the journals of a convicted pedophile, I thought this was an opportunity to begin a conversation. Are pedophiles human beings? How do we treat them? Where should they live after serving their sentences? It's clear that if we truly want to end pedophilia we need to stop sexually abusing our children, most of whom are abused in their families rather than by strangers who are pedophiles. Many, if not most, pedophiles were sexually abused as children.

"John," an inmate at Graterford and self-described sex addict, writes about pedophilia:

Hello my name is John, I'm a sex addict. I've been asked to write some words about pedophiles. Because I'm part of a recovery group of sexual addicts, I know three pedophiles. Each one of these men was molested sexually as a child. There's absolutely no doubt in my mind that that is what has created their problem. Their trust was betrayed as children, and that has created within them a longing for the world of innocence of children. To some extent, the only truly safe sexual partner that their inner child conceives of is another child. A very tragic situation.

None of these pedophiles are active. One had a very long career working in institutions and, unfortunately, molesting children he and his wife had adopted at the time (he no longer has any contact with these children). The other is in prison; he saw the damage he was doing to his victim and sought help. A very valiant act. The result is that he's serving a 20 year sentence in a maximum security prison. A brave and very confused man. And the third person has only had one slight incident of acting out, thank goodness, but his life is still continually plagued by the fact that some part of him longs for the purity and innocence of children and, in some ways, he sees them as a sexual objects.

I'm sure what follows will give you insight into yet one more pedophile's experience. It's easy to demonize these people, to think of them as monsters.

But they really don't fall beyond the bounds of humanity. They are apparently decent people with a very serious problem. The three pedophiles that I know realize how serious that problem is and are working on it. I think it's important that they have the space to do that work because it does keep other children safe. Obviously the state has chosen, in one instance, to lock up one of my friends, although he only molested one child and turned himself in. It's a difficult problem. I certainly don't condone pedophilia because that's what happened to all of these pedophiles, they were abused as children. That should be stopped as soon as possible. But I think I would leave to you the conclusion of what should society do with these people, how should they be helped or punished. What's the most effective and compassionate way to prevent the next generation of pedophiles being generated by the current generation of pedophiles?

* * *

"Coming into prison was pretty much like dying."

"Louis Mason"

One December evening, the phone rang in Louis Mason's house, and his life changed forever. Six months later he would lose his wife, his home, his business and his freedom because of what he believed was love.

The phone call was from JT, one of Mason's oldest friends, accusing Louis of sexually abusing his two sons.

There were other boys, it came out the next day. Four of them, hundreds of incidents over ten years. Louis confessed to his wife; then turned himself in and told the police everything.

He was sentenced to 21 years in prison. His appeal for reconsideration of the length of his sentence after six years was denied. Parole was denied after eight years, after ten years, and again after twelve years.

The name Louis Mason and the victims' names are pseudonyms, to protect the boys as well as Louis himself. He still uses a cover story to explain his crime: other prisoners don't treat child molesters very well.

Louis was my oldest friend's second husband. I had only met him a few times – they lived in a different part of the country – and I wasn't sure I liked him; he made me uneasy but I couldn't figure out why. When my friend told me what had happened, and that he was in prison, her words struck me. "He loved those boys," she said.

I had met one of them once when I was visiting my friend. He didn't say much. A typical teenager, I thought, except that he spent most of the weekend with Louis. Maybe that's what made me feel uneasy.

"He loved those boys." Her words haunted me. Was this just the rationalization of a perverted pedophile? What if the boys consented, as Louis maintains to this day? Would it matter if the boys loved him back?

No, says Richard Gartner, Ph.D., founding director of the Sexual Abuse Program of the William Alanson White Psychoanalytic Institute. Consent is not possible in the unequal power relationship between an adult and a child, even a teenager. And, as he writes in his book *Betrayed as Boys* (1999*)*, "the nontraumatic impact on the victim does not make the behavior less abusive . . . When the abuse is orchestrated as a loving, caring, or playful act, the child is betrayed not only by the behavior itself, but by the lies, mystification, and confusion surrounding it" (p. 18).

Patrick Carnes, Ph.D., a prolific speaker and writer on addiction and recovery, goes even further. It's not love, he writes in *Don't Call It Love* (1992). It's sexual addiction: "[A]ddicts know that what they do is different, that it has a power of its own, and that they are no longer in charge of their lives" (p. 48).

Louis had been a prisoner for twelve years when I visited him. The prison was surrounded by cornfields that stretched to the horizon, and by silver concertina wire shining in the sun. I was his first visitor in four years.

He was dressed in green, like all the other prisoners crowding into the visiting room. His hair fell in blond waves to his shoulders; his eyes sparkled as he hugged me. He seemed lighter than I remembered, and more open. I felt very comfortable with him.

We spoke for four hours. He *did* love those boys, but he also knew that he was out of control, and, at some level, that what he did was wrong:

(From the prison interview)

Q: Did any of the boys ever say, "Do you think what we're doing is wrong?"

A: "Sam" at one point was questioning it. And sometimes he'd say, "No, I don't want to do this." I'd say, "Come on," and I'd harp. Sometimes he'd relent and say, "All right let's just do something here quick." Other times he'd say, "No!" and I'd leave, and I'd be depressed all night. But in general what I remember saying to him when he questioned it was, "Well if it was so wrong why does it feel so good?" "Yeah, I guess you're right," he'd say. "But don't tell anybody," I'd say.

Q: When you said you were depressed all night why were you depressed?

A: Because I couldn't get what I wanted. And that's where it started becoming an obsession . .

. I wanted that physical fix, that high, that adrenalin, that sexual rush. And at that point, I was out of control. No question. I started figuring that this was something we could do, and I could get what I wanted, and if they didn't give it to me I'd get it from somebody else. And that's where it started becoming dangerous, and where I'm rightly locked up over it, I think, because I couldn't get help.

Louis entrusted me with his writings so that I could tell his story: five volumes of journals, which he started one week after he was led out of the courtroom in handcuffs; an autobiography; and a "Sexual Assault Narrative," which he had to write as part of his treatment program. In the beginning he longs for his wife and the life he lost; he describes what prison feels like after the first week, the first year, and now – fourteen years later. He attends group and individual therapy for sexual offenders, comes out as a gay man and falls in love. Through it all, he struggles to reconcile actions that hurt the people he most loved with his belief in himself as a spiritual being.

The following excerpts tell a small part of this story. As Louis wrote to me, "I am so hopeful it will be of value. This life is not one that I would wish on anyone, but since it's mine, let's make it helpful to others."

EXCERPTS

<u>Remorse</u> *(From a letter to his wife, returning the divorce papers she had sent him to sign, after nearly one year in prison)*

Well, here are the papers. I hope you know this: if I had any *real* idea that what I was doing was as destructive as it actually turned out to be, on all fronts; that it would cause the disintegration of the entire world – well, I would never, ever have started. Please know this. This has been a high price to pay for my ignorance. I'm sorry.

<u>Growing up</u> *(From the autobiography)*

I was a sensitive boy and cried easily about a lot. I was told to grow up and hold back the tears. I was also quite shy. Other kids called me a "sissy" and told me I threw a ball like a girl. Before I was five, I recall a great fear of the dark – including large snakes living under my bed that came up and frightened me. They were like large street lamps that lined both sides of the bed and would lean down and strike at me if I wasn't on guard.

From my earliest memories I was slated to become a priest. Throughout grade school, I embodied the whole concept of the "perfect boy." I didn't use cuss words (I didn't say the "F" word until eighth grade, and I felt real guilty), didn't smoke or do anything "bad." I was an altar boy from third grade onward, and had a real emotional experience with it all. I bought it, all of it, including the guilt.

Early sexual abuse *(From the journals, Year 2)*

I got up in front of the mental health group and gave my story last Thursday. It took an hour to give a complete rundown of my life. Not much time, actually, considering it's taken me 42 + years to live it. But a pattern did emerge, one of much living outside the normal. Seems there may have been some sexual abuse in my childhood. The first time I can actually remember being forced to do something I wasn't sure about was to suck an older kid at knifepoint when I was 12 or 13, at camp. That was the beginning of the "real stuff": hard, large dicks and me. Something burned deep into my psyche at that point – I can still feel it – a mixture of awe, fear, excitement and tremendous fascination with the darker forces of sex. And here I am, over 30 years later.

Spiritual life *(From the journals, Year 1)*

I am finding that living the spiritual life is the only life to live. Doing this in prison is, in one sense, maybe a bit trickier: one has very little control over very much. It is a very narrow band. But within that narrow band of possible experience, one still has the spiritual choice to be responsible – to reveal integrity. Once again it has taken an unpleasant episode to wake me up to further responsibilities – to continue to grow deeper roots in the spiritual life. Maybe I will begin to stay fluid, dexterous, sharp-witted in Truth without the need of such reminders from circumstance.

Tonight I watched the crescent moon set over the mountains. Its position in the sky was perfect to see through a window from my cell.

On Prozac *(From the journals, Year 4)*

Can it be that all this muddling through the days, forcing myself forward a step at a time has been a biochemical imbalance? If that is so, and the heaviness lightens, it will mean a change in myself that goes back at least 25 years. The dark days and nights of my mid and late teens. Those times that I described as "the front of my head caving in" during my early twenties. Those black rages later on through my thirties, bringing me here through all the swamps and caverns of the prison nightmare. I feel released

Prison Reflections, Year One *(From the journals, Year 1)*

I entered this system not a "criminal" by mindset. I respected authority, albeit not liking it. I believed in law and order, to a certain degree. Not any more.

I respect these guards as much as I respect a cockroach. Now that I've seen the so-called "justice system" at work, from the street cops to the courts, I spit in their faces. They deserve worse. It's crooked, self-serving, dishonest and corrupt.

Yes, I deserve some kind of punishment, in the eyes of society. In my own eyes, I think it wouldn't be like this. All of this has been nothing less than torture: mental, emotional and physical. I truly hope and trust that spiritually is of some use – to someone, and maybe to me, whatever good that might do at this point.

Prison Reflections, Year Fourteen *(From a letter to the author)*

SEDITIOUS PEACE

Sedition is a state of mind. Not all of us can (or want to) carry sticks, guns or bombs as an expression of our discontent. But all of us can be of the mindset of PEACE. Peace is THE most revolutionary, seditious option that we can represent. And it's one that the people in power don't seem to get.

If each of us stopped fighting, in and outside ourselves, and let go of the virulent anger and hate that even people committed to peace can become entangled in, then EMPIRE (and the emperor as well) would have no more fuel to feed the furnace. All those dried-up old men and women would look around, find no fresh faces to feed to their angry gods, and begin preying upon each other.

In prison, sedition can be as simple as refusing to go along with the crowd and choosing to be a person, not just a number. Act a little too independently, and you might find yourself hauled off to a segregation cell. Speak out just a little bit too confidently, too actively, too noteworthily, and away you go. Think creatively, challenging old ruts of behavior, even if those ruts are obviously headed right off a cliff, you better keep it to yourself, or, yep -- you guessed it; segregation.

So what can be done within the confines of confinement? (And aren't we all, in one way or another?) My answer is: BE PEACE. Don't buy into the control mindsets that prevail all around.

Sedition, choosing to live the different life of revolutionary peace, will bring about positive change. Let the old, fear-laden, hate-filled EMPIRE feed upon itself, and may the driest, most withered of them win -- and get blown away freshly of a new spring.

* * *

In his book, Patrick Carnes describes three stages of recovery from sexual addiction: "Grief," a time of remorse and taking stock of one's life; "Repair," when the addict begins to take responsibility and grow spiritually; and finally "Growth," a commitment to a different way of living. I see these stages in Louis's writings. But has he recovered? When he is released, will he re-offend?

According to a 50-state survey conducted by the Colorado Department of Corrections, it's unlikely that he will re-offend. Recidivism was significantly lower for sex offenders than for the general prison population, and lower still (below 10%) for those who had participated in treatment programs. Barry Maletzky (1991), in a study of 855 patients with homosexual pedophilia, reported a successful treatment outcome for 86.4%.

Even so, when Louis is released from prison, he will be required to register with the police and, in some cases, the FBI, as a sex offender. Depending on the state in which he chooses to live, the community may also be notified of his presence.

He hopes to live with the man he fell in love with in prison, who has now been released. As Louis wrote to me recently, "We shared love continuously, caring for each other's welfare and well-being. I've never shared my life with anyone else who knows and understands me from the inside out; who wants to be together till the stars fall from the sky."

REFERENCES

Carnes, P.C. (1992). *Don't Call It Love: Recovery from Sexual Addiction.* New York: Bantam Books.

Colorado Department of Corrections (2000). State Sex Offender Treatment Programs: 50-State Survey. (www.doc.state.co.us/programs.htm)

Gartner, R.B. (1999). *Betrayed as Boys.* New York: Guilford Press.

Maletsky, B.M. (1991). *Treating the Sexual Offender.* Newbury Park, CA: Sage Publications.

Postscript

Preventing Sexual Abuse
Bobbie Harvey

In late 2002, as the sexual abuse scandal in the Catholic Church was making headlines, the *New York Times* published an article by Linda Villarosa entitled "To Prevent Sexual Abuse, Abusers Step Forward" (December 3, 2002). The article quoted Dr. Keith Kaufman, chairman of the psychology department at Portland State University in Oregon and president of the Association for the Treatment of Sexual Abusers: "We have had a 20-year history of a singular approach to prevention with a focus on relying on kids to protect themselves from adults," he said. "This doesn't even make sense logically. Why do we think it's right to give children the huge responsibility of protecting themselves from sexual offenders?"

The national non-profit organization Stop It Now! was founded in 1992 with a similar premise. Their mission is "to call on all abusers and potential abusers to stop and seek help, to educate adults about the ways to stop sexual abuse, and to increase public awareness of the trauma of child sexual abuse." According to their website (www.stopitnow.org):

No prevention program has ever directly challenged abusers or those at risk to abuse to step forward for help and to take responsibility for a crime committed. No prevention program has directly asked family members of abusers or those at risk to confront inappropriate sexual behaviors within their families. Stop It Now! programs across the country and the United Kingdom are testing this idea. Based upon the successes of these programs we will modify and expand the media and outreach programs regionally and nationally.

Stop It Now! has websites and programs in Georgia, Philadelphia, Minnesota, Vermont, and in the UK and Ireland.

Louis Mason would agree with this approach. Shortly after his incarceration he wrote a proposal for "a new program developed to assist known and, as yet, undiscovered child sex offenders." He described the purpose as follows:

Because federal and state law requires that social workers, therapists, counselors, teachers, and many other professionals must turn over known child sexual offenders to law enforcement agencies, those individuals who might consider seeking professional help to stop their activities most often do not, for fear of the vast legal and socially humiliating consequences. Therefore, to provide a means for those people [child sexual offenders] to deal with this situation voluntarily would be the express purpose of this program. Also, it would seek to create a broad and vivid awareness of the damages caused to the victims of child sexual abuse.

Listening to and actually working with convicted child molesters is not an easy thing for most people to do. Judy Little, executive director of a non-profit organization for victims of childhood sexual abuse called Voices in Action, was quoted in the *New York Times* article: "The professional and humanitarian in me believes that if we are ever to stop this cycle, we have to help perpetrators heal and allow those that are healed to take part in prevention," she said. "But part of me is still hurting inside from the abuse that I suffered, so I don't care what they have to say. I don't want to hear the empty excuses for their behavior."

On the other hand, relying on children and their parents to prevent sexual abuse clearly is not working. Perhaps it is time, as Judith suggests, to begin a conversation – a conversation where we recognize pedophiles as fellow human beings who may actually want, and be able, to help.

* * *

"The person who doesn't fit in with our notions of who is worthy of love – the bag lady at the corner, the strange old man who rides through town on a three-wheel bike all strung up with flags – is just the person who, by not fitting into our patterns, insists that we expand not only our views but our capacity to love. Today, see if you can stretch your heart and expand

your love so that it touches not only those to whom you can give it easily, but also to those who need it so much."

Daphne Rose
Kingma

Chapter Four

The Hole

Many human rights organizations consider the use of "The Hole," or "Restricted Housing Units," cruel and unusual punishment. "E. M. Emerson," who wrote the following account of his experience in The Hole, is a pseudonym for a man who has been in prison for 35 years. He considers Ralph W. Emerson to be his spiritual father, and Emily Dickinson his spiritual mother. He carries a book of her poems in his back pocket.

OUT OF CONTROL IN THE BACK YARD OF CENTRAL OFFICE
"E. M. Emerson"

In the back yard of the Pennsylvania Department of Correction's Central Office sits one of the most brutal and inhumane restricted housing units (RHU) in the entire Commonwealth. Having recently spent over a hundred days there, I witnessed staff brutality and DOC policy violations on a daily basis.

It blew my mind to watch some inmates being denied meals for one and two days at a time, all because they were guilty of talking out loud or being child molesters. At every single meal I watched someone getting burned because he wasn't standing at the precise angle in his doorway when the food cart passed by, or he wasn't dressed properly, or he'd been observed having a conversation with his neighbor. Once a prisoner who'd been denied his meal shouted out this passage from the DOC Inmate Handbook: "Denying food will not be used as a form of punishment." The hateful guard shouted back, "This is Camp Hill, fellow. We do what we want here!" And they surely do.

At every shower period on Monday, Wednesday, and Friday, men are denied showers on a whim. First, the guards scoff at any prisoner who asks for a shower during his first week. Then if a man is in the RHU for violating some infraction against a staff person, he is further punished by being repeatedly ignored when he asks for a shower. They take nine men to the showers at one time. If there are eleven prisoners on a tier or section who want to shower, two of these men are going to be burned. They'll enter the cells and find some graffiti on the wall or some other excuse to deny men a shower. Then there's the matter of the water temperature – it's determined by the particular mood of the guard in charge that day! One day it may be scalding hot, the next day ice cold. If any man is heard uttering a word once the water is turned on, everyone is punished – they cut all the showers off, and everyone is forced to go back to his cell lathered in soap. Finally, when a holiday falls on a Monday, there are no showers that day.

Another violation of both PA and federal laws comes in the form of denying an hour of daily exercise. The exercise cages are all there, but not once in my one hundred plus days was I afforded the opportunity to go out in the exercise yard. When I asked a lieutenant why they don't allow yard, she said, "That's preposterous. All you have to do is sign up." My wife called the prison one day to inquire about my yard, and she was told that the log book showed I'd had yard that very day. That was a vicious lie. (A couple of men did get to go out in the exercise yard while I was there. These men were, I was told, on long term administrative custody status.)

Once I watched two guards enter the cell next to mine and beat a fellow until he couldn't cry out any more. All the while, a female lieutenant stood on the tier watching. When she said, "Okay, that's enough fellows," one of the guards shouted back, "We're not done yet , LT."

The sickness doesn't stop here. I personally saw them handing out confiscation slips to an inmate whose mail included a newspaper clipping or two. Once this same fellow was denied mail that was labeled "legal" and "religious materials." All of his confiscated mail was placed in his property. What about phone calls? Well, here's another blatant DOC policy violation.

In the words of the RHU's Program Review Committee chief, "We don't do phone calls." What about additional commissary items for men on long-term administrative custody status? "We don't do that either."

At every turn, Camp Hill's RHU is designed to break a man's spirit in every way possible. A building without air conditioning, the place is a festering hot box in the summer, with temperatures reaching 110 degrees at times. The walls of the cinderblock cells are covered in sheets of metal which serve to keep the heat intense. Men who try to write letters in this sweltering heat find themselves dripping sweat all over the paper. Thus, we learn to write in the middle of the night when it's not as hot. During the day those who have been there long enough have learned to flood the floor and lay in the cool water in an effort to bring one's body temperature down and make things a little more bearable.

Then there are the cockroaches and waterbugs the size of matchbox cars running around interminably. Once I awakened in the middle of the night to find one of these giant bugs crawling in my hair and after that, I made it a habit of sleeping with a towel over my head. Throughout the day you can hear several times in every hour the slap! of men's shower shoes as they kill bug after bug and curse like sailors in the process.

Every single day I spent in RHU, I thanked my lucky stars for my loved ones who kept me grounded in hope and restraint. There were days when the mail came to my door and I cried with gratitude, just for the reminder that I was loved. Feeling that love was the perfect antidote for the hatred and rage I'd built up inside of me all day toward these vicious guards. I have always believed that my spirit could withstand the harshest treatment and conditions that could come my way.

I don't believe that any more.

As vigilant as I was, I couldn't shield myself completely from their brutality. They confiscated a piece of my mail almost daily and placed it in my property, sending me a confiscation slip with an explanation that the envelope was too big or it contained religious materials. Twice, too, they came in my cell on shower day and denied me a shower after they found someone else's scribblings on the wall.

No. The oppression prisoners are subjected to in RHU would crack the toughest human's spirit. On those days when I would watch my fellow prisoners being physically and mentally tortured, I cried for them and thanked God it wasn't me. I was torn and dejected nevertheless.

After observing these guards for all those weeks and months, I came to realize how truly self-loathing they are. Treating prisoners cruelly is the way they validate their own existence; it's their key to power.

What amazes me more than anything about the brutality and inhumanity that continues to take place in the RHU is that it is condoned by high-level staff. All of these men are aware of what is taking place there, and each has his own spin tactics for denying the truth. These men are professionals, and they 're good at what they do. When they say brutality and inhumanity don't exist in their back yards, who's to argue with them? And who cares anyway?

* * *

"Louis Mason," profiled in the previous chapter, was sentenced to 21 years in prison for child sexual molestation. About six months after he arrived, a capsule of an antibiotic he had been prescribed for a cold was found in his cell, and he was sent to "The Hole" for a week. The following excerpts are from letters he wrote to his wife.

LETTERS FROM THE HOLE
"Louis Mason"

October 30

Hello from the dungeon. Yes, that's what this place, this particular section of The Hole, is called. It is all still quite a shock to me that I am here.

I'm now in the belly of the dragon. I guess I had to see this aspect too. It's majorly barren: the cell is about 6x9 feet, not much different from the others, but there is only a toilet/sink and a cement slab shelf with a mattress pad and thin pillow. No shelves, no table, no stool – nothing else. And I'll be in this cell day and night. The light is dim overhead and that's about it. The walls are a yellow-beige, with various graffiti, drawings and calendars drawn or scratched out. "Home" for seven days, which is actually a short span for this place. There are some men here for several months!

The guards in Unit 1 were very nice – the one who escorted me to the Seg wing said I was the last guy he thought would end up in the Hole. He said to take it easy and not make a fuss and I'll be out in no time. He pointed out that this could be a quick and easy lesson to be absolutely diligent in my behavior. He acknowledged that I was a model inmate otherwise, and this should sharpen me up even more. If I can get the coffee addiction under control, it will be all right. It's quiet here. I'm alone. I can see out of a window to the west somewhat – not much, but some. The sun shone into my cell before sunset tonight. It was good. A guy brought a book cart by earlier and I picked out a couple.

This Hole time comes just as I was exploring the options of college. Tomorrow I had an interview scheduled.

October 31

So what is this solitary hole time to accomplish? I wonder. It's very dark when the dim lights go out. It was almost too quiet – it *was* too quiet – during the evening hours. Yes, I can pretend the Zen monastery routine again; I can pretend this is a learning experience to sharpen my wits, but the facts are that I'm being disciplined for an offense DOC sees as very serious. On paper, this looks like I had *real* drugs, or needles, when the fact is it was a stupid pill. No matter, they tacked on 8 more points and it will take a few *years* for them to go away. I'm in quicksand in the belly of this dragon – stillness is the answer, but it's not easy to be still when everything is in a turmoil.

November 2

The hours here are so very long. It is very difficult to adjust to this snail-pace of time. I want to appreciate all of this, for what it has to offer: quiet (it is very quiet most of the time, an almost cavernous, echoing silence); space (there is nowhere to go and nothing to be done); and time (without any reference points like clocks, watches, bells, announcements, time has become very fluid – but so much so I fear I could drown in it).

This kind of opportunity gives me the chance to go deep in my thinking, and I have. It is an "intermission" time between, to look at who, what and how I have been handling my life thus far. I'm almost afraid to look deeper, for what is down there? Have I but covered over all those dark and tangled motivations that I acted on before, that put me here? In looking close, I think not. True, there is a numbness present when I look in that direction, and I believe that is good. There is no longing for the old ways.

The big event of the evening around here was one guy figured out how to get a spark out of a light socket to light a piece of toilet paper to light a cigarette. I was quite amazed to find that several of the men had cigarettes, papers and/or tobacco! How they get it in here, through all the searches, I'll never know. But in keeping with my "deliberately totally clean" policy, I didn't participate – not even asking for a puff. I can be right on purpose. It's the ghosts that seem to get me. Maybe they are all finally out of the closet, or almost. It is true that I had a long period of secrecy and double living – no wonder there have been so many ghosts around.

November 3

Being here is like being in some Grade B movie script, or more like radio I suppose, since it's only voices that you hear. Every so often, someone will say something, and a wave of comment will go through, then fade. Now and again, I get asked for a comment about a point; otherwise I rarely say anything. There's a certain bizarre camaraderie present here.

November 4

Approaching the end of Day 5. I have been enclosed in this 6x9 foot space continuously now for about 60 hours. I have not had a shower since Friday morning. Never, as far as I can recall, have I spent so much time in such a small, cold, smelly, hard-edged, inhospitable space. Less than 2 days remain. In the morning, I will be permitted a shower, and about noon, opportunity to go outside for an hour. I will go, no matter what the weather. This has been quite a marathon.

* * *

Albert Brown was sentenced to life in prison in 1945, at the age of 25. In the following interview, excerpted from *Life Without Parole* by Victor Hassine, he describes The Hole in the now-closed Eastern State Penitentiary in Philadelphia.

"Then there was what they called the Hole. I remember there was a guy they say cursed at the Deputy. They put him in the Hole for four days. Then they took him to the Deputy and they say he cursed at him again, so they put him back in the Hole for 30 days. When they took him to the Deputy again, they say he acted up again. But they figured he was crazy and so they just let him alone after that. The Hole was a four-by-four-foot cell with a solid door they kept shut. You couldn't stand up or lay down all the way. You'd get bread and water in there with a full meal every three days. No sir, that Hole was no joke."

* * *

"A well-ordered police state rests on the cornerstone of a cowed citizenry…an electorate sedated by the drug of fear."

Lewis H. Lapham

PART V
Friendship, Love and Sexuality

Ancestral Rhythms

Oil on canvas   Muti Ajamu-Osagboro

Chapter One

Sexuality and Relationships

"In here, babies die by the billions"

Anton Forde/Trevor Mattis

This was one of the most difficult topics for the men to address and again some of them just couldn't do it. Those that could were promised their privacy would be respected by not having their names revealed.

SEX IN PRISON
Anton Forde/Trevor Mattis

If you should ask the average inmate in prison to analyze the effects of his being incarcerated and ask him to pinpoint the single most painful punishment to him, he would say it's the lack of sex. Yes sex. Pussy is the most powerful force known to man. If given the choice between sex and freedom 90% of the inmates would choose sex. It's better to be able to have sex and no freedom than to have freedom and no sex. Sex is the undisputed master of all men's desires. How many men do you know, and I'm speaking impoverished men, who would give up their sex organ for ten million dollars? Most men would rather live a miserable life and die a pauper than give up their sexual function.

With this in mind, I have developed a revolutionary approach to the alternatives to incarceration. It is very cheap and would be much more effective than the present prison industry. Since the essence of punishment by incarceration is the denial of sex, let's just deny sex without the infrastructure and overhead costs of imprisonment. All we'd have to do is design a chastity belt for males and I guarantee you we would have the most conforming generation of men in the history of mankind. A six-month sentence to the chastity belt with no ability to have sex or masturbate would be more effective than five years imprisonment. Now a true deterrent would be in effect.

Sex in prison is prevalent. I would estimate, depending on the prison, at least 40% of the inmates are involved in some type of sexual contact within a year. If we include masturbation as sexual activity, it would be 99%. Homosexual contact accounts for 95% of the sexual contact in the most restricted of prisons and about 50% in the lesser-restricted ones. At least 15% of the inmates in the average prison population engage in regular homosexual activity and this is a very conservative number. In Pennsylvania, it's closer to 20% and as much as 40% if we include irregular homosexual contact. That is, inmates who engage in homosexual activity but on an irregular basis. These numbers would be even more startling if you look at inmates who had some type of homosexual contact over a five-year period; it would be close to 50%. The true number of inmates engaging is hard to determine because of the secrecy involved. You can easily see the relative numbers when a particularly feminine-looking homosexual is in the population.

In Pennsylvania, less than 5% of the general inmate population is overtly homosexual. When I refer to homosexual I mean anyone who participates in homosexual activity. Most inmates tend to differentiate between the giver and the receiver. They define a homosexual as the male performing the female role in sexual contact and don't include the male performing the masculine role.

A fact that may startle you is some of the types of inmates who engage in homosexual activity. I find that among those considered players on the streets, I mean the men considered the most handsome, those known to have had the most girls on the streets, a good 60% of them engage in homosexual activity in prison. There's no criterion you can use to judge which inmate is involved in homosexual activity. I mean none. I've seen the most venerable and respected inmates involved, from Imams to notorious gangsters.

On the issue of rapes in prison I'll only say this: It happens. It occurs more frequently than is officially acknowledged but much less than you think. Studies indicate one out of five prisoners has been raped.

Sex between inmates and staff does occur but it is relatively rare: 99% of the time it does not last for too long, since the parties are usually discovered quickly. This usually is due to: 1) the indiscretion of one of either party; and 2) to the prevalence of jailhouse snitches (officially referred to as confidential informants) and inmate jealousy. In prison, a mere note on a piece of paper placed anonymously, or mere suspicion is sufficient to have an individual inmate placed in The Hole (RHU) for months, then transferred.

Sex between inmates and their visitors: The visiting room where it can occur is where the majority of the heterosexual relationships occur. It is atypical sex, somewhat degrading to a normal person and most of all it has to be quick. Given the circumstances and the passion for human sexual contact, this, whenever and however it can occur, is always worth the consequences and possible repercussions and they are many to the average inmate.

There are a few other ways heterosexual activity can occur in prison. These are ways the most astute and creative inmates have developed. Only a few inmates fall into this category. I will not discuss any of these esoteric methods fearing I might reveal trade secrets. Everything isn't for everybody, and maybe one day, if I'm fortunate, I'll be employing them.

A final note worth mentioning: It is really strange that prison officials frown upon heterosexual contact between inmates and go to the utmost length to eliminate it; however, they basically look the other way on homosexual contact between inmates, sometimes even seem to encourage it.

* * *

Yesterday morning, an intense sadness came over me as I watched two guards, a man and a woman, patrol the yard during the two-hour recreation period. It was a beautiful morning with bright sun and gentle breezes. I noticed the carefree way in which the pair slowly walked around the yard, deep in conversation. Though I couldn't hear what they were saying, their facial expressions and body language clearly conveyed that they were discussing something quite intimate. The special way she smiled at him, tilting her head, listening and looking at him as he spoke, caused a painful stirring deep within my soul.

It's been so long since a woman responded to me that way. I envied the male guard, for he was experiencing something I've been denied for most of my adult life. Between them was an openness and intimacy that was simply beautiful to behold. As I stood alone in one corner watching them, I was overcome with a deep scnsc of desolation. This feeling was so intense it brought me to tears. Yes, dammit, I cried. I cried because something inside me longs to experience that level of closeness with a woman.

It's amazing how the small things that many men take for granted can mean so much to me.

Having been in prison since I was a teenager and thereby denied the opportunity for positive and healthy interactions with women has impacted on me in ways that mere words cannot accurately convey. Sometimes I dream I am free and in the presence of a beautiful woman. We are sitting beside each other, both of us naked. I say to her, "Please just let me hold you." As I hold her in my arms and feel the warmth and sensuality of my flesh against hers, I begin to cry. It is at this point that I always awaken. Lying in the dark cell, my face and the pillow wet with my tears and my senses alive with memory, I feel tortured by the vividness of the recurring dream and the intensity of my desires. And yet, despite the pain, I'm glad for the experience, if only in my dreams.

I know many men who've been in prison so long that they are no longer capable of dreaming. They neither have nocturnal dreams nor thoughts of ever experiencing anything beyond these walls. This is something I find amazing and sad. This inability to dream or see beyond one's present circumstances says a lot about the negative effects of long-term incarceration and the hopelessness and despair that can set in when human beings are locked in cages and treated like animals.

What can a society hope to accomplish through such dehumanizing methods?

* * *

One of the most difficult aspects of my incarceration is the pain I feel as a direct result of being denied access to women. Besides the forced celibacy, having little or no positive interaction with women has had quite an impact on my life and my development as a man. Even with the love and support of my mother, sisters and female friends who visit occasionally, not being able to share and grow in a healthy adult relationship with a woman has created an unnatural void in my life. Because I was only a teenager when I was sent to prison, I've never had a chance to have a real partnership which has really stunted my development. The impact is often quite painful. There are times when I cry for the love and inspiration that only a woman can give to a man; this is what I yearn for the most.

It is a myth that all men in prison are involved in homosexuality; such is not the case. Sure, because most prisons are all male environments, quite naturally there exists a certain level of homosexuality, but the level isn't high. There's also a myth that lifers frequently engage in homosexuality, but this too is untrue. Most of the homosexuals are men serving short sentences or are repeat offenders. Rapes are becoming less frequent as many more men are participating in religion, which is bringing about a remarkable change in the prison sub-culture.

For me, refraining from participating in homosexuality hasn't been that difficult. Having sex with another man isn't something I find at all desirable. Plus the sexual abuse I suffered as a child has left me with so many hang-ups and insecurities that I seldom allow anyone to get too close to me.

Prison has had quite a negative effect on me. In order to survive, I've become withdrawn and I know I have a warped sense of myself and others. As Anton Forde says in his book, *Contemplations of a Convict*, "Prison irrevocably changes a person. Much in the same way that war does. The experience changes you, but you don't necessarily have to show it. Though you feel normal and may act normal, you're not normal."

I often think of the difficulties I'll encounter upon my release. Readjusting to the world beyond these walls will present me with one of the greatest challenges of my life. Twenty-five years is a long time to be trapped in someone's prison. There are so many things I've lost touch with. How will I adjust? Who will be there to help me? Will I be successful and never return to prison?

These are questions I often ask myself.

* * *

Dealing with issues related to my sexuality during the past twenty years of incarceration has been extremely difficult. From the beginning, I've maintained communication and friendships with women on the other side of the wall. This has always been important because it keeps me in contact with the world. Also, I'm afraid I'll lose touch with my ability to relate to and interact with women. I've tried to stay in contact with women I knew before coming to prison, and though my circumstances dictate the limitations of what level of intimacy I'm able to experience, I've struggled to maintain as meaningful relationships as possible. Trying to maintain outside relationships is difficult; many men simply choose to do their time alone so they don't have to deal with the pain, disappointment and aggravation of trying to stay connected with family and others.

Then there are many family members and loved ones of men in prison who just aren't able to visit or can't afford the exorbitant cost of collect calls, the only kind allowed. I know many men who've been at Graterford for years and have never received a visit or even mail from anyone beyond these walls. It's not that no one out there loves them, but for some people it's easier to close their minds to the pain and struggle of others.

I'll never forget a friend of mine, Mike. He was a lifer, a few years older than me from my old neighborhood where he was well-respected and always had pretty women, nice clothes and fancy cars. His family came regularly and were very supportive. His four children came whenever anyone would bring them, but Mike didn't know how to love from prison. This was a source of great pain for him, because he wanted to be loving but just didn't know how. One day out in the yard I asked him how he coped with the pain of missing his children and family. He looked at me and said what he felt was the most humiliating powerlessness a man could ever feel.

Soon after our conversation, they found Mike dead in his cell of a drug overdose. I often think of Mike and how important it is for people, especially men in prison serving extensive sentences, to learn how to love in the face of extreme difficulty.

* * *

There are no conjugal visiting rights in Pennsylvania like there are in more progressive states. Prisoners are not allowed to have sex with visitors. As a heterosexual man, this has been very difficult for me.

To make matters worse, inmates are only allowed to briefly embrace or kiss visitors as they enter or exit the visitors' room. This embrace must be simple and brief, otherwise a guard will be quick to approach you and demand that you separate from your visitor. If caught kissing or hugging during the visit, an inmate is subject to receive a misconduct, which could result in his being sent to The Hole for a 60-day period as well as losing his visiting privileges for up to a year. Some men do engage in homosexuality and in many instances the institution promotes such activity as many guards just look the other way when they encounter such acts. It's accepted as normal behavior here.

I've always been afraid of being caught up in homosexuality, fearing that besides it not being attractive to me, it would damage my self image and take me too far away from who and what I am. I refuse to risk so much. Plus I have enough personal troubles and hang-ups without adding that shit to it. Therefore I have not had sex of any sort, except for a few encounters with a former girlfriend while in the county jail awaiting trial. Even that was against the rules, but guards were paid and rules broken.

My desire for sexual intimacy is as strong as ever.

During the early years in prison, not having access to women was the cause of a great deal of stress and tension. I sought release through strenuous exercise and sometimes fighting with other inmates.

The long nights are the most difficult.

Sometimes I lie awake as my whole body and soul come alive with a longing that masturbation can't quench. There's a crippling impact caused by the loneliness I often feel at the lack of access to a woman. Sometimes it's so bad that throughout the day I move around as though caught in a dark cloud of depression. I feel incomplete and stunted in my growth. Years ago, while on a visit from my mother, I shared with her my longing for a meaningful relationship with a woman and how at night I pray for God to send me someone to love.

My mother told me to just hold on because one day I'll find the proper woman and all will be well. She also told me that out there somewhere is a special woman who's praying the same prayer as I am, and God has already decided that the two of us will come together, but we have to wait until the time is right. So I wait, remembering what Mom told me. One day, when this nightmare is over, I'll be free to experience all that being in prison has denied me for so long. Sometimes I wonder how I will adjust after being alone for so long. I'll just have to go slow and give myself time. It is said that time heals all wounds. Perhaps it will heal mine as well.

One day I'll get my chance to be all that I can be. I just have to keep holding on. I will.

* * *

I can state for the record that I am NOT homophobic. I like all kinds of people in my life, and that includes homosexuals.

Things happen sometimes which are out of our control and one has to come clean. Just because I am not sexually attracted to another man doesn't mean I have hang-ups. It's just that the same sex doesn't do it for me regardless of the circumstances.

Yes, being incarcerated in a men's prison for many years brings on some desires one wishes could be tightly locked away.

When I'd only been in prison for five years, I recall a guy I got friendly with. Gay before he came to prison, he was very comfortable with who he was. The sexual dance started off very easily. In my mind, I will always see him as a nice person. He came to my cell every day early in the morning. We talked about everything under the sun, from sports to relationships. I'd never had any open sexual feelings toward another man; I was fresh meat for him.

That summer, my sexual yearnings hit an all-time high, though my feelings weren't about him. He took advantage of all occasions to touch me in a non-sexual way. I enjoyed the attention he showered on me. After awhile, he asked me if I'd like to have sexual relations with him. I told him I enjoyed our friendship but didn't want it to reach that point. He really wanted to have a sexual experience with me to endear himself to me, but I just couldn't get into the moment with him. So he backed away, and sat on the edge of the bed and we just talked the morning away, neither of us referring to what had almost happened. Instead of fighting over this, we became the best of friends. I think what he really did for me was to make me see that people who are gay are in a light that is all their own. To this day, I'm comfortable around all kinds of people.

* * *

Chapter Two

Those Who Love Prisoners and Those Prisoners Love

The Visiting Room

The wall of waiting women silently wails and weeps
as Daddyless children wander, their energies restless
in such a place where Daddy's treated like a thing.
Each woman holds a number, like a piece of deli
meat.
Hearts broken over and over; cruel guards treating
them
like the human garbage their loved ones have
become.

How did they come to be in such a place?

Recorded by cameras, the women and children
have just a few cherished moments with him.
Secret talk and silent touches under scrutiny,
trapped and guarded like wild animals in a cage.

Soon they must leave him again, going alone,
shivering
into the cloudy dusk, a half-moon peeking
from behind dark shadows, a reminder of the Light
as the sun sets on yet another day in Shadow
America.

Judith Trustone

No one more eloquently articulates the agonies of loving a prisoner than Asha Bandele, whose memoir *The Prisoner's Wife* has become a best-seller. Going into a New York prison to teach poetry workshops, she is seduced by the words of one of her students, words that men inside must cultivate if they want to communicate, words that all women hunger for that so many free men seem to lack. She says, "You haven't lived until you get a love letter from a prisoner!" Eventually they marry in prison, and, because New York is a state that humanely allows conjugal visits, they are able to spend a few nights together in privacy and intimacy every couple of years, though their lovemaking is interrupted when it's time for her husband to be counted.

After eight years, Bandele stops visiting him because she can no longer tolerate the abuse by the guards.

The stereotype of a woman in love with a prisoner is of someone with low self-esteem who is unable to find a man on the outside. This picture demeans the thousands of women (and unfortunately too few men) with the courage to care about prisoners. Connie DeLano certainly fit no such category when she married a much younger man of another culture and color in Graterford's visiting room. Connie's heart lives full time in Shadow America. Bright, gentle and articulate, her clear blue eyes sparkle with love as she talks about her husband, José Hernandez, twenty-one years her junior and from another culture.

Connie's late father was a minister who volunteered at Graterford. He was so taken with José, a young lifer, that he introduced him to his daughter twelve years ago. She was in an unhappy marriage and working in the corporate world when they met, and the connection they both felt immediately was puzzling. Under these unlikely circumstances, a relationship never crossed her mind.

As the attraction between them grew stronger, she was increasingly impressed with who he was despite the horrendous experiences of his young life. She says, "His spirit is mind-boggling. His thirst for knowledge and understanding constantly amazes me."

Her son and daughter, both in their thirties, aren't happy about their mother's commitment to José. Her closest friends are supportive; some have even been to the prison to meet him.

Their wedding took place in the Graterford visiting room on New Year's Day, 2000. She wanted the ceremony in order to reaffirm her commitment to José. She visits him once a week, though sometimes they cut back because the environment of the visiting room is "hard to handle." Because of DOC rules, they may hug, kiss briefly and hold hands, all under the constant scrutiny of video cameras and guards. Their phone calls, always collect, are monitored and recorded. Imagine some invisible stranger listening in on every phone conversation, often a prisoner's only link to the outside world, to family and loved ones. For the rest of your life.

Connie says, "The guards are either polite or disapproving of our age and color differences. One time we were sitting together, and José put his hand on my knee. The guard shot out of his chair, screaming, and grabbed José and took him away. When he returned, trembling, he told me the guard had threatened to write him up for making sexual advances to me."

José calls her two or three times a week, and their attempts at verbal intimacy always include a third, anonymous person. From his 41-cents-an-hour job, he sends her frequent gifts, and, at times, money, according to the values of his Hispanic culture. In networking with other women married to prisoners, Connie has found them to be intelligent, caring, concerned about racism and social issues.

"If I had it to do over, I would without hesitation. I have no regrets. I've become a much stronger person. I pray a lot, and have conversations with God. I stand by José and my belief in his innocence and his right to live a free life."

Sadly, Connie couldn't tolerate the life of a prisoner's wife, and they divorced.

The following "Visiting Room" stories, most by inmates who wished to remain anonymous, illustrate the poignancy – as well as the humiliation – of those moments when prisoners and their loved ones are reunited.

* * *

The scene is the visiting room at the Pittsburgh prison. An elderly woman is weeping as a young man tries to comfort her. She'd traveled a great distance to see her incarcerated son for the first time in years. She'd been through cancer and chemotherapy, and when she went through the rigorous search by guards, one of them snatched her wig from her head to see if she had any contraband. Weakened by the humiliation, the weary woman had to sit and try to regroup to regain the strength any mother needs to visit with her imprisoned child.

* * *

One Saturday morning the guard came and told me I had a visitor. I walked to the visitors' area, pulled down my pants and bent over before being allowed into the room. Once there, I waited an hour and a half for my visitor to be admitted. Then a guard told me my visit had been canceled. At that point I had no idea who'd come to see me. When I asked the guard why the visit had been cancelled, he arrogantly responded, "They left." Not wanting to give him the pleasure of humiliating me even more, I left the room to return to my cell, once again baring my butt to the guards.

As I walked back, a silent rage bubbled in me. But I knew if I exploded it would only make things worse. To react emotionally by throwing a tempter tantrum or demanding the guards provide me with more reason for the cancelled visit would accomplish nothing except for maybe a trip to The Hole and possibly a brand new case of "assaulting an officer." I kept my emotions in check and lay down on my bed, comforting myself with the knowledge that if the visitor who'd left was my mother, she wouldn't have left without a legitimate reason. Two hours later, the same guard showed up at my cell to tell me again I had a visitor. Once more I made my way to the visitors' room, once again bending over and showing my ass to the guards.

Forty-five minutes later, my mother and seven year old niece appeared. Once my niece spotted me through the crowd, she ran straight for me and flung her little arms around me in a warm embrace. I picked her up and held her in my arms and for several minutes I stood there oblivious to everyone and everything. Eventually my mother, my niece and I moved through the noisy, crowded room, searching for a place to sit.

Mom explained that she'd arrived at the prison at 9 am. After she'd been sitting in the waiting room for several hours the guards called her up to the desk and said she needed more extensive identification for my seven year old niece. They claimed that the two pieces of identification she'd shown them wasn't enough. And even though my mother produced a copy of the parental visiting approval form that my sister was required to fill out and send back to the prison ensuring that she had given my mother permission to bring her to see me, that wasn't enough. They still claimed more identification was needed. How much identification can a seven year old have? The parental forms are required before any child below 18 can visit. Without the forms, adults are not allowed to bring children into the institution. Despite the fact that my mother had the form and several pieces of identification for her, my niece was denied access. So my mother and my niece drove the 45 minutes back to Philly in order to get my niece's birth certificate, then all the way back to Graterford. By the time I saw them they were tired and stressed out, but we still managed to have a good visit.

What my mother experienced was typical of the way visitors are treated when attempting to visit their loved ones here. It's as if the guards go out of their way to harass and discourage visitors. This treatment has been inflicted on my family for the past twenty years. I can understand why some of the guys in here never get visits.

One time, the guards at the front desk denied an elderly aunt of mine a visit because she refused to strip naked and submit to a complete body search. She was 79 years old at the time. They claimed to suspect her, an old woman, of attempting to smuggle drugs into the prison. My aunt said they talked to her as if she was a criminal, taking her off to a side room and totally disrespecting her with all sorts of crazy accusations. But, as I said, such treatment is typical. Visitors are constantly harassed and discouraged from visiting. Some swear never to come back after experiencing Graterford's visiting room practices.

I've always wondered what it is that causes prison guards to treat inmates and their loved ones with such contempt and disrespect. This negative treatment and attitude isn't just in relation to white guards and black inmates. In some instances, black guards treat black inmates worse than white guards do. And most of the time, this ill treatment isn't expressed in the form of physical violence, for rarely do the guards actually brutalize inmates. The brutality is more psychological.

They play head games and constantly nag and harass inmates over the most petty things. It's as if many of the guards possess a deep-rooted hatred and resentment toward black inmates. Most of the time, when an inmate assaults a guard it's because he's been pushed so far he just can't take any more abuse. The guards know if an inmate pushes or strikes them, it will result in a new case and a new sentence, adding to time to be served. The guards know this and use it as a psychological blackjack to beat inmates over the head with. For me, a new case and sentence of any sort added to what I'm already serving would place me in a position where I'd never get out of here. This is why I can't afford to allow my emotions to dictate how I respond in any situation, be it with another inmate or with guards. Because of this I've grown into an expert at finding viable alternatives to violence. I simply can't afford not to.

My future freedom depends on it.

* * *

One recent evening, guards entered the cell in which I was housed and ordered me to strip search – get naked – to prove I wasn't concealing any weapons or contraband. After putting my clothes back on, I was handcuffed and taken directly to The Hole without explanation. Several hours later, a written incident report was dropped into the cell simply stating that I was being placed under "Administrative Custody," stating "inmate is a danger to some person(s) in the institution who cannot be protected by alternate measures." Now what this meant I still don't know.

On my third day of being held incommunicado in The Hole (unable to write a letter or make a phone call to anyone), a guard informed me that I was scheduled to be transferred to another prison. An hour later I was told I had a visit and was escorted in handcuffs to a small room separated in half by a thick Plexiglas partition. On each side of the partition was a row of stools and telephone receivers through which a visitor and prisoner could speak. Already seated on one side was my mother. Still handcuffed, I picked up the phone on my side and sat down.

My mother's first question to me was, "Are you okay?" I told her I was fine and asked how she found out I was in The Hole. One of my friends had called and told her what happened. I shared how I had absolutely no idea what was going on, and that I was to be transferred. Where to I didn't know. With those few details out of the way, I went on to assure my mother that I was okay. I hadn't been charged with breaking or violating any institutional rules or regulations. We were allowed only a one hour visit.

And despite the handcuffs and thick partition separating us, I reassured her that all would be well and I'd call her when I reached whatever prison they transferred me to. It was important that my outlook on the situation was positive because I knew my mother needed to draw from my strength and leave the prison knowing I was okay.

The next morning, around four o'clock, I was awakened by guards, handcuffed, shackled in leg irons and tossed into a van with no idea where I was headed. Looking out into the semi-darkness through the van's window, I was mesmerized by what I saw. As the small van exited Graterford's property and began to snake its way through the early morning traffic, I was filled with an incredible sense of fear and excitement.

Sprawled out before me was the world beyond the prison's huge walls, a world I had been locked away from for the past 21 years. The trees, the roads, the houses, the people, their cars, everything had an eerie look about it. I felt as if I was seeing these things for the very first time. Yet I was afraid because I didn't know where they were taking me. I was so emotionally overwhelmed by the experience, I didn't notice I was crying until I felt the wetness of the tears rolling down my face. I laughed when I went to wipe them and couldn't because the chains wrapped around my wrists and body prevented me from even the slightest movements.

For twelve hours I sat chained in that hot-ass van as it traveled all over Pennsylvania, stopping at prison after prison, finally reaching my new home. My entire body was aching from sitting chained in the same position for so many hours. Once inside the prison, I was fed and then placed in a temporary holding cell to await an official hearing scheduled for the next day.

At the hearing I was asked whether I knew why I was transferred. I told them that I had no idea. One of the hearing examiners, who had what I assumed was my folder in front of him, snapped "You were transferred here because you were suspected of being involved in a major drug ring." I responded that this was the first time I had heard such an accusation. Another of the hearing examiners then stated, "There's no report of any misconduct charges against you involving drugs. So they probably made such a claim to justify transferring you. They do it all the time. Apparently someone wanted you out of there, and quickly."

So here I am, all the way at the other end of the state. I've been placed directly in the prison's main population. And although I hate all prisons I hear this one isn't that bad. Some say it's better than Graterford. I guess we'll see, huh? One thing for certain is that I know damn near half the other inmates here. Having been in Graterford so long, I've mingled with some of the roughest prisoners in the state. And, since I've always been a man amongst men, I get a lot of respect from other prisoners. It matters not whether it's here, Graterford or any other prison.

So far, I kind of like it here. My younger brother from California and his wife came to visit me here last week. The visiting room here is a lot better than at Graterford, a much less oppressive environment. They've actually got beautiful trees and flowers in their visiting room yard. It felt so wonderful sitting under the shade of a tree with those I love. And the guards weren't walking around harassing us.

As far as visits go, my family will visit me even if I were to suddenly be transferred to China. My squad is tight like that. We've successfully survived 21 years of Graterford. Surviving anywhere else is a piece of cake. Plus, as black folks we're experts at surviving.

* * *

My visits have been limited these past three years. However, prior to that I was receiving regular visits from my then wife and two small children. Perhaps for the children there are drawbacks to the experience of seeing their father in prison. But this must be weighed against not seeing their father at all during the long years of incarceration. Even though I haven't seen them for the past three years, I believe the knowledge and constant reminders from exposure to media, prison literature, and their mother that their father is in jail has already caused irreversible damage.

I'm not sure how to describe the effects that visiting me here had upon my wife. Certainly it wasn't all positive. Of course, it helped to continue our turbulent connection, but overall, I think the visits created more problems than they actually helped to save. On many occasions, we would argue or I would poke or badger her about any possible extramarital affairs. Unfortunately, the reality of a wife or girlfriend having a relationship with another during the time of incarceration is a very bitter pill to swallow. The end result of a visit was usually a mixture of hope, denial, desperation and anger. It has always been exhausting for me and others.

* * *

In August, I got a visit from a couple of friends, Anthony and Elizabeth. I have known both of them since childhood. Elizabeth, who goes by the name of Bitty, came to see me because she would be going away for some time, working to retard alcoholism and drug abuse on Native American reservations.

Bitty came in with a white outfit with the top coming down to her knees to match the shorts. The guard pulled the top up without her consent to see if the panty line could be seen through the shorts. A female guard told her that she would not be allowed to visit me because she could see her panty line through her shorts. Luckily Anthony keeps his workout clothes in the trunk of his car, and just had them laundered.

I could see the pain and hurt on her face and I implored her to write or make an appointment to see the superintendent about the assault on her physically and mentally by this corrections officer. But she was afraid of what the guard would do to me later on. I told her I will be glad to have her report this guard so it will not happen to the next person. But as the visit went on, I could see that this would be the last time I would see her behind these prison walls. As they were leaving, Bitty pressed herself against me like it would be the last time I would see her in this setting again. Sure, she made a promise that she would see me when she got back, but I knew I'd never see her again until a miracle would occur and I would be released. Anthony promised he would come back to see me when he got another weekend free. As they left, I had felt it would definitely be the last time I would ever see Bitty.

The moral to this story is that the prison system claims it promotes the building of relationships with family and friends, but they seem to do all they can to break these ties down every chance they get by making women visitors feel so uncomfortable that some will have doubts about ever returning again to prison to visit friends.

* * *

"Wendy Pellinore" and Betty Jean Thompson both have firsthand experience with the visiting room. Wendy chose a pen name so as not to bring retribution on her imprisoned son. Betty Jean Thompson is a teacher and prison activist whose son was recently released.

The cost of imprisoning these two mothers' sons is, so far, close to $350,000 each.

THOUSAND POUND VISITS
"Wendy Pellinore"

I weigh 1000 pounds. I barely tip the scales at 120, but I am carrying the weight of years of accumulated stress. The weight is invisible, but it casts its shadow on every sunny day, taints every bite of food, and turns the earth to quicksand. It drags down every thought, tugs at every word. I have become scatter-brained, forgetful, routinely confused, distracted and disconnected.

It is my first visit to my son in jail at Chester County Prison. My husband and I visit separately in order to break up his weekly routine. My son has not yet been sentenced for his drug offenses. I am angry with him and resent having to take a place among the dregs of society that I expect I will find in the prison visiting room. I decide to put all 1000 lbs of myself into a bubble in order to avoid contamination. I try to attain a Zen-like calm.

My picture taken, I wait in the outer visitors' room. I notice random things: the guards' tattoos and pot bellies, how many people are speaking Spanish, the number of babies and toddlers, the absence of older kids. My name is called. I go to the double doors. It reminds me of the birdhouse at the Philadelphia Zoo. One door must close before the other opens in order not to let the birds escape. I mention as much to the woman waiting between the doors with me. She does not respond. I think perhaps she has never been to the Philadelphia Zoo. Maybe she doesn't speak English. I curse myself for leaving my bubble. I get back in it.

I sit at a table and wait. The room could pass for any corporate cafeteria without the food. I stare straight ahead, but I can see through my bubble. I notice the overwhelming number of young prisoners, but my attention is drawn to the older couple waiting at a table in front of me. I think they are there to visit their son or grandson, but I am mistaken. An older prisoner approaches. The gray-haired lady jumps up and exclaims, "How are you?!" They embrace and he replies, "Better, now that you are here." I turn away. I try to swallow.

My son enters the room. Our visit is strained. It does not go well. I look about the room. And then I see her: a middle-aged woman presumably visiting her spouse. The visit is over and she is hurrying to the door. She is trying not to cry before she can escape. She does not look back as her husband disappears with the guard wearing the bright blue gloves. Her mouth is set, breath held, eyes brimming. The bird door just can't open fast enough to let her out before she loses her dignity. I realize I am looking at myself.

Several months later I visit my son at SCI Camp Hill, a two-hour trip. I am still angry, but not with my son. My non-violent, drug-offending 21-year old has been sentenced to 4-10 years with innumerable years of probation attached at the end. He is at Camp Hill to be "classified." We find out he has been exposed to and/or has tuberculosis. He has also contracted a skin fungus. He is being treated for both in addition to another medication he takes. I am now worried that he could contract hepatitis. I send him newspaper clippings about the hepatitis epidemic in the prison system. I sign each letter, "Be Aware – Don't Share!" He pays for the nurse's visits out of the commissary money we send him. We are appalled to find out Montgomery County takes 20% of every cent we send him to cover "court costs."

I enter the outer visitors' area. The guard barks at me to get behind the red line. I look everywhere and can't find it. Another visitor points it out to me – it is on the wall, not the floor. I wait and wait. I notice random things: the girth of the guard at the desk where he sits, eating; the plastic bags that people bring their money in for the vending machines; the number of babies and toddlers; the lack of older kids. I note the racial makeup: I am the only white visitor in the room. My name is called and I go through the bird doors that lead inside/outside. I find the correct building and visitors' room. My son awaits. I hardly recognize him. He is 40 lbs heavier. He no longer does drugs so he has attained his proper weight for his height. Our visit flies by. He asks me for a TV, but I can't afford the $180 plus 20%. I tell him he has to wait. He understands the meaning of the word "wait."

It is eleven months since my son was first incarcerated. He is now in SCI Cresson, a four-hour trip. We go together now, my husband and I, because the visit requires an overnight stay. It has turned into a costly and time-consuming event. We try to make the best of it. We pretend it is the long weekend that we had been planning to take to see the change of leaves in New England. We note that this trip will be hazardous and impractical during the winter.

The next morning we drag our unspeakable sadness, our collective 2000 pounds to SCI Cresson. We enter the outer waiting room. There is not much to notice here. There are only a few people waiting. They all speak Spanish. At this moment I cannot remember one word of Spanish. I play peek-a-boo with the toddler. Another young mother enters with her baby. She tells me it is 5 weeks old.

We enter the inner visitors' room through the bird doors. Our son awaits. Now he has a beard and we joke and tell him he looks like a Dutch boy. He tells us his cellmates thought he was Muslim. I look at my beautiful, tubercular, fungified, ADHD-addled son and feel the weight of my 1000 pounds pressing me into my seat. He has his TV now. He shares it with 3 other TV-less cellmates. He has completed his citizenship course. He works in the kitchen. The visit flies. My eyes wander: I notice the father of the 5-week old baby. He is holding the baby on his lap and his eyes do not leave her. He stares at her in awe the entire time. I turn away. I try to swallow.

I discarded my bubble a while ago. I realized after the first few visits that I would not be "contaminated" by the people around me. There are only regular folks here in the visiting room: they are our neighbors, business companions, teammates, fellow taxpayers – all carrying their 1000 pounds of sadness. But I am still angry and confused.

When did we, as Americans, become comfortable making laws based on sound bites and clichés? **3 Strikes?** We must be satisfied with sentencing repeat offenders according to the rules of baseball. It does give new meaning to "The Great American Pastime." **Zero tolerance?** We must be content to absolve our leaders from looking at individual circumstances and taking responsibility for making decisions. **Mandatory minimums?** We must be endorsing the power of the District Attorney to decide the case instead of trusting our judges to exercise their powers of discernment. **Trying juveniles as adults?** Is this not an oxymoron?

One of the basic laws of science states that matter cannot be created or destroyed, only transformed. I add my 1000 pounds of sorrow to the 1000 pounds that each prisoner's loved ones carry. I come to my unscientific conclusion that there must be a way to transform this tonnage of sadness into the critical mass of energy needed to fix our broken system of justice. And I marvel that God forgives, but our astoundingly self-righteous society does not.

* * *

"A mother's love for her children, even her ability to let them be, is because she is under a painful law that the life passed through her must be brought to fruition. Even when she swallows it whole she is only acting like any frightened mother cat eating its young to keep it safe. It is not easy to give closeness and freedom, safety plus danger. No matter how old a

mother is she watches her middle-aged children for signs of improvement. It could not be otherwise, for she is impelled to know that the seeds of value sown in her have winnowed. She never outgrows the burden of love, and to the end she carries the weight of hope for those she bore. Oddly, very oddly, she is forever surprised and even faintly wronged that her sons and daughters are just people, for many mothers hope and half expect that their newborn child will make the world better, will somehow be a redeemer."

Florida Scott-Maxwell
The Measure of My Days

* * *

A MOTHER'S TALE
Betty Jean Thompson

My only son is an inmate. He has been in prison since 1992. One day in May of '92, an awful thing happened. A man was killed. My son was convicted of third degree murder in the man's death. I am sorry for the sorrow caused by my son's actions. I know that my sympathy will never relieve the family's pain. I still agonize over this terrible situation. My family was traumatized too!

Many people forget that as a mother of an inmate, I am sometimes made to feel like I committed the crime. I am not a horrible person. I am simply a mother who loves her son. I do not love my son any less because he is in prison. I can feel his pain and frustration, his fear, his guilt, his humiliation. He tries to hide it but a mother knows. I guess it's what we call "Mother's Intuition."

I have been grieving over and over with no reprieve. I try very hard not to show how scared and grief-stricken I really feel. You see there are times when I see my son fading away from life, wanting to slip away, just give up. I can't let that happen. He looks to me for strength, support and hope. There is no way I can allow myself to break down in front of him. I know he could not take it. I don't want him to give up on himself. He is talented and intelligent. I know most people don't care what happens to him, and fewer care what happens to me. I often feel that I am held accountable for the crime too! I am not ashamed of my son. I am saddened by the choices that he made as a very young man. Soon after my son's conviction, he was brutally beaten by some correctional officers at Holmesburg Prison. He was beaten so badly that when he came out for a visit, I did not recognize my own son. It was that beating that catapulted me into becoming an activist.

Betty's son, Larry, came home at last, and then co-authored a novel with her. A Candlelight in the Darkness was published in the spring of 2005 by Infinity Publishing.

* * *

The following is reprinted with permission from A Life for a Life (Roxbury Publishing Company, 2004) by James A. Paluch, Jr. Paluch was sentenced to life imprisonment for murder in 1991.

A WIFE DOING LIFE
Dianna L. Hollis

In 1982, little did I know that when I fell in love with my husband Mr. Peach, a lifer, I would face so many ups and downs because of his sentence. Our relationship grew from mutual respect and friendship to love, as we worked together in the Dispensary at SCI Camp Hill.

Being married to a prisoner, especially a lifer, is a very difficult situation. It is a very lonely life that causes a feeling of emptiness deep within. He is not there when I return home from a hard day's work to discuss how my day went or to have someone to vent my feelings to. There is no one to wait for, no one to greet at the door after his day's end.

When a crisis arises, he is not there to comfort me, to hold me, to offer his knowledge and wisdom, or to provide the emotional and spiritual support I need. When I call the institution to ask staff to have him call me, I am oftentimes told I have to go through his counselor, who is gone for the day. If he is given the message, or when he calls home, our phone calls are monitored with no privacy. He is not there to help me with household problems and chores too physically taxing for a woman to complete. He is not there to nurse me when I am sick.

At times, a sense of anger and frustration comes over me, but I have no helpmate to deal with the daily responsibilities that I alone face. Certain times of the year are more difficult than others. I see couples walking in the spring when the trees and grass become green with new life, new beginnings – wishing we could share just the simple things in life that other couples take for granted, feeling envy of others who have the opportunities that we sorely lack.

Christmas is a time to share with your loved ones, but my husband is clearly absent. On New Year's Eve, he is only in my thoughts as a new year begins. I wish he were here to kiss the New Year in, wondering if this year will bring him home.

Being married to an incarcerated man often forces me into secrecy because of people's insensitivity to prisoners in general. It is as though I lead two lives – one that people see and one that is hidden, making up white lies about what I do on my day off when I go to see my husband in a prison visiting room.

My loneliness is enhanced because there are few nonjudgmental people, even family members, with whom I can discuss my relationship. There is always the chance that I will be perceived as "crazy." People are easy to criticize but unwilling to learn about Mr. Peach and the reasons why I am committed to him. At work, it is difficult to hear women talk about plans for their vacations and holidays, the things they have bought their husbands for their birthdays, or vice versa, while having to deal with the reality of my own life. I feel myself being excluded from conversations with people who know my situation, or I probably feel that it is useless to engage in such conversations because of their insensitivity to me.

The financial responsibilities fall completely on my shoulders. From 1983 to the present, I have held two jobs. When Mr. Peach needs anything, it is up to me to supply his needs. I pay the overly excessive telephone rates that I am charged when he makes a collect call from a state prison. Because of the increased costs, we have to talk less often – increasing once again my feeling of loneliness and separation. The costs of weekly visits take a financial toll on me as well. Gas, car maintenance, the high cost of food from the visiting-room vending machines, and photographs are all personal expenses.

It is easy to say, do not visit and do not accept his calls, but those two very things, including Mr. Peach's letters, keep me going from day to day. When I leave him at the end of the visit, I immediately start counting the days until I can see him again. When I have a hectic week, I find comfort in knowing that I will see him soon. It is those visits that restore me, and quite honestly, they are some of the few times when I truly laugh and enjoy myself. I do things and go places, but I constantly feel the sadness and emptiness, that hollow feeling, all because he is not there with me. I picture in my mind how we could be doing things together. I find that even though I am in the free world, I am merely "existing," going through the motions but not living. For me, it is not what you do but who you do it with that matters.

Dealing with the incarceration itself is very stressful, causing physical problems like hypertension for both of us. The threats of bogus misconducts that could separate us permanently, retaliation, racism, and harassment in the visiting room over petty things are constant.

I worry about Mr. Peach's health, because the medical care and treatment he receives is below the standard for those of us out here in society. Medical policies in prison constitute pure negligence. I worry that, should he ever injure himself or have a life-threatening condition, will he get the proper care? I seriously doubt that he will.

I worry about Mr. Peach's safety, should there ever be a riot or a disturbance inside the prison. Will he become an innocent victim? He was supposed to call, I think, and he did not. Is he okay? The anxiety I feel disturbs me, until I am able to hear his voice. Oftentimes, we lose the means to communicate. When I call the prison, the staff is sometimes unwilling or too incompetent to give me the information that I need. There is also the anxiety of a prison lockdown, which happens from time to time. I am never sure when the lockdown will end or when I will be able to visit again. Will it resume on my day off, or must I wait until I have another day off?

As happened four years ago, I worry that he will suddenly be transferred, perhaps farther away from me, because I have spoken out against injustices and wrongs perpetrated within the system. Unfortunately, retaliation and racism are often difficult to prove.

I remember reading about one lifer, Reginald McFadden, who was given the rare gift of freedom via executive clemency, and how he failed. McFadden, who was not a meritorious lifer, was only granted a commutation of his life sentence because he provided testimony against some alleged participants in the 1989 Camp Hill riots. McFadden's undeserved release, then his later crime of rape and murder in New York, has caused deserving Pennsylvania lifers to pay dearly because of the government's irresponsibility.

I think of Mr. Peach's commutation papers sitting on the Governor's desk for a year and a half, waiting for a decision, only to be denied, no reasons given. Yet, someone like McFadden was granted commutation. So now my husband is being held accountable for not only McFadden's criminal actions but for some politicians' and bureaucrats' irresponsible deeds. It haunts me to think that Mr. Peach was just a signature away from freedom. I ask myself, will it ever happen again? I long just to share some of the best years left of our own lives together.

Despite the negatives surrounding my husband's incarceration, our relationship has indeed grown stronger over the years. We have experienced many trials and tribulations, but our love for each other has sustained our marriage. Mr. Peach has great faith, and it is because of our faith in the Creator that we have survived. I have often told him that if he were not the man he is, I would not have stayed in the relationship, because it is too difficult. Consequently, I believe that we know each other better than most married couples do in the free world.

We use most of the time we share together to learn about each other, discussing issues and reading the Holy Scriptures without the distraction of outside influences like television. We have grown in mental love, and each of us usually knows the other's thoughts and feelings –often writing about the same things in our letters. He treats me with respect, and I feel like a special, loved woman. I feel warmth, and I am aglow in his presence. He is my emotional and spiritual support, as well as my advisor in the many hardships that I face, offering his unique wisdom. He has a good sense of humor and he lightens the heaviness I so often feel.

I could never walk away from our love, despite all the negatives. I have devoted myself to him and to our 20 years of marriage. To let another woman reap the rewards of my hardships would be wrong. Perhaps that is selfish on my part, but that is how I feel.

Mr. Peach and I have great faith in the Creator. We believe that if He says, "it shall be," it will be. We pray that He will fulfill our prayers, and that Mr. Peach will come home.
Until then, I too am "doing life."

For most of the SageWriters, their feelings about their loving and loyal mothers (and occasionally fathers) reach almost mythical proportions. Here are just a few testimonials.

* * *

MOTHER
Danny Haggard

When I think of my mother, it is often with sadness and appreciation for her undying years of love. She is no longer with me, but I can now look back and know that she gave to me what I can never have again. Unconditional love. Although I didn't understand the hardships she faced throughout her life as a single mother and deaf-mute, I now can see how much she sacrificed for her only son. She always gave without question. Even though I didn't have the best clothing or the latest sneakers, as least I had them. No matter the poor decisions I made in life, she never turned her back. She made sure I went to school and showed her love the best way she knew how. She was always there for me. In the end, I wasn't there for her. This is a cross I must bear for my life and would change if I could. We are only given one mother in this lifetime and I shall always miss mine.

Tears in Paradise

If the souls of the righteous are
allowed to grieve once they physically leave...
I know my Moms is cryin' at this very moment cause
She's missin' me just a sure as I breathe.

Muti Ajamu- Osagboro

MAMMA I NEVER TOLD YOU SORRY
Anton Forde/Trevor Mattis

It's been twelve years since they found me guilty
and took my life from me. Mamma, I know how much
you cry and stress yourself with worry about your only
child, the apple of your eye, in whom you vested your
future, wasting away your dreams in a prison cell.
When friends ask you where's your son, you're too
ashamed to tell. You know you brought someone
great into this world, a lawyer, a doctor or a world
leader, only to see him become nothing but a
common prisoner. I know you fell because I let you
down – Mama I never told you sorry. You did
everything for me, sacrificed your own self, only child
– single parent, you went hungry to see me eat
properly. You went poor to make sure that I had all
that I needed. Many times you gave up a vacation to
ensure I got an education. You delayed your life until I
became an adult, but look at the result: in your eyes it

must be an insult. Mama, I never told you sorry, I know you had aspirations and dreams to live through me. I had the ability but lacked the opportunity; it's a sad reality, but life brings with it no guarantees. You did good, did all you could, made me into a good person, don't be ashamed of me for any reason, my situation being locked up in prison, in no way reflects upon you as a person. Don't cry; hold your head high, what was meant to be must be. Mama, I never told you sorry. I promise that one day I'll make you proud; as long as I have life, you'll live to see a day when the world recognizes me. The day will come, when you'll be proud that I'm your son for what I achieve, because you always believed you brought someone special into this world, believe me – Mama now's the time to say it: "I'm sorry."

* * *

Onc day I'll make it home, baby, one day I'll be free
Then I can thank you for all the times you've loved me.
I'm doing life without parole, but I'm still hoping
To get out of this hole and find you waiting…

Anton Forde/Trevor Mattis

The Message

Gentleman, we stand here before God and
Ourselves, as witnesses of the utter
Devotion of motherhood.

To the very tips of the follicles that grace
Our crowns, to the lines that crease the
Soles of our feet – we men should proclaim
All our mothers' nobilities.

She, and she alone, my grateful equals,
Carried your flesh and your soul for nine
Laborious months.

She is as much a part of you as the solar
System is to the Universe. Your very flesh
Should remind you constantly that you will
Never escape her protective uterus.

Your presence is still felt in her womb.
She still screams for joy when you kick.
She still remembers her lack of the "now" as
She rubs her stomach.

The mothers are with us. Can you hear them?
"That's my Baby." "There's my boy."
"My Baby has grey now." "Mine has a beard."
"Why is my son wearing brown?"

If you but take a moment to listen to your
Heartbeat, their conversations can be
Heard. "Thump, thump!" "Thump, thump!"

I'VE TOLD THEM MAMMA!   *Christopher R. Murray*

MY FATHER
Tony Harper

My father has been there for me for most of my time in prison. He's been with me through the good times and bad, when everybody else in my life couldn't stand the test of time. Yes, it takes a very strong person to stand by someone you love who's incarcerated. Because time, as well as some of the staff, will do everything imaginable to turn them away from you. But my dad is a strong person because he laughs in their faces, because our love for one another is stronger than the evil that dwells in the people who have me locked away.

* * *

John Griffins's eloquent memoir, <u>A Letter To My Father</u>, was published in 2001 by Xlibris.com. Written just before his brother died, it captures what it was like growing up in North Philadelphia in the tumultuous sixties, his relationships with his children, and his involvement with the Nation of Islam. In his book, he documents the events that have affected his family since his father's death as a soldier when John was four years old.

John is still in prison and has just published a new book..

MEMORIES
John Griffin
($1,140,000)

My mother raised my brother, James, and me to be respectful to everyone, especially women. We never heard a curse word, or the dreaded 'N' word in our house. She was an exceptional woman. From the day my father died – he was killed on my fourth birthday – she became both mother and father to us. She exemplified love, confidence, and courage, and taught us about our father's love for us.

My love for my father, my respect for him and all that I know about him came from her. She saved all his pictures for us; little mementos and letters he had written to her while he was serving in the army during WWII. It was because of her efforts that my brother and I learned the true value of family.

From *A Letter to My Father*

A collection of past events
Coexisting as images.
Some are mine,
Others are borrowed
From those who knew you better than I.
Sometimes I confuse the two. Their memories
Become mine. Their time with you

Became my precious moments. My personal
Glimpses into a mirror, shattered,
Each piece reflecting a different view,
A separate part of the same puzzle
In the mind of a three-year-old. Fragmented
Images of a tall, dark man
With a white, toothy grin,
His outstretched arms
Reaching down over a vast distance,
Lifting me, picking me up,
Rubbing his cheek against my skin. And,
Through another shattered piece,
I see his large hands,
Rope-like veins pushing up
From beneath black, leathery skin,
Wiggling like fat worms as I
Play with them, pushing them
This way and that way.
But it wasn't just the memories
Though we cloaked ourselves in them.
As if they were a shroud rendering us safe,
we anchored them around our necks so that
no other man would have our love.
It was her devotion to you, a display
Of loving that never changed
Even after her life had been tragically altered.
Like a poetic griot, she gave you life in death.
She excited our young minds with accounts of you;
Like an artist, her words the brush,
our minds the canvas, she brought you into our world.
With a voice more enchanting as she spoke,
Sometimes pausing, an intense hush adorning her
As she seems to relish and appreciate the taste
of her thoughts. Like the food a mothering eagle feeds
to her young, her words rolled around in her mouth

before she'd drop them, unselfishly,
into our minds. No, it wasn't just
the memories, Dad, it was her love.

John Griffin

* * *

Toni Cyan-Brock, who is married to a prisoner.
Prisoners of Love   www.prisonersoflove.com.

MAIL CALL IN THE PENITENTIARY
Timothy John Brock

The prison is hot and humid tonight. The cement that makes up the walls collects the humidity like the outside of a drink glass on a summer's day. Inmate Tommy Jackson nervously paces the day room. It's been a long weekend, four days with no mail issue, and he's burning for a dose of his baby's love.

"Pass out the mail, punk!" he hollers out angrily.

His voice was loud enough for the guard to hear, and Tommy looks around like he's also wondering who hollered. He wipes his nose with the back of his hand, then folds his arms across his chest, scanning the dayroom for somebody to vent his frustration on.

Mail call is running late tonight due to having an asshole cop working on his cellblock, and the tension is so thick that you could cut it with a shank. Attitudes crack like so many firecrackers on the Fourth of July. Easygoing inmates are not so easygoing. Sundays and holidays are dreaded because there is no mail issue on those days, transforming the prison into an even grayer, more somber place.

Tommy can barely contain his apprehension. This gradual wasting away of his life is such a terminally pointless malady, as inexorable as blood dripping tick-tock from the slit wrists of time.

Minutes sink like days, days seem to press on forever and nights . . .

"Nights? My goodness!" Tommy thinks. The nights are spent feeling held by chains and darkness both real and symbolic.

Personal letters, to a prisoner, are quite like birthday presents, but only a thousand times better because if you get a letter every night, then you celebrate life every night with a present from a loved one. Too, there is no love floating amongst the prisoners, it's either business or play. If love is felt, it is carefully guarded, protected. Love is looked at as a feminine trait, and feminine is considered fragile and delicate. It can be mistaken for a weakness and, in these chains, a guy needs all the strength available inside to shield himself from the fools outside and keep the wolves at bay.

Unless they're totally devoid of feelings, a prisoner's entire day revolves around mail call. Tonight the guys are really open-eyed and hopeful as they anticipate some news from home. Those few who are indifferent to mail issue usually are professional chowhounds. Their life revolves around the dining area and food.

Tonight, the boys are really on edge. After four long days of sweating, this asshole cop wants to make them sweat a little more, for no reason other than he has the power to do this; the proclaimed self-righteous making life more miserable for those already down and suffering inside a concrete tomb of melancholy. Not all guards are this way, just those who are guessed to be either insecure of themselves or living somber lives outside the walls.

"I'll pass out the damn mail when I have time, INMATE!" screams the guard with added emphasis on "Inmate." It's the kind of emphasis that lets the inmate know he is looked on as scum. The guard is doing nothing but strolling around in circles with his hands in his pockets, knowing full well that he's putting the men through another needless night of torment.

"Lazy bastard!" scowls an older inmate as he paces, agitated by the wait.

The air is sliced with obscenities mumbled in frustration. The guard finally prepares the mail for issue. The tension in the building has scared him, and he realizes that if he presses too far, the situation could rip out of control, perhaps even escalate into a riot, with him at the center. Once the guard steps inside the dayroom with a stack of mail and newspapers, the atmosphere radically changes from loud and hostile to quiet and humble. Everybody stops what they're doing, and, as if by magic, a large crowd appears around the guard. Some guys who never come outside their rooms float over to the crowd. Even macho guys cock their heads in the direction of the crowd as they post-up in the back of the day-room, appearing to watch TV; yet their direct attention is toward the mail issue.

"Sixty-five cell, Ramirez!" hollers the guard.

Jesse usually receives more mail than anyone else on the block. Being a member of a close-knit family, and having loyal friends who write several times a month, he receives four or five letters a week. Some guys do their time doing nothing but watching the TV or walking around hustling a puff off cigarettes all day. Most of those guys wonder why they never receive any mail. Some will get angry and stop around and threaten to disown all their family members and friends.

"I get mail every day because I write every day!" Jesse tells them. "If you want letters, you've got to write letters."

Jesse does his time writing instead of wasting away like so many friends who live and die for contraband cigarettes and coffee. He contributes to the outside world, his world, and has love unlike those who crumble and have nothing but addictions and bad habits to nurse.

It's a great feeling to receive the present of love from family and friends. Everyone who gets a letter is thrilled to receive them. It's an exhibition of love and affection, a gentle knowing that the inmate is cared for and thought about even in their absence. They are filled inside with glowing warmth of emotion that makes them feel significant while in the midst of such utter disrespect. It's painful, yet comforting to have loved ones who share with you out there on the other side; people who are cheering in your corner for you and waiting for you to come back home.

"Franco, 67 cell!"

Another name is called out and the letter is snatched with an ardent swipe and ripped open eagerly on the spot.

The once fat stack of letters is now down to three. Tommy feels a lump of despair climb from his heart and lodge itself inside his throat. As each name is called his chances dwindle. He desperately looks at the left-hand corner of the remaining letters to see if he can recognize any handwriting on the return address. Just a small peek of a number or letter written from his wife's feminine hand would ease his aching heart.

Erickson, a little guy covered in tattoos, rushes forward to receive his letter from the guard and struts off tapping it on his leg. Bailey, a young skinhead, leans against the second tier railing, laughing at the crowd of nervous and excited faces. He thinks them fools all gathered around the guard like newborn chicks hungrily waiting for mama bird to feed them. He thinks himself wise for having shut out his family and friends before they could shut him out again; his tired motto being, "Do unto others before they do unto you." He has no need of anyone on the other side, and that's all it is to him. "The other side." It's not the "free world" like they say. He learned that a long time ago: "Ain't nothin' free." He is totally indifferent to what's going on out there. He doesn't care.

He laughs again at the many faces of expression, either of pleasure or panic that stroll away from mail call each night. The truth is, before he shut out the outside world, he was also one of those faces in that crowd. He was down there anxiously waiting to hear from somebody/anybody, but after spending seven brutal months in silence, something inside him broke. He hadn't heard a word from anyone, and he became so despondent that he vowed to himself to puke up that place called Home and refuse to respond to those rare letters that he finally did receive. Some of those letters still go unread.

The last letter was handed out, and Tommy didn't receive a letter from his wife again tonight. This makes the eighth night in a row. He clears his throat and stands alone with his thoughts. He is upset and worried because he knows that she writes to him every night.

"Maybe she's ill and in the hospital, or has been kidnapped or has left him for another guy like Fisk's girlfriend did. She just stopped writing him without even saying good-bye." Or worse, "What if she was raped and killed?"

In this city of chains those possibilities are not spawned by empty paranoia. Daily, Tommy sees men who have done those things and worse, and he hears them talk and knows that they are not the last of their breed. He worries, powerless to protect her. He begins to tremble as he climbs the stairs to his row.

He is a stranger to his cellie with whom he has shared the tiny space with for the past year and a half. He digs through a box of his personal belongings in a choking silence and pulls out the last few letters she has written him. He rereads them over and over again searching for any clues that might help him better understand what has happened. In bed that night, he puts her letters under his pillow and holds them tight and spends another sleepless night wondering, waiting and praying that he'll hear from her tomorrow night at mail call. Her essence pervades the envelope and haunts him as he lies in his bunk and waits for daylight and another mail call.

* * *

*"Our goal is to create a beloved community,
and this will require a qualitative change in our souls
as well as a quantitative change in our lives."*

Martin Luther King, Jr.

* * *

Patrick Middleton, Ph.D., is the first prisoner in American to earn his B.A., M.A., and Ph.D. while in prison. He is the author of <u>Healing Our Imprisoned Minds: A People's Guide To Hope & Freedom</u>, a columnist for the Human Rights Coalition, senior editor of SageWriters.com, and a frequent contributor to <u>Graterfriends</u>.

He has been in prison for 33 years.

LESSONS IN LIFE: FRIENDSHIPS IN PRISON
Patrick Middleton
($1,900,000)

One annoying cliché repeated so often by prisoners still green behind the bars is: "A person doesn't have any friends in prison. Only acquaintances." I used to argue passionately to convert these macho fellows: "How can you say that? I have several friends." To a man, it all came down to trust: "You're crazy if you trust anybody in prison." I never changed a single mind. I came to pity them instead. I know that if they're here long enough, they'll learn the truth about another cliché – no man is an island.

When I was a teen, my grandfather would often remind me to choose my friends carefully. I never did though. I had one real friend and he chose me. I was a delinquent, whereas he was an upstanding boy. Throughout all my skullduggeries, my friend was there for me – never embarrassed, never judging, never giving up on me. Forty years later, he's an engineer and I'm a seasoned convict. And we're still friends. There's a lesson here. It has to do with loyalty.

Prison has taught me some precious lessons about life. I've learned, for example, that there are two distinct worlds in which humans live – the internal and the external. Each has its boundaries of freedom. My external world now consists of the walkways and hallways, the prison yard, the chapel and the buildings, and this little room of a cell. There is much more freedom, though, in my inner world. The walkways can lead to just about anywhere, and I am free to believe. I am free to believe in a God or none at all. I can choose algebra or geometry. I can see the glass as half empty or half full. And if I wish, I can cultivate love and goodwill in the hearts and minds of others and my own.

And then there are lessons about friendship. How life is so much better when we have a few good friends to share it with. It takes time – sometimes years – to cultivate lasting friendships. It starts with trust. We take chances, we show our vulnerabilities, and it's a beautiful thing when it's reciprocated. Along the way, we learn to listen and encourage, we share our histories, our hills and valleys, we laugh and tease and sometimes cry together, and so much more.

Many of the friends I've gained over the years are fellow musicians. We worked hard together. We argued. We fussed. We created lots of good music and many special memories. We grew as musicians and as human beings. We came to depend on each other for a smile or an ear when we needed it. There was a spiritual comfort in knowing that they had my back and I had theirs.

What do you do after you've shared years of your life with a friend who is suddenly transferred or goes home or dies? How do you deal with that "missing you" feeling, that homesick feeling you felt when you first went away?

We stay strong. We wait for time to lessen the pain. We work on new friendships. And from time to time we rearrange the pictures of our friends in our photo albums; we relive the memories of them in our minds. And if that's not enough, we talk to our old friends when we're alone. We tell them how much we miss them.

And then we remember that in having known them, life has been good to us.

PART VI
Two Ways Out

Untitled by Leonard Jefferson

Chapter One

The Death Penalty

Donetta Hill was convicted and sentenced to death in 1992 for a double homicide she says she did not commit. She is one of 46 women on Death Row in Pennsylvania. Her court-appointed inexperienced attorney failed to investigate, failed to call witnesses on her behalf, failed to get DNA testing and withheld evidence proving her innocence. The prosecutor and police also withheld evidence. Yet court evidence and testimony showed she had an ironclad alibi for the time of the crimes, and no ballistic or fingerprint evidence was found connecting her to the crimes. Hair and blood samples have recently been found not to be hers and other witnesses have actually identified another perpetrator.

She's already won one appeal in the courts, allowing evidence to be introduced that was withheld at trial. Despite another appeal, her conviction has yet to be overturned and she knows her fight for freedom is long from being over. She has not seen her two teenage daughters in seven years, has no family or outside support, receives no money, visits or mail. Her outspoken activism marks her for constant retaliatory attacks by prison officials. Her time on Death Row is marked by cruelty and betrayal.

The conditions of women in prison and on Pennsylvania's Death Row were dramatically described in a four-part series by Carol Williams that began June 5,2002 in the Philadelphia New Observer. The focus of the series, from which the following is excerpted, was on Donetta Hill.

MUNCY HORRORS REVEALED BY DEATH ROW INMATE
Carol Williams

Donetta Hill, a Philadelphia native, has been on Death Row for ten years for a crime she insists she did not commit. She has already won one appeal. Her prison experience has been filled with cruelty, betrayal and inhumanity. Calling for the end of torture of prisoners, she describes life at Muncy:

"It's horrible. We are subjected to strip searches every time they take us out of our cells. You have to be strip searched before you shower, after you shower, when you go into the yard, to the library, to a visit, before and after everything you do. It can happen fifteen times a week depending upon how active you want to be. I feel raped every time they do it. They hold a mirror between your legs..."

While she says there are many good guards at Muncy, some of them play "mind games," part of the conditioning process meant to "break you."

"It's all about power," she said as she described a recent incident when she was brought to another facility for an appeals hearing: "They told me that the police van was coming at 1 pm. I was told to strip, lift (raise the breasts), spread my legs and cough. I was on my monthly and it was particularly humiliating. I complied anyway. They told me that they saw something in me."

She was asked to repeat the procedure two more times. Then she was told to "wipe from front to back and show them. They said that maybe there was some tissue in me." The experience, she says, left her feeling frustrated, humiliated and demeaned. "I almost cried."

Rather then continue the torture, Donetta Hill says that she initially decided not to go to her hearing. I said, "Then I guess I won't go, but my lawyer and the judge will know and there better be a good excuse. After a while they told me that the van left anyway."

After being returned to her room, she experienced a severe anxiety attack. Then she was told to get dressed, that the van was back and she would receive a misconduct charge upon her return to Muncy for resisting the trip.

She says that when she got to the Sheriff's gate, correctional officers asked her why she was refusing to come to court, that they had received a call from Muncy to that effect. Ms. Hill says that she explained that she was told that the van had left. They told her the van had never left the institution.

She went on to talk about the mysterious deaths of two prisoners at Muncy. In April 1992 a transsexual named "Jennifer" arrived at Muncy. The prisoner was in transition and still had his testicles. Ms. Hill says that this was the reason why he was at Muncy, a female institution, rather than a male facility like Graterford.

To complicate matters, Ms. Hill says that he was so emotionally tortured, taunted and harassed by the guards because of his difference that he committed suicide.

The death of "Denise Wallace" especially troubles Ms. Hill, who was in the room next to hers. Ms. Wallace was a "mental case," Ms. Hill said, who used to swallow pens, spoons and forks.

"The guards and the staff would not help her. She kept throwing herself against the big steel door in there and you could just hear it all night long. I asked them to please take her out of there before she hurt herself. One night, around 11:30 pm, they took her out and she had a huge knot on her head from banging it against the door. They laughed at her. They still did not take that little girl out of that cell. I asked if they could tie her down but they refused. I would like to find out who her family is. I want to tell them that they killed that little girl. They said that she hung herself, but she was just a little thing. White folks go to the state hospital or a mental facility, but they put that baby in here. They might as well have their own cemetery up here," she said sadly.

"There is a blue code of silence. My lawyer said that he is worried that something will happen to me for exposing this to the public, but I'm not worried about that right now. For me, the important thing is to bust this thing open."

She complained about green mold on the bread, mice droppings and mice nibble marks on the trays. She said that in January, she contracted food poisoning from the food. She complained about huge bugs and rats in the water closets and food unfit for human consumption.

"You're looked down on, judged. They make it so hard for you. The loneliness is the worst part. I need somebody that I can trust, to go to with these problems. I need somebody that I can talk to about what is going on here. This is why I am giving this interview, so that people will know on the outside. No matter what they say, all of this is true."

Ms. Hill stated that it is a known fact among the inmates that every day the women prisoners engage in sexual activity "behind the books." "And they get no misconducts for it. It's horrible up here."

Bob Esking, the Public Information Officer for the Philadelphia Prison System, had this to say about her claims of brutality: "Upon investigation, we found Donetta Hill's allegations to be unfounded."

* * *

Letter from Carolyn King on Death Row
SCI Muncy, Pennsylvania, USA
April 3, 1998

I came to SCI Muncy in 1994 and I am writing this affidavit to let you know what I have had to endure here since 1994. When I got here I was placed in the infirmary for 8 days for medical clearance. While there I was not allowed to have any writing material, legal material or access to a law library, no reading material.

After 8 days I moved to the Restricted Housing Unit (RHU) which is located outside the compound. I was placed in a cell that had paint peeling off the walls and floors, feces stains, blood stains, filth and so dirty I could not clean the walls and the windows were so dirty you could not see out. When you flushed the toilets feces, urine, and tissue came up in the neighbor's cell and vice versa. There was absolutely no proper ventilation or heating. The windows are not insulated or caulked, the winter wind would just blow in and you are only allowed 2 blankets.

Food would come cold in a Styrofoam container w/hair most of the time. And it was served by the officer after they opened a wicket with feces on it to feed the person. I received 3 showers/shaves a week with peeling paint from the ceilings, 4x5 area, no proper ventilation forced to carry shower items while handcuffed from behind. The showers and halls were cleaned by GP detail workers who didn't sweep or change mop heads. The only time the building would be scrubbed down is when the Commissioner was coming or Land I or Board of Health.

I am a practicing Catholic and was denied confession until August, 1996, although I was in and out for court, the RHU stayed the same. I was also denied extra religious prayer books. Also in the RHU they housed mentally ill people who had misconducts and were basically barred from the Mental Health Unit or refused to be 304 to a State Hospital. One of the mentally ill patients was stripped down and she would run from the back of her cell and run head first into the door until she knocked herself unconscious, when she came to, she resumed the same behavior. Nobody did anything for her. She earned her stuff back and hung herself from the door on approximately February 25 or 26th, 1998 at 2:30 PM in the The Hole. Her name was Denise Wallace and she needed mental health help. Also the mentally ill or behavior problem inmates would kick and bang on the doors, scream at the top of their lungs for hours, smear feces all over the room that we had to smell, throw urine through the door or wicket, flood the rooms and hallways, and kick cinderblocks out of walls. So they made a steel room, everything is steel, the walls and all.

When they would come to strip these people they were subjected to mace or capstun. I was placed across the hall from these people and I was constantly subjected to this. I personally witnessed a number of people eating feces and relieving themselves on the floor. There were some rooms that were so bad that when the officers finally removed the inmate from the cell, the feces and maggots were swept in the hallway. Officers call us "Death Row bitches" and taunt us with things like "I hope you get the needle first." They ask us if we are afraid to die and laugh and talk openly about executions in front of us.

I was afraid to write anyone and tell them about this because I didn't know what the administration or officers would do to me because I know mail was being opened before going out. I thought the officers would read it and maybe hurt me.

When I arrived here I was not given an inmate handbook. I didn't know about the Grievance Process etc...and especially the ICU or Austin Decision until now. I have officers come in geared up with their masks, body equipment and shield and video cameras. In August, 1996 the Superintendent moved all 4 capital cases (women) round each other and finally installed cabinets to put our stuff in and electrical outlets for two Death Row inmates who did not have them.

When making phone calls, for some period of time we could not use the telephone without the officers hearing every word of our conversation. But they built the non-contact booth for confession and one side was for the telephone. There was sick call conducted at your cell door, if a referral was made to see the doctor. It was not guaranteed because the transport cars were busy and it could be canceled for any reason and without telling you. They finally put an examining room upstairs that consists of a table, a scale, desk, chair and sheet. That's it. When a doctor would order us medication as a PRN, that means as needed, they would not bring it until medline which could be hours away, and even then we could only get aspirin/Tylenol and Tummy after meals.

75% of the law library books are outdated and anything current that comes in is destroyed. At one time we had indoor recreation where we could play board games during inclement weather but that has been taken away. Recreation outerwear consists of a very thin state corduroy jacket, hat, gardening gloves and holey (with holes) boots – one set which everyone wears and which is only washed once a year – people who relieve themselves in them and have scabies also wear them.

On November 17, 1997 the four of us were moved to a unit within the compound called "Sones B." But it is not our unit like we were told. It is the BAU (Behavior Adjustment Unit) so they got us away from the mentally ill and behavior problems and now plan on bringing them down here to the BAU. The only thing separating us is a fenced in area that is not soundproof. So when they bring them here it will be the same thing all over again, except we have been told they will have programs which we cannot participate in.

On November 19, Superintendent Byrd came to meet with us and made a lot of promises. She stared down Donetta Hill whom they have housed in the Phase II Room (she has had two death warrants signed) which is pure mental torture. She asked to be moved from the Phase II Room and the Superintendent told her "As long as your head rolls around on your shoulders you will remain in that cell."

Our shower area is a steel cage which reminds us all of a gas chamber. We are permitted 3 showers a week and one haircut every 6 months.

On January 2, 1998 Donetta Hill experienced a breakdown, so they stripped her and came all geared up with the shield. They threatened to shock her with the shield and then demonstrated it. After they threatened her she let them strip her room. She was not allowed to go to the Mental Health Unit but was handcuffed, naked, to the wicket and shackled. All of this was videotaped and Lt. Maietla was doing the strip. Men officers were in the room when she was stripped. Lt. A. Smith told her there would be no Mental Health Unit: "This is the end of the line." Donetta had told the Lt. that she would remove her clothing in front of the female officers, but they did not listen to her. They took all her clothing, panties, socks, comb, hygiene items. She was naked and had nothing in the room, no mattress, no blanket, nothing. We are not permitted interviews with the news media. I write this letter to beg for help for those of us on Death Row at Muncy.

Sincerely,
Carol King OC7210

All mail is open and read.

* * *

WHY ABOLITION OF THE DEATH PENALTY IS A QUEER ISSUE

Kay Whitlock
AFSC National Representative, LGBT Issues

In the wake of the 1998 death of Matthew Shepard, the Wyoming youth who was murdered in the act of anti-gay hate violence, numerous lesbian, gay, bisexual and transgender (LGBT) activists and organizations throughout the United States reacted with shock and anger as Shepard's murder immediately developed an iconic force. Now there was a human face to symbolize the cost of anti-LGBT bigotry because, unlike most hate-motivated murders, the killing of Matthew received a great deal of international media attention. Many people in LGBT communities called for the death penalty for those who murdered Matthew. Yet on February 9, 1999, in the midst of this highly charged political atmosphere, eleven major organizations representing LGBT communities stepped forward to announce their joint opposition to the death penalty. Since that time, other LGBT organizations, including the National Youth Advocacy Coalition and the National Coalition of Anti-Violence Projects, have spoken out against the death penalty.

For the past several years, American Friends Service Committee (AFSC) has produced resources about and worked to address the linkages between hate violence and state violence, pointing out that within the criminal justice system, the violence of the state is most clearly directed to those who are also most vulnerable to hate-motivated attacks and harassment – including people of color and LGBT people. AFSC emphasizes that harsher penalties for those who commit hate-motivated acts of violence will compound, rather than reduce, violence against vulnerable communities.

The criminal justice system is a disturbing mirror image of the hate and violence that is directed against people of color, poor people, queers, youth, mentally disabled people, and women. In fact, given identical acts of violence, race and class are the single most important determinants of who will be arrested, charged, tried, convicted, and sentenced to death in the United States. Strategic use of homophobia and rigid gender stereotyping by prosecutors often play an instrumental role in persuading jurors to sentence particular defendants to death. It is not illegal to use a defendant's actual or perceived sexual or gender identity to try to sway the sentence in a capital case. Homophobia is used to demonize defendants and appeal to juror bias, and this anti-queer bias is furthered by issues of poverty, race, and prosecutorial misconduct.

Rather than addressing complex social, economic, and political problems that increase violence and crime, the United States increasingly has relied on correctional facilities, jails, prisons, and execution chambers as the "solution" to those problems. What then is the framework necessary and large enough to respond to the needs of victims of violence, their families and communities while simultaneously holding accountable those who perpetrate acts of violence – without reinforcing the violence of racism, misogyny and poverty? The

Universal Declaration of Human Rights (1948) affirms that the foundation of human rights is respect for the inherent dignity of all human beings and the inviolability of the human person. These principles should inform all our work to end violence and to create authentic justice that not only holds individuals and institutions accountable for violent acts against others, but also addresses the social, economic, and spiritual roots of that violence.

For more information on the death penalty as an LGBT issue, please order JUSTICE VISIONS Working Papers, "Why Abolition of the Death Penalty is a Queer Issue," and "In a Time of Broken Bones; A Call to Dialogue on Hate Violence and the Limitations of Hate Crimes Legislation," or visit www.afsc.org/lgbt/criminal-justice.

* * *

"Prison systems throughout the world are generally ugly, barbaric, counterproductive and insane. Someday our descendants will look back on our time with shock that such sophisticated people could have treated prisoners the way we do."

Bo Lozoff
Human Kindness Foundation

A Kinder, Gentler Murder?
By Judith Trustone

The silver needle is loaded with
society's venom of vengeance,
an arrow aimed at ravaged veins
by a bureaucrat in a crisp white shirt and tie,
a political appointee, a civil servant
for this most uncivil of acts.

Does he sleep at night,
dream, or sedate himself
with alcohol and sports?

Does he talk with his children
about his job?
Are they proud or ashamed?

Does he pray and to whom?
Does he think about killing
while making love to his wife?

Nearby on a lumpy mattress
in a cheap motel with tired pillows,
a grieving mother ignores
the press pounding on her door
as she waits for her condemned son's spirit
to be ripped from her,
releasing them both
from decades of unbearable anguish and agony.

Years of hot tears have burned
deep furrows into her brown cheeks
like dry arroyos in a vast wasteland.
She wears her constant fatigue

like a dusty, gray cape wrapped tightly
around her hurting heart.
Sadness and poverty are all she's ever known.

He had only been a squirt of sperm
to his father,
dooming him in the womb.

His siblings turned away long ago,
weary of his endless appeals
and brief spurts of hope.

His grandmother blissfully smiles
at her memories of him as she tiptoes
a tiny step at a time to the other side.

She knows he will be waiting for her.

Where are the "pro-lifers,"
the religious zealots, friends of fetuses
who care so little about life once born?

His birth became
a one-way ticket
to the silver needle.

At the nod from the warden
with the pale, frozen face,
the chemical switch is thrown,
and a tidal wave of poison,
the politicians' kinder, gentler murder
ravages cell by cell as it rushes
to his battered and bashed heart
that never had a chance
to beat with the fullness

of love
except from his Mamma.

No matter if he's innocent as so many are.
His crime is being born poor and having
black skin in a country that hates him.

A violent and deliberate death
gallops around the arterial bend,
closer and closer to its target,
suffocating his last breath
while watchers struggle
with the impulse
to vomit.

Justice weeps beneath her blindfold,
her naked breasts shrouded
in a six thousand dollar drape
by men fearful of being distracted
from their imperialistic wars.

Now freed from his tortured body,
his soul hovers briefly above the fishbowl,
then rises above the demonstrators and TV crews
outside,
pauses for a moment over the no-tell-motel
where his mother weeps dry tears,
until angels surround him,
gently lifting him upward ,
away from his tragically short life
to a place of final peace, leaving us to just ask
WHY?

PART VII
Transformation

Chapter One

Visions of What Could Be

This section includes comments from a wide range of prisoners, activists, teachers, guards and families who responded to two questions:

First, what do you think of the current criminal justice system? And second, if you had no political, legal or budgetary restraints, what kind of a new system would you build from the ground up?

WhIle dozens of people said they wanted to write something, not all who promised did. A couple of guards decided it was too risky. Many of those I interviewed or who wrote are not included in this printing due to space limitations.

Anton Forde/Trevor Mattis, Inmate
($545,000)

The justice system is comprised of three parts, and each must be changed if we are to effect change in the total system. One common theme running through all arms of this system is racial discrimination. Racism unites this system into a cohesive body.

Law Enforcement

Seventy-five percent of people in prisons across the nation are in there for drug-related crimes. Legalize drugs and you would save billions of dollars annually; cut the prison population from 2.3 million to 500,000; eliminate the violence associated with drug selling; remove the profit motive from the drug trade; and make it easier to identify drug abusers so we could precisely target those in need of drug treatment.

This is based on the premise that at all times there will be a certain percentage of the population who use and abuse drugs, and that it is the abuse, not the *use*, of drugs that creates the problem. With easily accessible treatment and an aggressive educational program, I think this society can handle safely legalizing drugs.

With non-violent offenders out of the way, prison would function to contain, control, and rehabilitate the most violent and incorrigible offenders in our society.

Contrary to popular belief, the easiest prisoner to rehabilitate is a violent offender. More than 50% of all violent crimes are either spur of the moment crimes of passion, done under the influence of drugs, or were unintended. More than 50% of all violent offenders would not repeat their actions even if they were never ever convicted.

Next, I would implement a system of neighborhood policing where only people who grew up in or live in the neighborhood would be hired to police those districts. These individuals would have a better feel for who has committed a crime and whom to arrest. I would give these police officers wide latitude as to when to make an arrest, when to reprimand or warn, and when to turn a suspect over to parents, counselors or a treatment program.

I would set a high standard in the area of investigations. The police would have to investigate all cases thoroughly before bringing charges. A suspect charged for a crime could plead guilty for a reduced sentence but could not get a reduced sentence by implicating or testifying against a co-defendant.

I would make illegal the tactic of police officers who coerce confessions from a suspect by promising them leniency. I would make it mandatory that all defendants and suspects get counseling prior to making any statements to the police and that counsel be present during any and all debriefing.

The Judicial System

Judges should not have been prosecutors or lawyers before being on the bench. All judges would have to spend one week in anonymous identity in the following a) county jail b) medium security prison c) maximum security prison d) Death Row. Juries would be mandatory for all cases where the defendant faces a sentence of ten or more years. I would repeal mandatory sentences and return to a discretionary sentencing scheme. All sentences would carry automatic time reduction incentives determined by the convicted person's progress and development while incarcerated. I would allow for more creative sentences like house arrest, banishment, conscription for humanity work in impoverished countries and disaster areas, work on farms, natural reserves and wilderness areas.

Sentencing for conspiracy would be according to individual culpability. I would abolish the death penalty. The maximum time any person could continuously stay in jail would be 25 years. Teenagers could not be tried as adults.

The Penal System

I would redefine those who offend society's laws as patients in need of treatment. All incoming inmates would be evaluated to see where best to place them within a variety of programs and institutions. Great emphasis would be placed on the reconstruction of self-esteem and the correction of deep-rooted emotional problems stemming from socio-economic conditions.

Within the penal system the emphasis should be on education. The daily routine would be structured around such programs, many of which would be mandatory. All of these programs would also be tied to time reducing and financial incentives.

I would increase the volunteer programs where people from the community participate with inmates in various rehabilitative programs. All inmates would have to participate in a victim's awareness program where they come face to face with crime victims to fully understand the effects of crime on victims.

I would have many of the educational programs designed and implemented by ethnocentric instructors who would cater to blacks and Hispanics, the majority of the people now in prison. I would have families and loved ones work closely with prison officials in monitoring inmate progress.

Inmates who are parents would be given the opportunity to actively participate in the parenting of their children, and I would develop programs to maintain and strengthen family ties.

All of these suggestions address the symptoms but not the root causes of crime. To address these causes we would have to radically change the inequities of this capitalistic economic system by changing it into an egalitarian socio-economic system, eradicating racism and oppression in all its various forms, and allowing all citizens fair and impartial access to good education and good job opportunities.

* * *

William Ayers, PhD

William Ayers is a school reform activist, Distinguished Professor of Education, and Senior University Scholar at the University of Illinois at Chicago. A former member of the Weather Underground, he is the founder of the Center for Youth and Society and founder and co-director of the Small Schools Workshop. His books include *A Kind and Just Parent: The Children of Juvenile Court* (Beacon Press, 1997); *To Teach: The Journey of a Teacher,* (Teachers College Press, 1993) which was named Book of the Year in 1993 by Kappa Delta Pi and won the Witten Award for Distinguished Work in Biography and Autobiography in 1995; and *Fugitive Days: A Memoir,* (Beacon Press, 2001). His latest book is *Teaching Toward Freedom* (Beacon Press 2004).

"The U.S must commit its considerable wealth and resources to healing the racial nightmare that is at its core. This means reparations, redistribution, reinvestment. It means popular mobilization for full participation in democratic life, and the creation of institutions that encourage the engagements of citizens. And it means reversing the current treacherous tendency – instead of retreating from education and promoting a criminal justice solution to every problem, we must embrace education in all its forms as the great humanizing enterprise that it can and should be, and reject the criminalization of society.

The criminal justice system should be based on principles of fairness, equity, and democratic participation. Concretely, every effort should be made to divert citizens from prison. Principles of restorative justice should guide us, and institutions like peer juries and community councils should be generously supported. Prison should be the last resort, not the first option, reserved for violent offenders, and still built around notions of participatory democracy, community-building, and engaged human capacity. There should be a commitment to education, to creating art and culture, to community craft, to treatment and counseling. Prisoners should emerge more able to participate in all the decisions that affect their lives: economic, social and emotional."

* * *

Ernie Preate, Esq.

When Ernie Preate was Attorney General of Pennsylvania, he was one of the nation's toughest. Then he went to prison and learned how justice really works. Once a prosecutor who sent defendants to long prison terms and even Death Row, Ernie Preate is now a defense attorney who works for prison reform.

With the election of Ed Rendell as Governor of Pennsylvania, Preate is convinced that Rendell, as he promised to inmates, will make the Board of Pardons more functional. He also supports the Parole for Lifers movement. Based on these hopes, inmate James Taylor, founder of People Against Recidivism (PAR), has raised $10,000 through his supporters to hire Preate to take his case before the revamped Board of Pardons when that occurs. All Lifers in Pennsylvania are watching carefully.

The following is excerpted from an article in *Hope Magazine*, May/June 2002, by Scott Westcot, reporter for the *Erie Times-News*.

JAILHOUSE SHOCK

Ernie Preate's epiphany came the first time he entered the mess hall of the federal prison camp in Duluth, Minnesota. After shuffling through the chow line, Preate turned to find a seat. What he saw stopped him cold. Table after table was filled with African American and Hispanic men. As Pennsylvania's Attorney General, Preate was aware of the disproportionate number of minorities behind bars. While serving time himself for mail fraud, he saw it firsthand. "It was just a sea of black faces," Preate recalls of that January 1996 day. "I said to myself, 'Oh my God, I helped create this.'" The moment was pivotal in Preate's transformation from Pennsylvania's top law enforcement official to the vocal prison-reform advocate he is today. Preate still believes that criminals, particularly violent offenders, should serve prison time. But his own jailhouse experience convinced him that our criminal justice system largely warehouses human beings, discriminates against minorities, and is pathetically inadequate in its rehabilitation efforts.

Preate's first reckoning with the skewed aspects of criminal justice came in the months leading to his guilty plea. The charge of mail fraud – a federal felony – hinged on campaign contributions he had not disclosed a decade earlier. It might have been reduced to a charge of campaign violations. But when the feds threatened also to charge Preate's brothers in the case, he began to see the difference money makes in our legal system.

"If you have money you can get a fair fight in court," says Preate. "If you're poor, forget it. I wasn't poor, but I by no means had the resources to take on the government. I talked it over with my family and said let's end this right now. We don't have the money to fight it." Preate pleaded guilty and was sentenced to 14 months in federal prison. While in prison he soon learned "...While the system claims it's trying to rehabilitate, it's really about tearing people down. What I was finding was there are a lot of good people in prison that made mistakes. Contrary to public perception that they are a menacing evil, the vast majority are not. Frankly I was shocked by the number who had not received effective counsel," says Preate. "Even the simplest things, some of those lawyers didn't do. They didn't ask for discovery; they didn't call witnesses; they didn't make the appropriate motions. Our whole system is based on advocacy, and it was clear many of these prisoners had not had competent advocates."

Once he gained his freedom, Preate acted on his promise. "There were some people who knocked me as having a so-called jailhouse conversion," Preate says. "When you've fallen as far as I fell, it's not that you're a bleeding heart. It's that your eyes are opened. Going to prison was a freeing experience for me. For the first time I could think without constraint and without jeopardizing my political career." His main thrust is that the criminal justice system stacks the deck against minorities, the poor, and the disenfranchised. Preate thinks the first imperative is to concentrate on education and prevention.

"What I see is America being destroyed from within. We haven't built a single new university in Pennsylvania in decades, but since 1984 we've built 19 new prisons, expanded one, and have two more in the works. We know that the greatest preventer of crime is education. If we truly committed ourselves to education we would have a much safer society. But we are investing in warehouses of humanity instead of investing in people."

"My life is no longer about achieving power or political success," Preate often tells people. "It's about bringing hope to the hopeless. The most rewarding thing is I am getting to see that I can be an agent for change," says Preate. "I think our country is at stake, and we have a system that is breaking down.....I'll never stop fighting to change that. Never."

* * *

La Chae Singletary, Inmate

There are so many underlying problems that cause us to come to jail, that I would have to incorporate in my ideal prison setting more professionals geared to helping individuals discover the root issues that keep them from living normal lives. Because despite what politicians think, most of us *don't* want to live like we do.

* * *

The following excerpted interview with the Honorable Richard J. Nygaard, United States third circuit court judge, is reprinted, with permission, from Life Without Parole, *edited by Robert Johnson and Thomas J. Bernard.*

PRISONS AS I SEE THEM
The Honorable Richard J. Nygaard
Third Circuit

When I became a judge over two decades ago, my sense of frustration with the sentencing of offenders began almost immediately. I felt that I was "shoveling sand against the tide," that there was something terribly wrong with our entire system. And I felt powerless to facilitate real change in anyone who appeared before me for sentencing. What was needed, I thought, was a tough, no nonsense approach. I was quite content to think that each person has a free will, and that each person was free to choose to commit or not commit crimes. This is what our system is based on, and I worried little that it also may be the reason for our system's failures. I short, I was content with the maxim If you do the crime, you do the time.

That impression did not last, however. It began to change, as I learned about the real world from which offenders came; as I saw the real milieu into which I sent them and the communities to which they would someday return. . .

First, I began to look at what prison does and is doing to the people I send there. . . As I talked with offenders whom I had incarcerated, and others with whom I had become acquainted through my prison visits, I was appalled. Although many professionals within the penal system struggle mightily to make something productive out of it, all too many have simply given up. Prisons, which began as penitentiaries (places to do penance), have become human warehouses. Beneath it all, these warehouses are evil places, populated in substantial percentages by people whose evil is not sufficiently controlled; and being staffed by "watchers" who are insufficiently "watched" to prevent them from harassing or emotionally, even physically, tormenting their charges. The result is predictable: prisons are rife with uncertainty, fear, and their concomitants – anger and violence. . .

Second, I began to wonder what exactly prison does to us, to society. The way we treat our fellow citizens is a reflection of our self-worth, serving to create our self-image. I suggest that with respect to both sentencing and prison, we must ask ourselves, "Is our action a negation or an affirmation of our own humanity?" Are we proud of what we are doing?. . .

I must confess my own initial apathy to the fact that such an enormous undertaking was being so effectively, efficiently, and bloodlessly carried out. Not for long, however. Some outlaw spirit within me, some rebellious fire in my belly that covets personal freedom and liberty, was anguished, unsettled, and concerned that the incarceration super-machine has encountered so little resistance to its insatiable appetite for imprisoning human beings. . .

To date, the debaters of crime and punishment have generally been bifurcated into those who believe that convicts can be healed of their criminality and those who believe that convicts must be punished into absolute and unconditional obedience. . .

Recently, in this post-modern age of advanced technology, a third possibility intruded itself into the long-standing feud between those who would cure and those who would punish con-victs. Locking away offenders indefinitely suddenly became an achievable possibility, and the warehousing model soon became the most widely used and accepted penological purpose in the na-tion. The broad-based acceptance of this warehousing model can be attributed to its seductive logic, winning over even the most devoted proponents from both the cure and punish camps.

The "honey-trap" logic of the warehousing model goes something like this: since we have yet to develop an effective treatment against criminal behavior, the most logical thing to do is to quarantine criminals until an effective cure or punishment for crime can be developed. Additionally, by safeguarding our law-abiding citizens from the malice of disruptive elements, we will be more willing and able to seek and develop a more effective treatment or cure for crime. This is the "leper colony" approach. Once banished, these social lepers are easily forgotten, and society finds it easier to embrace apathy, even antipathy, toward these social pariahs. . .

I myself accepted this seemingly foolproof logic. . . Stubbornly, I continued to hope that warehousing criminals meant increased safety for my family and myself. Behind it all, though, I suspected that I was ignoring a greater truth.

That truth is now becoming known to me: the warehousing model does not make anyone safer. If anything, it exposes us all to certain harm as a result of the false sense of security it provides, benignly inhibiting our resolve to discover real and lasting solutions to the problems of crime. . .

Think of criminals as 50-gallon drums of toxic waste, inexplicably and unavoidably produced as a by-product of some manufacturing process that your company is engaged in. . .

As you consider this example, think about what is happening every time a bigger and better prison is built that promises nothing more than warehousing inmates indefinitely and inflicting upon them more severe punishment. Would you consider it reasonable for a waste manager to pay good money to have people shake up a drum of toxic waste, making it even more dangerous before releasing it to the community? No? Neither would I. Yet, that is what is happening to prisoners in our mushrooming, understaffed institutions.

If I wish to be truly safe, I must apparently invest in developing an antidote to the toxic by-product being produced by our growing, prospering community. More important, I must invest in developing a way to break down toxic waste into its elementary components, so that I may make productive use of them again. This means that we must conduct research and require prison managers to direct their efforts and resources toward correcting convicts rather than tormenting them. Consequently, we must staff our facilities with persons who care about the by-product (convicts) they store and want to neutralize their dangerous propensities.

If no antidote, treatment, or cure exists, then we will be no better or worse for trying to discover them. However, if cures do exist, if treatments are effective, if antidotes can be used, and we do not try to discover and use them, or if we do not seek to apply them, then we condemn ourselves to the inevitable human equivalent of toxic waste spills – the release of more dangerous individuals into our communities.

* * *

"Trying to change a culture is lonely work, but this is more important than anything now."

Vina Drennan

* * *

David Mandeville, Inmate

With more than 95% of inmates returning to prison, the current system is an obvious failure. No business with this high a rate of failure would survive.

The current attitude of hatred and anger society feels about inmates must change, for it only creates rage among inmates that is projected onto other inmates, those in authority and society as a whole. The attitude needed is one of love, acceptance and understanding. Love is the most powerful force that exists.

Prisoners should not be isolated from their communities. Families and communities should be key in their rehabilitation so both parties in a conflict face their responsibilities for bad behavior and make necessary restitution so forgiveness can take place.

Education in institutions should be focused on self-discovery, helping prisoners identify their values, their physical and emotional needs, their dreams.

Counselors should have very small caseloads and see their assigned prisoners weekly.

The goal of incarceration should be to enlighten, not punish. Incarceration should work. Prisoners should come out reborn, responsible and wise, full of love and compassion for others.

There is no need to incarcerate non-violent offenders; they belong in rehab or community programs. Only violent and explosive offenders need to be incarcerated, and the family and community should be active in their habilitation.

Long-term sentences should be done away with. No one should spend more than ten years in prison unless he refuses to change his behavior and continues to be a real and violent threat.

The Department of Corrections has not rehabilitated me. Through my own efforts I've come to understand life differently. I've found meaning and the key lies within my own heart.

I would start a new system by changing the approach taken to prosecute an offender. Instead of a myriad of charges, there would only be two possible charges, violent and non-violent unacceptable behavior. Cases would be prosecuted for the best outcome for the offender, the victim, the community and the family. Upon conviction, violent offenders would be sent to a habilitation center. This center should be followed by a period of house arrest and then a parole-like system.

Non-violent offenders would be sent to a three to six month educational program focused on reflection, self-seeking and internally-focused education so the offender can understand himself and what led to his past unacceptable behavior. He should take full responsibility for his behavior and make restitution.

Offenders would have to do community service and go to town meetings in addition to weekly counseling sessions with psychologists. The whole process should last about two years: three to six months in the center, three months house arrest and eighteen months on some sort of parole.

Violent offenders would go through the same process after their incarceration. The staff would be well-trained and well-paid, treating prisoners with love, respect and understanding.

I think these ideas would work, though they need more fine-tuning and deeper exploration. This system would not only be more effective but would cost much less as well. I have faith in the resources of this country. Psychologists, former prisoners, behavior specialists and social workers have much experience which could be utitilized to fix this horrible problem.

* * *

William DiMascio, Executive Director, Pennsylvania Prison Society

Many of the "tough on crime" policies adopted over the last decade have helped to pave the way, or at least condition us to respond as we have in our current "war on terrorism." In the name of protection against crime – public safety – we have discredited the judiciary and adopted mandatory sentences, weakened prisoners' constitutional access to redress of abuse, and accelerated an execution process that continues to display its defects.

Terrorism and crime are not geographic entities with physical features that can be occupied. They are concepts – often arbitrarily defined in political or partisan terms – and acts that violate the dignity and vitality of humankind.

No amount of military might will eradicate terrorism any more than unlimited police powers will eliminate all crime. Look at the never-ending violence in the Middle East where military force and terrorism seem to feed on each other. Look also at the criminal justice system in this country where decades of prison building and incarceration have done little to assuage the public's fear of crime.

The time has clearly come for us to consider other strategies in both these conflicts. Shore up our defenses, improve our policing and security, but then let's also address the root causes of these problems. Let's put our sense of fairness and equality to use in leading nations of the world to recognize the problems that breed the kind of hatred that led to the September 11th attacks. And let's also understand that demonizing people caught up in the criminal justice system does nothing to repair the damage done by crime.

The legacy of the United States is steeped in humanistic ideals, ethical and moral values, and democratic principles. These are the armaments of the citizenry. They help to keep us focused when terrorism or crime fan emotions that blind us to the benefits of dissent and compassion. They are all the armaments we need to take the high ground against the "poverty of dignity" that motivates criminal activity nationally and internationally.

* * *

Joan Gauker, Director of Volunteers, Graterford Prison
Founder and editorial writer, *Graterfriends*

As the wealthiest, healthiest and most progressive nation on earth, we should hang our heads in shame for the way we've developed and maintained prison systems that are unhealthy and unenlightened for prisoners and for those still on the street. We have the know-how to do a better job of caring for those who offend and preparing them to return to society (and most prisoners will return) as responsible citizens. Yet, we squander that know-how to salve our need for punishment and retribution – which ultimately harms the prisoners, those who guard them and the society to which they will return. The continuance and expansion of our uninspired, punishment/retribution-oriented prison systems are fueled by unenlightened politicians, a complicated intertwined social justice political agenda, and an apathetic, uninformed electorate.

The new system I would build would be a Day-One system. The concept is that from Day-One of an offender's confinement, everyone in the system, including the offender, is working on a program that will prepare that offender to return to society as an emotionally healthy, contributing member. In this dream, governments would define the object of imprisonment to be removal from society for the purpose of providing the offender with the incentive, the skills and the support system to return to the community as a responsible person able to work, be a good family member, and have a healthy outlook toward society's rules of behavior.

The government would implement restorative justice programs, help people work at reconciliation, and provide the treatment and support programs needed in and out of prison. If there were a parole system in this dream, it, too would be a Day-One system, in that from day one of a person's release, everyone, including the offender, would be working to keep the offender from re-offending. Such a parole system would be staffed by people who care about helping, not policing, those in their charge.

* * *

Bonnie Kerness, Co-Director American Friends Service Committee, Criminal Justice Program

There is no way to look into any aspect of prison or the wider criminal justice system without being slapped in the face with the racism and white supremacy that prisoners of color endure. If we dig deeper into these practices, the political function they serve is inescapable. Police, the courts, the prison system, and the death penalty all serve as social control mechanisms. The economic function they serve is equally as chilling. I believe that in the U.S. criminal justice system the politics of the police, the politics of the courts, the politics of the prison system and the politics of the death penalty are manifestations of the racism and classism that govern much of our lives. Every part of the criminal justice system falls most heavily on the poor and people of color. Involuntary prison slavery is real.

I've heard people say that the criminal justice system doesn't work. I've come to believe exactly the opposite. It works perfectly as a matter of both economic and political policy. I don't believe it is an accident that the young adolescent of color worth nothing in the country's economy suddenly generates between 30 and 60 thousand dollars a year once trapped in the system.

The expansion of prisons, parole, probation, the courts and police systems has resulted in an enormous bureaucracy which has been a boon for everyone, all with one thing in common: a paycheck earned by keeping human beings in cages in human warehouses. The criminalization of poverty is a lucrative business and we've replaced the social safety net with a dragnet.

What's going on in the name of all of us needs to be stopped. Poverty and prisons are state-manifested violence. I think that whites have to consciously wash off the racism that infects us daily in a society where we are privileged in relation to people of color. I think people of color have to become specifically involved in fighting the bottom line expression of racism, classism and oppression that the prison system represents. Each of us needs to use any forum that we have available to describe the connections between slavery and the criminal justice system, between U.S. domestic policies toward people of color and U.S. international policies towards countries of color. We need to stand up and say "Not in my name!" will you commit these atrocities anymore.

I have worked with many United States political prisoners and their families for decades. I have never seen anything like what I'm now seeing in U.S. prisons. My soul is shaken by what I read in my daily mail.

* * *

Elizabeth Quigley, Coordinator, Pennsylvania Association of Learning Alternatives

We have the best justice system in the world. On paper. In theory. No other country in the world has a better record for the promise of justice, yet we have the worst justice system in the world. When the rich buy justice. When the corrupt walk. When a parent grieves and an abuser goes free. How can we change so that our justice system lives up to our ideal? By becoming activists. By speaking out. By letting our legislators know that we expect the system to work. By living and practicing justice in our own lives.

With no limitations, financial or otherwise, I would start with the children. I would see that each child was fed, sheltered, loved and listened to, and then a sane justice system could begin. It is the inequities of our larger system that corrupt our justice system. We all have to work on ourselves like Buddhists in order to fix our larger social system, we have to listen deeply like Quakers, and we have to love all society's children so much that we never let any child be hurt. That is where and when justice will begin.

* * *

John Griffin, Inmate
($1,140,000)

The current prison system is the result of centuries of hate and ignorance. This system is maintained by lies and deceit. The walls that keep us in also keep John Q. Public out.

The state and federal governments have a captive audience. Prisoners are constantly being programmed, through abuse and neglect, to return to prison after their release. Who holds the wardens and superintendents accountable for the failures they release back into society?

This country's hatred and total disregard for minorities and the poor has led to the greatest deterioration in history: the mass incarceration and neglect of its own citizens.

In order to build a more humane and effective system, one must tear down the old one, brick by brick, exposing the antebellum criminal justice mentality that was created at the end of slavery and is continued under present-day legislation. Of all the political and social burdens weighing heavily on minorities and the poor, none is as onerous as the impediment to equal justice under the law.

My first act would be to establish a criminal justice system that operates within the community. Those individuals found guilty of non-violent crimes would be indebted to the community for service. Those with drug addictions would be given treatment instead of incarceration. There would be effective follow-up programs.

Those committing crimes requiring incarceration would be placed in community owned and operated facilities. These would be retraining centers with both educational and vocational courses, which are updated as there are advances in technology. All prisoners would be required to work and earn a wage adequate enough to pay their own way.

Prisoners would also have to meet their responsibilities toward their families by paying reduced child support and taxes. Those released from confinement wouldn't be referred to as ex-convicts and denied the rights of full citizenship.

However, without a fair and unbiased court system, judges who are willing to review the progress of those they confine, and a community willing to get involved and hold accountable those superintendents and wardens entrusted with the care of our young men, women and children, no change will be effective.

* * *

Philip Curcio, Inmate

The current system cannot function as intended because it's inconsistent. State institutions are labeled "rehabilitative" and "correctional," while the incarcerated are labeled "filthy" and "incorrigible." Prisoners internalize the revenge that society administers through ostracism and law. "Restoration" is the politically correct term to use when presenting prisons and prisoners.

There are too many mixed messages. The only way a broken relationship can be restored is by incorporating a method that classifies prisoners according to background/history, education, age and disposition. Rather than indiscriminately forcing the younger inmates to house with the older ones or the violent kind with the docile type or allowing the outgoing personality to override the reflective one, I'd organize units (like learning centers) that are conducive to each group. Incorporated in each "grade level" would be academic education, social etiquette and ample opportunity for creative expression.

Another common misconception is that by releasing "non-violent" offenders on parole and denying parole to "violent offenders," society is safer. Non-violent offenders can be more destructive to communities – not only as drug dealers or burglars, but also as the ones who most often return to prison. Violent offenders usually act out of passion and rarely re-offend when released. Prisoners need to be evaluated on a case-by-case system rather than by categorization. Shortsighted judgment by an impersonal Parole Board must be improved.

* * *

Sally Scattergood

A longtime inspirational activist, Sally serves on the board of PAR and is the co-founder of "Educating Children for Parenting," a unique national program based in Philadelphia that teaches parenting skills at the middle school level.

"My vision of a new system would be to have small prisons, no more than 50-60 inmates in each, divided into small groups. Inmates would do their own housekeeping, buy their food in the community, study with nutritionists and cook their own food. Educational opportunities including college courses would be offered. Everyone would learn skills relevant to the current economy and how to budget. They could be mentored and return to prison at night. The focus would be on conflict resolution, practicing non-violent methods in groups. Children would be in treatment with their parents, for I believe it's terribly important for children to be with their parents. Even abused children would benefit.

For the hard-core inmate and the mentally ill, I'd create hospital-like treatment."

* * *

Tony Harper, Inmate
($965,000)

No one has asked the real question: Where did racism come from? How can it be healed? The government has pitted rich against poor for so long to keep the poor in check, so that we will not rebel against a system whose only interest at heart is its own.

Prisons have the same effect as slavery.

A lack of jobs for years contributed to prisons being filled by people of color. There are some people behind these walls whose only crime was that they were in the wrong place at the wrong time, with dark skin color – which always plays a part in someone's presumed guilt. Look at the average place where people of color live: the housing is in deplorable shape, there are drug markets and gun shops. On every corner there is a bar or some place selling spirits to people. The states and the U.S. government, despite mandates to rehabilitate, refuse to educate people in prison because what better way to employ its masses than by keeping them coming back, keeping men/women locked up until their dreams die behind these walls.

As for the healing process in building a legal system from the ground up, Afrocentric and cultural education is the moral fabric from which most people of color get their direction. We need to keep God at the top of our lives so our decision will be based on wanting the best for one another.

Most of us won't be put off and will continue to fight the good fight.

* * *

Emmett Fulford, Inmate

What do I think of the current system? In many cases, those addicted to power in this country will do the unthinkable to have things their way. They will tell any lie necessary in an attempt to cover up their sick and evil deeds.

Our Department of Corrections, our Parole Boards, our Board of Pardons, our halfway houses, and our criminal courts have degenerated into a bunch of greedy people. We allow ourselves to be manipulated by our own anger and frustration because when all's said and done, we elect these little people instead of people who not only can identify the problems but offer solutions to these devastating problems.

What would I do to change our DOC systems?

What we need now is human beings working within the operational apparatus of the DOC to implement progressive policies instead of manipulating them in a cynical and sometimes sadistic manner.

Another suggestion for improvement is to look at the model of Dr. Mimi Silbert, co-founder and president of the Delancey Street Foundation, the nation's leading self-help residential education center in San Francisco. Her program has managed to help thousands of born losers since 1971, turning them into productive, responsible, mature and moral members of our American society.

Some of the principles of the DSF program are: each one teach one; there will be no violence, no threats of violence or intimidation at Delancey Street. You must learn three marketable skills, get a high school diploma, have steady employment, and not hang around glorifying criminal behavior. DSF is a solution.

Why aren't we or our elected leaders knocking on Doctor Silbert's door to find out how DSF could be duplicated in every city of our "drugged out" nation?

Is It because our 30-year drug war and the over one trillion dollars that has been wasted has our law enforcement and elected officials addicted to the waste of tax-payer money?

* * *

Robert Muhkam Hagood, Inmate
($1,175,000 when he died several years ago)

THE IMPORTANCE OF CULTURAL EDUCATION

"When people went to schools and became scholars in Greek, and scholars in Latin, and scholars in the ancient civilizations, but with total ignorance of their own civilization, those people were miseducated."

Dr. Carter G. Woodson
Miseducation of the Negro, 1930

The importance of a cultural education is that it prepares one to move through the socialization process of one's tribe, village, or nation, equipped with the knowledge of the "Ways" of one's ancestors. By having the ability to apply the knowledge and learn the arts, skills and crafts, one is accepted and acknowledged as a social peer with both the ability and commitment to make a difference in the lives of one's own people.

As a descendent of African People who were the slaves and property of European Americans, and as a student of both the Parochial School and the Public School Systems during the 1940's and the 1950's, I never saw an image of myself or someone that I could identify with ethnically in the center of the education process. Nor did I hear a discourse in any of the schools that I attended about African people being contributors to civilization.

All education is cultural. Thus I am compelled to ask: In which culture has one achieved his or her education? Also, does their education adequately define the genetic and hereditary nature of the human being that he or she was created to be? Likewise, did he or she learn to think, believe, speak and perform academically and socially in a manner that is alienating from one's true self? Or did they learn the history, values, music, religious and tribal rituals that guide provide guidance toward their own cultural identity through the education process?

Armed with the knowledge of one's own culture, people can redefine themselves, and they have the tools to reevaluate the society that they live in.

The importance of a cultural education is that one receives the skills and the knowledge necessary to make a difference in one's own life and the lives of others. One is accepted as a social peer based upon one's achievements as opposed to just being born.

Thus a lack of a cultural education will lead to a lifetime of mimicking, emulating and serving a people other than one's own. The descendants of African people should make a conscious effort to bring their own culture into the center of the education process, thereby preserving and defining their own cultural identity.

* * *

Chaka Turner, Inmate
($440,000)

I would not build a new system from the ground up for it already exists. It is known as a THEOCRACY. Government ruled by God. Jesus Christ preached of this government throughout his ministry on earth and referred to it as the Kingdom or the Kingdom of God. It is based on the foremost attribute of God, which is love. The quality of love is really and truly remarkable. In the Greek that the New Testament was written in, it is called Agape love. This is a special kind of love that while it includes basic affection is more motivated by principle, a sincere appreciation for God, his purpose, and his fellow man.

Jesus said, "You must love Jehovah your God with your whole soul and with your whole mind." This is the greatest commandment. The second, like it, is this, "You must love your neighbor as yourself." On these two commandments the whole Law hangs. If every person loved God and other people with an Agape, or unselfish love, there would be no need for a criminal justice system.

* * *

Aaron Christopher Wheeler, Inmate
($510,000)

Aaron Wheeler is serving a life sentence. His crime? He was in a sandwich shop with another guy who got angry at the clerk and pulled out a gun and shot him without warning. Aaron had no idea he was going to do this, has never held a gun in his life, and due to mandatory sentencing laws, is considered a co-conspirator. In Pennsylvania, his only recourse is the Board of Pardons.

"I am a black male who first got involved with the Criminal Justice System when I was fifteen years of age. I served about two to three years off and on in various juvenile facilities. As a juvenile, I noticed how the Criminal Justice System was biased against people of color. I saw how a white youth could commit the same crime as a person of color and the white youth would get probation while the person of color would always be sent away for months at a time.

In 1991, at the age of 22, I came to prison and have been here ever since. I am not convicted as the perpetrator of a crime, but as a co-conspirator. I never killed, shot or robbed anyone in any of the crimes I am convicted of. I never even touched or possessed a weapon in these crimes. There was no money taken and the majority of the witnesses do not even remember me being present at these. However, despite all of this, I am convicted of two counts of second degree murder, robbery, aggravated assault, possession of an instrument of crime and criminal conspiracy which has resulted in a sentence of double life imprisonment with a consecutive sentence of 27 ½ to 55 years ($945,000-$1,825,000).

Unless the system changes dramatically, I will die in prison.

The Criminal Justice System was created to benefit white men. We must remember that people of color had no rights when this system was created; we were considered property.

As years went by, we were given certain rights, but institutions (within the system) that were created to benefit white men remain the same to this very day. None of these institutions know how to deal with people of color. Despite the fact that there are now black judges, jurors, prosecutors, police, correctional officers, legislators, security guards and lawyers, all were trained by the old supremacist policies that have been embedded in these institutions since their creation.

The only way that the system can be improved is if the old foundation is destroyed and a new foundation is created where both whites and men and women of color are treated exactly the same for offenses committed.

To improve the system would take a lot of doing.

I would construct a system that is not based on the color of one's skin or on one's financial status. The system would treat everyone the same. All persons would be treated as human beings who just made a mistake at one time or another; rather than as outcasts, banned from ever enjoying life again after they have paid their debt to society.

Second, there would be no life sentences, death penalties or parole. No person would be sentenced to more than ten years in prison at one given time, despite the crimes s/he has committed. Any sentence given would have to be served in its entirety and would require the person's family and community to play a valuable part in his/her rehabilitation and recommitment back into society. It would also require the offender to make amends with the victim where possible or the victim's family.

Third, there would be no classification of crimes such as felony or misdemeanor; and once you pay your debt to society, that crime will never be held against you again.

Fourth, there would be no such thing as conspiracy. A person would only be held accountable for his/her own actions and not the actions of another.

Fifth, rather than being removed from the community, people would be sentenced to community work. This way they will be an asset rather than a liability to the community they were helping to destroy.

Finally, there would be a juvenile system where children are treated as children and keeping the family united is strongly practiced despite any crime that a child has committed. "

* * *

Rev. Peyton Craighill,
Former president of the board, *Graterfriends*; Board member, PA Prison Society

The present system is inherently dysfunctional. Its purpose is to reduce the amount of crime in society. But instead it promotes the growth of crime by turning loose people who are, if anything, less capable of coping effectively with life in society than they were when they were brought into the system. It wastes huge quantities of taxpayer money and chews up the lives of millions of people inside and outside the system, with little if anything to show for all the resources committed to it.

Any new system should include the following:

1. Crime prevention, focusing on youth-at-risk, especially in districts with high rates of juvenile delinquency. Prevention includes efforts such as programs for alternatives to violence, after-school education, family counseling, anti-drug campaigns, and job opportunities.

2. Community policing: improving relationships between police and the communities they serve. Young people often develop self-destructive attitudes towards social responsibility and authority as a result of what they perceive to be the misuse of power by the police in their neighborhoods.

3. The judicial system: moving from retributive to restorative justice, including citizens' reparative boards and conferencing. As long as the victims of the present judicial system experience justice primarily as a system used by the dominant authority in society to oppress them, they will have great difficulty developing positive attitudes and actions in dealing with that authority.

4. Corrections. Of the budget for corrections, 96% goes into custody and security; only 4% into "corrective" programs that help prisoners move towards greater success in dealing with their lives in society. We need to find examples in the most effective corrections systems of programs already functioning that serve as alternatives to the present dysfunctional system and then adopt them widely. The absolute minimum would be to supply literacy and G.E.D. programs for all prisoners who need them.

5. Post-release support: What can be done to reduce an 85% rate of recidivism? How can parole and other post-release programs become more supportive than punitive? These questions merely open the discussion of how the 600,000 prisoners a year coming out of our prisons can be helped to move more smoothly back into the wider society.

A major problem with efforts in the criminal justice system to bring about reform is that they are almost always focused on one of the areas listed above without reference to the other four. Because all five are so closely interlinked, such efforts have little hope of success. Due to ignorance, indifference, and protection of bureaucratic fiefdoms, each of the five areas tends to be isolated from the others. An endeavor to break through these barriers and to develop a comprehensive approach to justice reform encompassing all five in relationship to each other is greatly needed.

* * *

"Of hatred and ill will may not a trace remain.
May love and goodwill fill body, mind and life."
Dhammapada

Joseph Betz, PhD
Department of Philosophy
Villanova University

I am a teacher at Villanova University who began teaching philosophy courses in Graterford Prison thirteen years ago. I have gotten to know a little about the prison and about my students, some of whom I have taught in five different courses. The overwhelming impression that one gets is that this prison is only for "blue collar" criminals, that crime is only "blue collar" crime, that the institution is only for members of one social and economic class, only for poor urbanites, mostly African-American and Latino, many of whom are school-dropouts who can barely, or, only at a very low level, read or write. Of perhaps 3,300 in the prison, only about 125 can qualify for and are enrolled in our Villanova college-level courses.

When I think of why this is so, I am forced to imagine the following. These inmates are examples of what is likely to happen to a person who, through no fault of his own, grows up in urban poverty. As the whites left for the suburbs, they took with them their stores, factories, businesses, and ability to pay taxes. The poor, often black or Puerto Rican, were sucked into the vacuum: they could not get jobs or could not get good jobs, for the white employers were gone. When jobs disappear, crime appears. When jobs disappear, fathers disappear from their wives and children. If men cannot spend their time working, they will spend it drinking, gambling, and finding ways to make a quick and often dishonest dollar. If one in the ghetto cannot get work, he can still get drugs, and opportunities with drugs replace opportunities with working for Fortune 500 companies.

One way out of the ghetto is the army, and I have taught many prisoners who were in the army, but the army usually lasts only a few years, and then, back to the ghetto.

Not all of the inmate-students I have taught at Graterford came from absolute poverty. Some came from more prosperous families in nicer neighborhoods. But, even so, the ghetto and its ills often affected them, because they dared to experiment with the drugs that they learned were for sale in the poor neighborhood which they visited on drug-shopping expeditions.

Overwhelmingly, to visit the prison is to visit a poor neighborhood. To concentrate the poor in a prison like Graterford, just as they were concentrated in their old inner-city neighborhoods, is to continue the criminogenic conditions which caused their crimes in the first place.

I feel much more concern for the conditions in American society which have brought so many members of our lowest socio-economic classes to prison, and concern for the continuation of concentrated poor people in prison, than I have for the conditions which the prison authorities create within the walls of their institutions. But I can recommend changes, and one can think of them as treating those in our lower socio-economic classes as if they are invited to enter the middle class when they leave prison.

- The federal government should adopt something like the "Freedom Budget," which A. Phillip Randolph, Jr., head of the black Brotherhood of Sleeping Car Porters, designed for the Johnson Administration but which was never implemented. In Randolph's vision, however the federal government decided to spend its money, it would do it in such a way that it generated the maximum number of jobs for those who really needed them, especially in economically depressed parts of the country. We would spend our money on labor-intensive projects, and employ the labor of the poor recompensed by a living wage.

- Control the flow of capital in the economy so that it is prohibited from leaving the cities or the country. There are many ways a strong government could bargain with business to get jobs back into the inner city.

- Realize that drug selling occurs in its most virulent form only where there is no other employment, and drug using only where there is no opportunity or demand to use one's time productively. Treat drug users, not punish them, and give decent jobs to ghetto residents so that they can make a living without drug selling. This should come when good business and employment opportunities for all, regardless of race, return to the inner city. Then, the work ethic will crowd out the drug ethic as it has for most suburbanites.

- If prisons are bad because they continue to concentrate the poor in the same criminogenic conditions which the ghettoes had which originally caused the problem, then this sort of concentration in isolation should be broken up by various sorts of integration. Get more concerned, successful citizens into the prisons to work with the inmates. Get the non-violent inmates out of the prisons to mix at work with people from whom they will acquire the habits of solid citizens. In fact, get all of those whose future conduct is not likely to be a threat to society out of prisons quickly, with shorter terms, or perhaps with half-way houses.

- My vision, more integration of those without with those within prisons, for quicker release and partial release and for the treatment rather than imprisonment of drug addicts, means two other changes – shorter sentences and fewer prisons.

- In the 1960's, Governor Milton Shapp announced that there would be no execution of death sentences while he was governor. This magnanimous act should now be repeated. The isolation of death-row incarceration is inhumane. Inmates condemned to death should be given a chance to prove they are not dangerous to the other inmates in the general prison population. Having done so, they too should enjoy more integration with the decent and concerned citizens from outside now more present in the prison.

Prison should be a place where there is a more effective and sincere chance of correction. There should be meaningful work for all in prison related to occupations in demand in the outside world. There should be more mentoring, with training related to the newest tools and techniques now used on the outside. The 70% in prison who cannot read or write on an adult level should get the literacy training they so desperately need to be productive and responsible citizens. Having learned to read, they need better instruction to get their G.E.D.'s, to pass their high school equivalency exams.

Is there really any hope that my suggested reforms will be instituted in the American prison system? There is the present opportunity to go in directions favoring them because of the widespread anger at "white collar" criminals and the new realization of the enormous financial harm they have done to the whole economy. Since it is unlikely that we will begin to treat the influential "white collar" criminals as badly as we do the "blue collar" criminals, maybe a sense of fairness will induce us to treat the "blue collar" criminals as gently as we treat the "white collar" criminals.

* * *

Carol-Anne Riddle, PhD

Carol-Anne Riddle, who has served on the boards of *Graterfriends* and PAR, wonders why the media has focused so little on what goes on in prisons.

REPARATIVE BOARD PROCESS

I have been a volunteer in prison reform groups in Pittsburgh and Philadelphia for over 20 years and one thing I have learned is that the DOC –

Department of Corrections, the perfect oxymoron –
is in desperate need of an intense examination:

How can it cost almost $2 billion to support 28
prisons with a population of 35,000 men and women
in a system defined as a failure? The first thing I think
of is the amount of corruption there.

One odd side issue of that budget is that the
DOC receives money for each telephone call made by
inmates to their families and friends. All calls must be
made collect. So we see largely poor families
subsidizing the imprisonment of their fathers and
sons, mothers and daughters.

There are a variety of educational programs
offered mostly by volunteers but the basic foundation
of prison life is cruel, vile and immoral. "Prison" exists
as an unknown world for the average American, an
underground horror rarely examined.

The most vile aspect is Death Row. In Illinois
during several years time, the governor realized that a
total of 13 men on Death Row had been released
because they were found to be innocent and at the
same time 11 had been put to death. Illinois has
stopped putting people to death.

Consider the following:

- Supermax. The new super maximum
  isolation prisons from which "no one leaves
  alive." How many have been built in
  Pennsylvania? What does each one cost and
  does the state totally fund it or does the

federal government pay part? Why has the media not investigated this whole idea? Have state legislatures had any voice in the planning and building of these concentration camps?

- <u>Addiction to drugs and alcohol.</u> Inmates who are addicted to drugs and alcohol, estimated to be 70% of the incarcerated population, continue to use them in prison. Who brings them in – the guards? Vendors who deliver trucks full of goods? Who else? How much treatment is available?

- <u>What does a life sentence mean?</u> In all states except Pennsylvania and two others, lifers can be considered for parole after some years served and a clean record in prison. In Pennsylvania, a life sentence means the rest of your life and leaves lifers totally without hope: the past two governors have declared no possible parole or probation for lifers. We are paying to keep more and more elderly men in prison at a cost of over $65,000 each.

And 95% of inmates are released from jail and prison. Margaret Thatcher said, "Prisons are an expensive way to make bad people worse."

Since the American prison system is widely regarded as a failure, what would an adequate criminal justice look like? One possibility is the Reparative Board Process.

The Reparative Board Process, now being used in Vermont, parts of Canada, Australia and in some other nations, is based on how some native cultures deal with the problem of law-breakers. The philosophy of Reparative Boards is the opposite of "correction" which is the process of warehousing humans with a minimum of preparation for their return to the outside.

In the reparative process, inmates have four jobs to perform as restitution:

1. They have to do something to indicate they realize and acknowledge their wrongful actions.

2. They have to make restitution to their victim, if there is one, by expressing remorse – in a letter, phone call, personal meeting or through another person, etc.

3. Some restitution has to be made to the community as a whole.

4. They have to work out a plan for a course of living to avoid previous failure, i.e., entering a drug program.

First offenders start with a clean record after going through this program. This requires effort by the offender and needs support during the process but it has been very successful in stopping recidivism. We are spending almost $2 billion in Pennsylvania alone for our current failure. Why not try a pilot program?

* * *

THE NATIONAL EMOTIONAL LITERACY PROJECT FOR PRISONERS

Robin Casarjian, Founder
Lionheart Foundation
(*www.lionheart.org*)

With more than 70,000 copies of her *Houses of Healing* distributed to state and federal prisons nationwide, Robin Casarjian is a well-respected international leader in bringing powerful and effective emotional literacy rehabilitation curricula to prisoners and prison staff across the country and abroad. This prisoner's guide to inner power and freedom, also available in Spanish, has brought both hope and powerful, practical tools for rehabilitation to prisons since 1995. The book, which has an accompanying training manual for facilitators, offers hands-on exercises for developing emotional literacy skills, which help break the cycle of violence and addictions. In addition, the foundation offers an educational and training video series and professional training at institutions. They are currently working on an edition dealing with juveniles which will be distributed free to every juvenile detention facility in the U.S. Massachusetts is now implementing the first "Houses of Healing Therapeutic Community" in the country. This is an intensive, contained unit of 32-40 men within the larger inmate population of 1,000. Over twelve weeks, these men will participate in a comprehensive Houses of Healing Emotional Literacy program, which will include a research component measuring behavioral change and recidivism.

Robin Casarjian has sent copies of the book to the current 40 members of the SageWriters network at various prisons around the country, where it is hoped that seeds of empowerment and change will be planted and blossom.

* * *

VIPASSANA PRISON PROJECT
Vipassana Meditation Rehabilitation and Research Trust for North American Correctional Facilities
(info@prison.dhamma.org)

Imagine a consecutive 10-day silent retreat being held for twenty inmates at a maximum security prison in the deep South. In January 2002 at the W.E. Donaldson Correctional Facility in Bessemer, Alabama, 20 inmates successfully completed the Vipassana course. Vipassana, also known as "insight" or "mindfulness," means to see things as they really are, and is a logical process of mental purification through observing physical sensations. The non-sectarian technique enables one to achieve peace and harmony, freeing the mind from deep-seated causes of suffering.

The practice, which is being studied for effectiveness by the National Institute of Health, is taught in 10-day courses where participants sit in silence, learning the step-by-step technique for eleven hours a day. The goal is freedom from mental negativities. While the course considers the essential teachings of Buddha, it is taught in a universal, non-religious fashion and does not require one to be a Buddhist. Priests, nuns, rabbis, imams and even atheists all benefit from learning the technique, which is now a part of many prisons in India. Thousands of police cadets there also take the course as part of their training.

There are two videos about Vipassana in prisons: "Doing Time, Doing Vipassana," an award-winning documentary about prisons in India, and "Changing from Inside," about women prisoners taking the course at Seattle's North Rehabilitation Facility. (Pariyatti Book Services, www.pariyatti.com) The technique can be practiced by people of any culture. All courses are free, led by volunteers.

* * *

ALTERNATIVES TO VIOLENCE PROJECT
(www.overcomingviolence.org)

The Alternatives to Violence Project is an organization of dedicated volunteers formed by Quakers to help people develop effective ways of dealing with conflicts creatively and without violence. Its programs are offered only to voluntary participants. Each course consists of a 22-hour intensive program of exercises and discussions designed to develop self-esteem and self-confidence in a trusting and supportive atmosphere, which creates a sense of community. The courses teach principles of cooperation with co-workers, skills in listening, speaking, and observing and explore the many nonviolent solutions that are possible in almost every conflict when approached with a caring attitude toward others.

* * *

Chapter Two

What Other Countries Do

The following reports about international prison conditions are taken from articles from the February 2002 *Corrections Today*, a publication of the American Correctional Association (reprinted in *Graterfriends*).

FINLAND JUSTICE NOT POLITICIZED
Tapio Lappi-Seppala
Director of Finland's National Research Institute for Legal Policy

The Finnish criminal policy is both humane and rational. Elsewhere in the world – most notably in the United States and the United Kingdom – criminal policy is less rational – a toll of general politics, a way to transmit symbolic messages, take a stand, etc. Instead of balanced reasoning and weighing pros and cons of different strategies, criminal justice interventions often are decided by a simple political authority, the more simplistic the approaches advocated – thus one sees programs and slogans compressed into two or three words, such as "prison works," "war on drugs," and "zero tolerance."

This, then, leads to a tendency to offer simple solutions to complex problems and to pander to a punitive (or presumably punitive) public opinion with harsh tough-on-crime campaigns. A common feature of these campaigns is that the solution to social problems is sought in places where it cannot be found – the penal system.

However, the ongoing total reform of the Finnish Penal Code has been executed throughout in the spirit of "humane neoclassical crime policy," regarding principles of due process and legal safeguards. The penal system reform moves in the direction of the expansion of community-based measures and focuses on situational and local crime prevention. For now, it still is difficult to imagine that the claim that "prison works" will find its way into Finnish political campaigns.

* * *

Adam Stapleton is a UK criminal lawyer who has worked as a consultant in Malawi with Penal Reform International for the past six years. He has also

consulted on human rights and penal reform issues
for donor agencies in other African nations.

AFRICAN REFORM: PARALEGALS
Adam Stapleton

Prisons in Malawi, an English-speaking country in sub-Sahara Africa, are antiquated, fortress-like structures where men dressed in rags sit in the sun with nothing to do; where more than 100 men sleep on the floor of a dormitory, packed in like sardines in a space designed for 30; where windows are two or three slits high on the walls, and the air is stale; and where the toilet is usually a bucket by the door. The smell is stunning, as is the human degradation and the poverty of it all. More than 50% of the prisoners are remand prisoners awaiting trial – some have been waiting for years. Women prisoners are separated from men, and have their children with them, but have no special treatment or diet provided, unless from outside sources.

In 1996, 40 African nations' representatives met to discuss the continent's prison conditions. Heads of prison services, law commissioners, police officers, judges and governmental officials sat with non-governmental representatives to discuss problems, which boiled down to just one: crowding. The conference produced the Kampala Declaration on Prison Conditions in Africa, whose preamble calls African prisons "inhuman." With it was drawn a plan for penal reform in Africa that highlights the "special role" of nongovernmental agencies (NGOs) in safeguarding inmates' human rights. It also urges inmates' access to lawyers and accredited paralegals; special attention to vulnerable inmates such as juveniles and females; and regular reviews of the time detainees spend on remand – recommending closer attention to alternative sentencing such as the use of local, customary practices for settling disputes through restorative justice processes.

This declaration, adopted by the UN in 1997, and others developed throughout Africa, influenced a 1999 UK international penal reform conference when representatives from more than 50 countries called for a new agenda on penal reform. The document's common theme is that criminal justice systems worldwide need reform and prison services are in crisis. The new agenda for penal reform developed at the UK conference argues that criminal justice should have a "well-defined and limited role to play in any democratic society and should not be use to resolve problems not relevant to it."

In May 2000, the Para-Legal Advisory Service (PAS) was created in Malawi as an innovative project seeking to apply the principles and recommendations of the declaration, and to give poor people access to the formal justice system. Since then, paralegals have instituted positive changes, earned the trust and respect of prisoners and criminal justice professionals and made themselves indispensable.

* * *

Bertel Osterdahl was formerly a Major General in the armed forces who became Director General of the Swedish Prison and Probation Administration in 1994.

SWEDISH PRISONS: POSITIVE
Bertel Osterdahl

It is an important aspect of Swedish criminal policy to reduce the suffering that is inescapably linked to deprivation or restriction of liberty. It clearly is beneficial for inmates to return to the community as law-abiding citizens. To achieve this, their time in prison must be used positively and creatively so they have more of a chance to do so. This requires an investment in a range of active treatment programs that allows them to address their offending behaviors.

Also, it is well known that incarceration has damaging effects. While incarcerated, inmates tend to discuss crime, improve their knowledge of ways to commit crimes, enlarge their criminal contacts and plan future crimes. Thus a prison can become unsafe for inmates and staff. Further, prison life is highly regulated and tends to remove opportunities for personal responsibility. Prisons can become colleges of crime that reinforce criminal identity and diminish capacity to adjust to the demands of community life.

An initial task for the Swedish Probation and Prison service is to counteract these negative effects. Prison leave and visits are granted to maintain contact with families and community organizations.

Correctional staff develops relationships with inmates to have a positive influence in their lives. Specific programs are developed to allow inmates to address their social inadequacies. Life in prison should approximate as closely as possible to the social conditions of the community so inmates can maintain a sense of personal responsibility.

Alternatives to incarceration are used to the greatest possible extent. Incarceration not only puts offenders' capacity for leading law-abiding lives at risk, but also is an expensive sanction.

Legislative changes were made recently to reduce incarceration by wider use of probation and community service. Life-sentenced inmates rarely serve their entire sentences. The practice is that government, following the granting of a request for clemency, usually transforms the indeterminate life sentence into a fixed term. Thereafter, the provisions on conditional release apply. Since 1995, life sentences have been commuted to between 18 and 25 years of fixed incarceration.

The role of the prison officers is changed. Formerly, the uniformed officer staff only had custodial duties. Social work assistants and psychologists carried out social work and treatment activities. A late 1980s study showed prison officers often manifested stress symptoms as a result of being seriously under-stimulated and uncomfortable in their passive role. Consequently, social work assistants were transferred to other branches, and prison officers' staff given new tasks with greater responsibility. Staff has become contact persons for granting prison leave, entry into personal change programs, etc.

In their new role, prison officers resolve conflicts among inmates, which threaten prison security and order. Close contact with inmates allows staff to know the underlying reasons for inmates' negative actions. Hence technical security in the form of high walls and closed-circuit TV, alarm devices, etc. now is supplemented by knowledge derived from closer inmate-staff contact – dynamic security. As a result, escapes diminished steadily and the home-leave misuse rate is low.

* * *

David Daubney is general of criminal law policy and coordinator of the Sentencing Reform Team in the Policy Sector of the Department of Justice of Canada in Ottawa.

CANADA ENCOURAGES COMMUNITY CORRECTIONS: LESS PRISON
David Daubney

Canadian ministers, made aware of the increasing numbers of Canadian prisoners, in 1995 called for a strategy to contain the prisoner growth rate and associated costs. They chose one that combines crime prevention, tough treatment of serious crime and greater use of community sanctions for low-risk offenders, over a shift toward a crime control and punishment policy. The legislative centerpiece of this Canadian venture, Bill C-41, also created the "conditional sentence of imprisonment." Given a conditional sentence (less than two years), the offender is permitted to serve in the community with certain conditions.

Among other versions, framers of Bill C-14 noted more than 30% of prison admissions were for failure to pay fines. They established two alternatives to prison for failure to pay fines: the non-issuance/renewal of licenses or permits and streamlined ability to register the outstanding fine as a civil judgment. Several provinces have fine-option programs for offenders to work off fines through community service. Also, it is required the judge inquire into the offender's ability to pay before levying a fine; the fine be calculated on a formula that reflects minimum wage levels; and there must be a default hearing to determine if the offender has a reasonable excuse for nonpayment before a warrant of committal can be issued. These changes contributed to dramatic decreases in the number of offenders imprisoned for fine default.

Canada's revisions also reformed aspects of probation, parole (accelerate it), and prison (moving to a restorative justice model). Among the new principles are: to assist in the rehabilitation of offenders; to promote a restorative sense of responsibility in offenders and acknowledgement of harm done to victims and the community; to not deprive an offender of liberty if less restrictive sanctions may be appropriate in the circumstances;

and to consider all available sanctions other than incarceration for all offenders, with particular attention to the circumstances of Aboriginal offenders.

* * *

SCOTS INDEPENDENT PRISON INSPECTIONS:
Aim for Decency; Changed Lives
Clive Fairweather
Scotland's Chief Inspector of Prisons

The principle of independent prison inspection has a long history in the United Kingdom, but some might ask why this should be of any relevance to corrections in the United States. The answer is the inspection reports inform the community, which is unable to see what is going on behind prison walls, while highlighting poor performance and good practice at the same time. This approach is an important tool for promoting correctional excellence.

Its origins in the UK can be traced back to at least 1773, when John Howard was appointed high sheriff, or judge, of Bedfordshire. Along with magistrates, he was responsible for prison inspection, and was appalled by the conditions and injustices he found. Consequently, he became an advocate for the reform of the penal establishments, and began to visit prisons, not only in the UK, but also around the world, in a quest to improve standards.

After the Napoleonic Wars ended in 1815, the Quaker Movement, which included Elizabeth Fry, persuaded a parliamentary select committee to agree that one uniform system of prison discipline should be established in every jail and house of correction in England and Wales. Also, prison inspectors were appointed to visit and report on them. Howard and Fry's vision of reform through independent inspections, enshrined in the Prison Act of 1835, still is relevant in the 21st century.

In 1981, a non-governmental independent inspectorate for English and Welsh prisons was formed, and a similar body was established in Scotland. The objective given to the chief inspector is a deceptively simple one: "To inspect or arrange for the inspection of prisons in Scotland and to report to the secretary of state on them...In particular, on the treatment of (inmates) and conditions in prisons."

The chief inspector, appointed by the queen, is independent from those in prison operations. His or her inspection team consists of several inspectors or consultants, and two advisory senior prison governors, and a $300,000/year budget. The inspection process is dynamic. It reflects the nature of each particular establishment, while retaining a core set of issues for use at all inspections. When a particular issue arises from a certain inmate group, the inspectorate examines it in detail and, if required, carries out an inspection focusing solely on that issue. Following the inspection and weeks of redrafting, detailed reports are published and made available to prison management, staff and prisoners, and distributed to the wider public via nationwide media outlets.

Each penal establishment, even private ones, receives a full formal inspection every three and one half years, which can last between seven and fourteen days depending on the size and complexity of the establishment. All aspects of the prison are examined for safety, decency and its contribution to crime prevention. The team is interested in assessing outcomes from the public's point of view. The reports that emerge, therefore, are a detailed snapshot of the establishment and, although politicians and prison authorities may not always act on their contents, the subsequent media coverage can be a powerful instrument for change. Eventually this gets officials' attention.

Full inspections are followed each year by intermediate visits, which may be unannounced. These reports are made public, ensuring that progress is continually monitored. The chief inspector is required to submit a written annual report to the Scottish Parliament and may be called in to provide verbal evidence.

Some reports in recent years led to wider improvements, for example, in conditions for remand prisoners – those awaiting trial or sentencing. Through inspectorate pressure and the efforts of individual governors, remand prisoners throughout Scotland now receive the best of prison conditions, whereas previously they were a disadvantaged group.

There also are improvements in conditions for women prisoners – who until recently in Scotland had an appalling record of suicides. Scottish politicians now accept that the number of women in prison should be greatly reduced – dealt with in the community through alternatives such as electronic monitoring, which allows mothers to look after their children.

The main female prison itself has been transformed, with its health center now entirely restructured to address the physical and mental health needs of the vulnerable and often bewildered women who regularly arrive at the prison from court. Better working conditions have been introduced, as well as televisions in every cell to reduce the time for morbid contemplations. This may seem incredible, but it is only during the past year that prisoners have had access to TV because of public disquiet about an apparent luxury. Also, prison authorities are uniformly concentrating their efforts on measuring and dealing with individual drug problems.

The first questions any chief inspector of prisons must ask when stepping into a jail are brutal: "Are they injured? If so, why and what can be done to prevent this?" This applies equally to staff and prisoners. To the questions: "Are conditions decent here?" inspectors use the rule of thumb that prison conditions should be no better or worse than those found in public institutions such as schools or hospitals. However, increasingly, the inspectors are asking: "What does this particular establishment try to do to prevent future victims or crime?" This refers to escapes and rehabilitation.

The one thing prisoners have is time, and such time should be used constructively to help offer individuals new opportunities and change inappropriate behavior patterns. Prisoners need to learn to lead more useful lives and to be properly prepared for release. Here the importance of role models in the shape of experienced and mature correctional officers cannot be underestimated.

Thus, the central aim of imprisonment and inspection is not only about incarceration, but also about trying to change behavior as a practical crime-prevention measure. This requires careful assessment of offenders at the start of their sentences to determine their problems, their histories of offending and reasons behind it, as well as if there is any family support and whether they will have accommodations after release, etc. Induction should not be regarded as an event, but rather as an ongoing process. Staff must keep returning to "measure" and obtain more detail from offenders regarding what will help bring about significant change. They should create a sentence plan for the individual who, while in prison, tries to address these issues, ending up with a workable release plan.

Each prison also has an independent body (descended from the original magistrates of the 1700's), now called the Visiting Committee. This body scrutinizes its prison on a regular basis and members are appointed by the first minister or local authority. They represent a cross-section of the community, are volunteers, and organize their visits in such a way that someone is inside a prison each week to monitor the treatment of prisoners and report to the governor or politicians what is found. These laypersons lack detailed training but more than make up for it through their fair, open-minded approach. These watchdogs are by no means "toothless and barking," and the concept of independent prison inspection is as applicable elsewhere in the free world as it is to the UK. Visit website: www.scotland.gov.uk/hmip for ideas.

* * *

NETHERLANDS: NEIGHBORHOOD PRISONS
Kees Boeij
General Director of the Penitentiaries Noord-Holland Noord in the Netherlands.

In the Netherlands there is an increasing effort to detain offenders in their neighborhoods, rather than the former practice of detention where the crime was committed. Also, placing detainees near their home facilitates family visits.

This effort stems from the realization by penitentiary leaders the system had to come out of its isolated position – where everything was done to build small societies within the prison walls – which had its own kitchen, library, educational staff and employment provisions. Once officials realized this was not always efficient, and by no means a guarantee of good quality, they started looking for partners in society who were willing and able to provide these services.

When they realized they were not only isolating the detainees but the prison itself, they began putting new prisons in industrial areas – where citizens rarely try to prevent their presence. The search for partners was based on the understanding prison governors cannot rehabilitate or reintegrate inmates into society alone. In fact, prisons do not want to do it alone because a variety of authorities and people are needed during detention to assist and guide detainees. Also, for the system to do it alone makes it too easy for society to hold the prison system solely responsible.

In the Netherlands, ex-detainees are entitled to housing and government benefits. Municipalities like to cooperate to arrange this. Moreover, there are subsidies from the Ministry of Social Affairs to the municipalities to compensate the costs for former detainees assisted with housing, benefits and education.

* * *

KAZAKHSTAN: From Totalitarianism in Prisons to Human Rights
Pyotr Posmakov
Chairman of the Committee for the Penal System of the Republic of Kazakhstan.

During the Soviet era, Kazakhstan was a land of forced labor camps. The republic's prison service, a component of the Soviet Union's system, had a punitive criminal policy that caused severe crowding. After the 1991 Soviet Union breakup, Kazakhstan became independent and established its own penal system. In 1984 the number of prisoners surpassed 100,000. Since then, three amnesties and decriminalization of about 70 criminal code articles caused the number to stabilize at 84,000 in recent years.

Studies show no direct connection between the number of crimes and the amount of incarceration. The incarceration rate is determined more by general conditions of reliance in society and balance of political forces. Indeed, the rate of imprisonment seems to depend on criminal policy, the application of laws and traditions that have taken root in public consciousness. An offender eventually will be released, and it is no secret that incarceration does not help re-educate inmates. In fact, during incarceration inmates become saturated with criminal ideology and take it with them upon release. Thus, by passing a significant part of the country's population through detention facilities, the society deteriorates. It is not difficult to calculate the continuation of such a criminal policy toward incarceration during the next ten to twenty years may result in irretrievable consequences.

Thus, "Limitations of Freedom," a new kind of punishment that does not require the offender's isolation, was introduced in Kazakhstan by 2003. Those sentenced to limitations of freedom retain their active and passive electoral rights to the state and local government bodies as well as the right to participate in the republican referendum.

Currently, Kazakhstan is making efforts to humanize its approach to punishment and move closer to the international standards and norm, but the changed socioeconomic situation in Kazakhstan limits the work. Still, officials and non-governmental organizations interested in penal reform are exploring many options. Prison Reform International has been working on a Kazakhstan project introduced in 2003, that includes prison reform; alternatives to prison; and tuberculosis treatment and control.

* * *

Andrew Coyle, director of the International Centre for Prison Studies, University of London, U.K., was formerly a prison warden for 25 years in Scotland and England.

"LAND OF THE FREE" DEPRIVES MANY
Andrew Coyle

With less than 5% of the world's population, the U.S. has 23% of the world's inmates – more than 2.6 million men, women and children in federal and state prisons and local jails. This is a greater proportion than any other country in the world. Include those on some sort of parole, and the figure rises to 6.6 million: 3.8% of all U.S. residents.

These figures set the U.S. apart from the democratic world and are a constant source of wonder for academics, correction professionals and public commentators in other countries. Why should it be necessary for the "land of the free" to deprive so many citizens of their liberty? Who are these two plus million men, women and children? What happens to them while in custody? What happens to them after their release?

If a correctional system exists to serve its community, then it makes sense that this community should be able to judge the extent to which this mandate is being observed. For better or worse, prisons are a part of the democratic process in all countries. Those of us who work in them carry a heavy burden on behalf of our fellow citizens. The world of corrections is generally self-contained, with practitioners rarely looking beyond their own borders for points of comparison or learning.

"All that is necessary for evil to flourish is for good men to do nothing"

Edmund Burke

Chapter Three

Why Write? Why Art? Why Music?

Frank Ross

Graterford lifer Frank Ross, 70, says he didn't begin writing fiction until 1982, the day the penitentiary gates closed behind him. According to Leslie Pappas, a reporter for the Philadelphia Inquirer, *his son, Frank, thought his father would totally shut down. A month later, the father told the son he was writing a story.*

It didn't come easily: With only a ninth-grade education, Ross knew little about literature let alone grammar and punctuation.

"He was a pretty dreadful writer," said Kathryn Fanning, an Oklahoma editor and writing instructor whom Ross paid to critique his early work. "But he took criticism well and paid attention."

Ross points to Fanning as the person who helped him the most, but says it was painful.

"She destroyed my work," he said. "She crushed me." He recalls large X's slashed through entire pages of writing and "little taunting notes" in the margins, such as, "Have you ever considered driving a bus?"

Fanning said she edits line by line, and insisted she would never make such comments on a writer's work.

Fanning said she didn't know Ross was a prisoner until several years later, when he sent her a newspaper article about himself.

It was a shock, she said. "I had envisioned him as a wizened little white man with rimless glasses."

Ross also credits Doris Patterson, an Ardmore writer who tutored Graterford prisoners for about twelve years, with helping him to develop his work.

After several months of writing, he was startled one day to hear one of his characters talking to him. He feared he was going mad. But when he told Patterson he heard voices, "she didn't flinch," Ross said, 'Next time it happens, just tell them to speak up. If you can't see their faces, tell them to turn around.'"

Patterson worked with Ross for about five years. Eventually he discovered his own voice.

Now that his first book, *The Leaf Strewn Path & The Interview,* is in print, Ross has bigger plans: four screenplays that he hopes to sell.

In the meantime, he writes in longhand, on legal pads that he buys with money earned from cleaning his cellblock. He calls writing "humiliating," something that "bares your soul."

But he plans to keep doing it. "I'm obsessed," he said, adding that he wished he had discovered writing earlier in life.

"If I had, I wouldn't be here," he said. "You don't see too many writers that end up killing people."

Leslie Pappas, the Philadelphia Inquirer
March 24, 2003
Reprinted with permission

* * *

A USELESS LIFE IS AN EARLY DEATH (GOETHE)
James Bauhaus, Inmate

Nunio Morales, tired of the silence of our cage, asked me with exasperation, "You are always writing! Why are you always writing?"

Nunio was a good man, but perhaps too wrapped up in inmate culture. He was well respected for honorably following their code, but he was unable to see the big picture of how it was based on hatred, anger, opportunism and self-interest. Following the inmate code cost him 25 years of his life on a sentence that could have been quenched in thirteen years. Because he was honorable, plus he was open to new ideas, I thought of how to explain to him the advantages of writing over talking.

Nunio saw the disadvantages: why write when talking is so much easier? Also, with talking, you get to see the listener's reaction. You don't have to gather up pencil, paper, sharpener or eraser. You don't have to arduously write down words or stop everything to find out their correct spelling and meaning. You don't have to worry about them laughing about your grammar or ideas. If they do laugh, there is nothing they can show to others for them to laugh at. From his perspective, writing was a one-way street of trouble.

So, I wondered, why do I write? I write because writing is so very much more powerful than words. Words vanish into space as soon as they are said. If someone hears them, they exist in the mind only until the next of many petty distractions. Words are easily forgotten. They are hard to remember, there is always a cacophony of other words yammering for attention. This constant yik-yak chaos of goalless free-association makes words cheap as dirt. Words are weak, too: Because words are weak, countless crucial ideas are regularly lost and critical inventions had to be constantly re-invented. This is why it took four million years for man to domesticate animals, tame fire, learn to farm and put the wheel to work along with the sling, bow and javelin.

By contrast, writing is valuable and strong. The invention of writing allowed even more valuable constructs to quickly follow such as math, geometry and physics. They enabled us to perfect our environment and enhance our natural state. We built

castles, cathedrals, canals, highways and bridges.
Writing preserves good ideas. Information and invention no longer die along with the people who created them. Good ideas get passed around. Other inventive people improve on them. They get passed further on. Everyone benefits. Since the invention of writing, history began. In only hundreds of years we have progressed farther than we had in all the millions of years since we stood erect and grunted hunting signals to one another.

So, why do I write? I write because it is the most efficient way to get my ideas across to the most people in the shortest time. I write because writing lets me contribute as much as Albert Einstein or the inventor of the wheel. I write because it *gets things done.*

* * *

I first discovered SageWriters when I did a book review of *Celling America's Soul*, written by some of the writers in the group. While reading it, I was so deeply moved that I immediately felt inspired to become part of the organization.

Judith suggested that I start by writing to some of the SageWriters. I did this and felt a strong connection to them instantly. For years, I had wanted to reach out to the imprisoned, especially those who didn't deserve to be there in the first place. Through the letters, I got to know several of them. I learned about their backgrounds, their hobbies, their habits, as well as the numerous challenges they face everyday. Overall, I got to know them as *real* people.

Last winter Judith sent me the autobiography of one of the SageWriters. The book was self-published by the author, who has been imprisoned for over 25 years. The book was truly an inspiration to me. I learned so much just by reading about this man's life. He really opened up and shared an amazing story. And after reading it, I could only imagine the abundance of talent among all of the writers. I couldn't wait to read the manuscripts of other prisoners as well.

For the last four months I've been serving as a volunteer editor. This has been an eye-opening experience for me. Working with prisoners has given me a greater understanding of what they experience. I've been able to see them overcome the challenges placed before them, in order to see their work through to completion. Whether it's how they deal with typing their manuscripts without access to a computer, being transferred to another prison, being placed in The Hole, relying on snail mail as their primary method of communication with outsiders, lacking monetary funds to get their work published, or lacking the necessary tools to market it effectively, they all seemed to face their problems and difficulties head on, with tenacity and self-reliance.

This confirmed my belief that these individuals are not looking for sympathy, handouts, or luxuries that they don't deserve. They simply want to be treated as human beings. Their minds, bodies, and spirits require the same caring and attention as anyone else's. I really believe it's as simple as this. And one only needs to read the work of a SageWriter to see how writing can be used as a powerful tool to nourish these three elements, not only in prisoners but in all of us.

Stacian Gordon
Mentor, Volunteer Editor
Washington, DC

* * *

SageWriters allows me to let go of some of the pain of my past while preparing me for a transformed future. It allows an internal healing process to occur by writing down my secret feelings and sharing all I was holding in with others who may or may not have been suffering from similar conditions. I was permitted to see the humanity in others unlike myself and in return I was able to reconnect with my sense of dignity and self-respect amongst all humans, despite petty animosities and large adversities.

Most of all, SageWriters offered me hope in a time of despair and uncertainty. When I write I am able to channel powerful emotions that are wandering out of control. Poetry pushes me to practice patience and perfection. In essence, I am discovering the source beyond my thoughts and life conditions. I've become more aware that I must master this uncharted reality within myself. In summation, SageWriters gave me a mirror to reflect the True Me to the world!

Alfonso Percy Pew
Inmate

I'm a SageWriter

As my thoughts get blacker
My words transmit a fear factor
The spit from my lips were fire
Bubbling from the sips of "**BLACK POWER**"
But now it's **NATION TIME** building higher
Then the other side of that state razor wire
And guerrilla's around that bond fire
Thoughts that throw thrillers
To transform born killers
Into healthy healers
As I breathe my poems
Love into the hearts of natural losers
With each breach of security in my stanza
This **SAGE WRITER** is mega gangsta
Brighter yet stranger than the wall of steel
Enforced by a platoon of pigs
Nesting up on KKKoruption over the hill
Trying to infiltrate and create a cipher
But these devils can't break a **SAGE WRITER**
As I come forth of age
A prolific writer and a **sage**

Ndugu Askari Safrika
Inmate

* * *

WHAT WRITING DOES FOR ME

By Hasan Shakur (Derreck Frazier)

When Judith asked me to participate in this project I jumped at the moment to do so. I must admit, however, that at first I was somewhat apprehensive as I have been around enough to know, that sometimes people do not have a high morality code.

For me, it's more of not why I write, but; why not write as it offers so much for me. All my life I have been more of an orator then anything. Being imprisoned really halts that. Writing has become more of an alternative to me speaking.

With my writings, I have opened up a new being inside of this shell that wish to call a body. I am able to overcome any and all boundaries presented in front of me. It is more of a pleasure when I am able to touch someone in the process.

Being in a world where your physical being means so much, to be able to illustrate beauty in the form of words; makes one unique person. I being an activist I take my word and from them in such a way, you can actually sometimes feel them! What a beautiful feeling to read something and get chills down your spine!

What if I didn't write? Well, first of all you wouldn't be reading this. Am I correct? Words are some of the most powerful weapons we have in a situation like our. We are imprisoned, held captive within the bowels of a beast that is bent on devouring an entire generation of people that once thrived on being totally ignorant to the society around them. To strike back, one must use then words and make them cut to the core of the beast. Words are emotion in black and white meaning. I can cry a river and you can read it. It gives me the chance to reach out to you and you in return can reach back within yourself and reach back to me through a barrage of words written to become a paper of emotion.

In this sea of black and white one can easily get swept away into it and in most cases, I never want to return. I think this is the only way I can really escape without the barks of the bloodhounds, shots of the police or the reward on my head. I can for that moment in time get away and get within my thoughts and even develop a world all within itself. I can get away from the ignorance, which has become African People in America's most deadliest disease. Not only that but it gives me the chance to reach out.

At this very moment, I am having the sounds of jazz filtered into my ear. I have the tapping of this typewriter, drowned out by the jazz. I am sitting here but I am not here. I have been poured out of this shell and onto the piece of paper in which you are reading my very thoughts, my brain waves and my soul. Writing is all I have in the way of communicating to the masses of the people that seems to be somewhat interested in reading what a person in my situation wishes to say. To me, writing is a marriage in which I wish to never see end in divorce. It has become something beautiful and it becomes even more beautiful as time goes on.

If I would have to sum it up I would have to say that writing in itself is love to. Love that I have always wanted and a love that will never disappear as this is a love that will continue to flourish.

What does writing do for me? It shows me love. It is love. It resonates love and it incubates love therefore allowing me to offer love to you in return.

Hasan Shakur, another innocent man, was executed by the state of Texas on April 27, 2006.

* * *

"Why Write?"

The great abolitionist Frederick Douglass stated that human speech is a great miracle by which people are enlightened, and by which evil is exposed and ignorance dispelled. The same can be said for the written word. Taking this train of thought a few stations further I see words acting as a magical elixir. With well-crafted words we can heal the malignant cancers of ignorance, and human discord that has been deeply entrenched into society's consciousness. As the bible, says, "…in the beginning was the word…"

As I asked myself the question "why write?" a lot of answers came to mind. For me writing is therapeutic. It is a form of meditation that allows me to see myself and others clearly. Writing allows me to give voice to the million plus captives who are unable to articulate their own stories. These are just some of the answers that came to mind. As I combed through them I realized that they were not in line with what I really wanted to say. Then it hit me. I write because I want to shake people to the core. I want to take them away from their apathetic comfort zone.

I want my words to leap off the page and peel back the lids on society's third eye so they can see us clearly. I want people to look beyond our ebony, mahogany, banana, and coffee brown exteriors. Get a glimpse behind the stoic expressions we have been forced to wear for the majority of our lives. Can you see us yet? Glance beyond the network of veins, tendons, ligaments and bones that make up our tear stained faces. Stretch your vision to see pass the ugly that we have allowed ourselves to become.

I write to show you the little boy who once had dreams of being a doctor. I want you to see the little kid who always felt he had to work extra hard to fit in and be accepted. I want you to see the little child that is still hurting and full of fear. He's in there behind the mucus of toughness, hood savvy, and prison bitterness. That's him curled up in the fetal position hoping to be loved and appreciated. I want you to see him clearly.

Expand your grey matter like a rubber band; protract your view so you can see things outside of your peripheral vision. I know it's ugly and that is the beauty of the whole thing. When you can see all this ugliness maybe you will understand and maybe you won't. But you will have an option to choose.

Can you see that battered and torned woman balled up under the table trying to ward off the blows from her abuser? When she scrambles to get a pistol in defense of her life, can you see her? Allow your thoughts to travel like a bullet through her barrel into the heart of her tormentor. Can you se her children clutching at her legs as the authorities drag her away? Where were they before she was driven to fight for her life?

I write so you will know we are living, breathing people. We are not statistics and we most definitely are not inmate numbers. Maybe that sounds a bit haughty considering we are in prison. But look at it this way, if we become numerical statistics we may as well commit suicide because we have surrendered our humanity.

On a personal level I write to show how a little boy so full of hopes, dreams, and potential fell into an ocean of hurt, anger, and self-destruction. Like lava bubbling in a volcano, my anger erupted in four gun-blasts, consuming another life. I write to show you that there is hope for me and hope for you if you believe in the power of change. Within every negative situation there are seeds of positivity waiting to blossom. Through words I want to show you that I am caring father, son, brother, and friend. If you can see this in me, when you meet a young boy or girl who was like me you may feel compelled to stop and really look into them, and not just at them. Maybe you will tell them some of the things I wished to be told when I was growing up. This is why I write.

By Shaka Heru Khuti Senghor
Captive Name: James White

PRISONERS AS WRITING MENTORS FOR COLLEGE COMPOSITION STUDENTS
K. Limakatso Kendall, Ph.D.

Twenty-eight highly motivated teaching assistants help me teach two sections of first-year composition each semester. I call these teaching assistants "Writing Mentors," because they do more than assist me in teaching. They develop caring relationships with students, entering into dialog about the *content* of students' essays as they comment on organization and writing style. Each mentor spends hours reading students' essays and then crafting written responses which are often longer than the original essays. Each mentor carries between two and five students, and each student has two mentors. Yet none of us has ever met. Students and mentors know each other only by first names. All our interactions occur through correspondence. Each of the mentors – twenty-five men and three women – is a convicted felon serving time in one of fifteen prison units in Texas.

There is a pool of 164,000 potential teaching assistants in Texas alone. Prisoner's minds and creativity are going to waste; students are sitting in our classrooms staring vacantly into space. This project has more potential for changing lives and the educational process than I dreamed when I waded into it.

The development I see in my students causes me to reexamine the whole premise of first-year composition. There is something numbing to students about writing essays for English teachers. At worst, it's an exercise in futility. A student writes several pages about something she doesn't care about, to a teacher who doesn't want to read it and who only has time to make cursory remarks on the student's paper. Everyone loses. At best, first-year composition provides a minor outlet for creativity and offers a few survival skills for students who may later have to write essays or essay exams in other college courses. But after years of teaching composition, I have begun to doubt the validity of the whole rigmarole.

The writing mentor program restores validity to the course. In this program, students write essays, not as an exercise for an English teacher to read, pick apart, and slap a grade on, but as a communication of life experience to someone who really wants to receive it, who is hungry for stories of life in the free world, who has long been cut off from free world people, and who will read each essay and respond to it thoughtfully.

Most powerfully, for me, the program has provided wave after wave of insight and empathy, as I have watched the writing mentors grow in confidence, have seen the students wake from their habitual school-induced stupor, and have been privileged to read life-altering exchanges. Jason tells his mentor, Bill, that this program has saved his life; he was struggling with drug addiction, and Bill, who is himself in recovery, has pulled Jason through – at least for now. Bill has invested himself in Jason's recovery much as an AA sponsor or a fond uncle. Another student says her essays have been therapy for her, and her mentor affirms they have also been therapy for him. That mentor, a man named Jesse, attaches a note to me that says, "I've learned that teaching people to write is a very difficult job. You can't just say do it like this, the way I used to show my students in martial arts. You have to pull their own truth out of their minds."

Only one of the mentors plans to be an English teacher. John W. is determined to acquire as much education as he can in prison and then to pursue a Ph.D. in Welsh Literature when he's set free. This program has given John a taste of what's in store for him, and he pushes up his sleeves and attacks his responses with gusto. He's sure now. He can feel his future calling to him.

Will every project involving prisoners and college students work this well? Probably. I'd like to brag about my insight in the selection process, but I can't. I think self-selection is the magic. Prisoners who volunteer to spend hours helping college students do their homework, who are willing to go through an intensive training program that involves reading, writing essays and introductions, and corresponding about college course material, for no credit and no material reward, must be a special breed. I dreamed this up, but I couldn't make it work. My students had the most to gain from it: grades and credits. But they didn't make it work. The writing mentors made this program the deeply stirring, sometimes profound, often hilarious, transformational success it is.

Having teaching assistants who are eager to read and respond to students' work, and who have hours to focus on that work, restores to the business of education some of the heart and spirit the Romans had in mind when they coined the word, *educare*, based, as I understand, on the Greek word for "to draw out." As Jesse says, "You have to pull their own truth out of their minds." This drawing out of what is in each student takes us back to the medieval ideal of the university as a place where tutors and students engage in dialog about content, even as they hone their skills in rhetoric. I treasure my connections with these twenty-eight prisoners, and I intend to continue working with them for as long as they want. I have a waiting list of prisoners who are ready to take over when one of the original group is set free or gets tired. What we are doing together is profound for all of us.

* * *

The late Carl Hirsch, Ph.D., was adjunct faculty member at several colleges and universities in the Philadelphia area. He used Celling America's Soul as supplementary reading for his classes in social problems, violence and criminality.

As a sociologist teaching students from protected backgrounds of the lower middle or middle class, the groups my classes study who are not of their communities too often become the "theys" and the "thems": somehow different from "us" whose identities remain within the legitimate in-group; the "us" of the scientific community or of the student body. This is especially true when teaching about poverty, U.S. subcultures, crime and imprisonment.

I have used *Celling America's Soul* for the purpose of breaking down barriers that have both protected students from the harsh realities of life but which also have blocked their understanding of the prisoner as a human being, as a person. Indeed, discussion based on this book has led one student to share her own difficult experiences including the feelings of estrangement when visiting a loved relative under prison conditions that are so limiting to a close and feeling interaction. She also described the difficulties in trying to have her uncle's "story" reach the right ears for an appeal. In another case the frustration shared with the class concerned trying to get a relative's story told in order to correct an injustice suffered while they've been imprisoned.

One student shared having been a prisoner. The perception of other students in the class that this person who now sits among us, who has been given the trust that we extend to others in our college classes without a second thought, was once a prisoner serving a sentence in a state prison led to an altered view of who the "prisoner" is. This new view was a more open and objective one. The possibility that these "prisoners," portrayed in the worst light in the vast bulk of mass media entertainments, might be victims as well entered the students' thinking.

One student who was somewhat offended by the "non-academic" style of the book felt challenged by the assertions concerning the reported abuses of women prisoners and undertook her own research on this topic. She reported to class that the reports in the book were totally reinforced by every source she located and admitted to shock and dismay, not only concerning the situation she had uncovered, but also by her own previous ignorance of anything of this sort occurring in U.S. prisons.

In addition, in two of the three classes in which the book was used at least one student was a prison guard. Much to the dismay of one, but with a sigh of relief by the other, both had to acknowledge that the negative role of too many prison guards was accurately portrayed in the words of these men.

The reality that most prisoners will return to live among us, following alienating experiences behind bars, took on new meaning for the students. Concern replaced their previous ignorance of this reality. When coupled with materials from newspapers and book reviews describing the stigma and discrimination that makes it hard for these "human beings" to take a new direction and succeed in the "straight" world, students themselves raised the issue of the injustice of such a "no-win" situation.

Although the book is a "broadside" in favor of penal reform and not a scholarly study of contemporary prisons, it is quite useful for presentation to students. It succeeds in stimulating their reconsideration of the nature of imprisonment as the primary means we use to respond to criminality in our society and their thinking about the people who are prisoners, who do not find rehabilitation either on the inside or when they come out.

Chapter Four

Music in Prison

By Darrel Van Mastrigt

The phone rang for the fourth time that morning. Reluctantly getting out from under the warmth of the covers, a student stumbled into the wall to pick up the phone in his dormitory room.

"Time to get up. It's 7:30.", his mom cheerfully stated.

He was a freshman music student at Carnegie Mellon University on a full scholarship for technical brilliance on trumpet. Despite all he potential, his grades were terrible. Class attendance was declining. Wake-up calls were needed to get him out of bed in the mornings.

This weekend was going to be like every other one. Drinking, getting stoned, and stripping. He was drinking and smoking his life away. It would all catch up to him in the next few days.

February 9, 1987: "I was the only one with her. I must have killed her."

Detective Flaherty wrote these words in his notebook. Sitting across from him was a crying, shell-shocked, and confused 18 year-old. After being awake for 80 plus hours, the last twelve without food or water, there was no remaining will to resist. Five-ad-a-half hours of accusations, threats, and promises of death had deteriorated any care for the truth. A physical blow to the jaw, his head bouncing off the wall before being thrown to the floor by Detective Markel, made it clear to the former student that the torture would continue until he told the lies his interrogators wanted to hear. All that mattered was to end the suffering. To stop the abuse. The 18 year-old spent the next three hours telling lies to get the ordeal over with so he could finally sleep. When he couldn't produce another lie, the helpful detectives were always willing to give a hint. No video tape recorder was used to show the process and context of how the alleged confession was created. Just three detectives making a typewritten statement for the student to sign.

Even with no evidence to support the statement, this talented 18year-old music student was destined to die in a prison cell with no regard for truth or justice. No blood, no witnesses, no footprints, no forensic proof, no matter. His attorney told the judge his client was guilty and presented a charlatan of a hypnotist to insure that the sentence was life. Case closed. The truth be damned. Simply another silenced victim of America's justice never to heard from again. Thus far they have been right about silencing and ignoring the true facts about Darrell, the former student, and his innocence.

That should be the end of the story. However, it turned out to be the beginning of a new journey of growth, determination, spiritual discovery, maturity, and purpose in life behind bars. This is a compelling look at salvation through music and the quest for truth.

Darrell found himself in prison with no future. On his 19th birthday, he was sentenced to life without parole and the state took over the care, custody and control of his body. His fear was overwhelming. The nagging desire to be dead was strong. Drugs were freely available so Darrell returned to what he knew best – staying stoned to avoid facing the problems and realities of a life no worth having. Those first six months were a haze-filled nightmare with an attempt to end his life thrown in. Being strapped down in a mental ward with other patients freely roaming around his bed convinced him that suicide wasn't for him. Life wasn't quite that bad yet.

Upon transfer to another prison, things began to look brighter. His trumpet was sent to him. Music had always been a refuge, a safe world without pain or judgment. The ability to play alone, in groups and even in talent shows became a means of maintaining sanity in a world of chaos, violence and oppression. Despite being wrongfully incarcerated, he found solace in music.

In an unexpected turn of fate, another prisoner had a Bachelor's Degree and Master's Degree in music. This prisoner, Gary, was close to completing his Doctorate degree work. He was aware of Darrell's arrival and they met. Gary took Darrell under his wing.

To play trumpet, Darrell had to join bands. There were no classes or opportunities for a prisoner to learn about music unless he was already able to play. He joined oldies bands, R&B bands, rock bands, and the Catholic choir even though he wasn't Catholic. He could play anything musical put in front of him. By joining groups, he was able to learn from Gary all he could absorb. Gary agreed to teach Darrell everything he knew with the sole condition that anything taught for free must then be shared and taught to others for free. Over the next six years, Gary taught advanced trumpet techniques as well as theory, singing, directing, composing and other instruments. As the years and their friendship grew, Darrell could never learn enough.

During these years, Darrell also obtained his GED and an associate degree in business from Saint Francis College. (Darrell left high school after his junior year to insure a full scholarship. His failure to complete the first year of college negated the agreement for receiving his high school diploma at the end of the school year. Going from a full scholarship at a prestigious university to being a prisoner without a high school diploma was a traumatic shock that Darrel had to remedy.) To learn how to prove his innocence, he took paralegal courses and studied law cases.

Despite these educational successes, the courts still steadfastly refused to hear the truth in Darrell's case. Time after time, his case was denied on technical and procedural issues and relied on the false facts presented at the trial. Darrell continued retreating into his drug addiction to avoid facing the reality that he will never get out of prison, regardless of his innocence.

The Catholic choir went through a transitional period of losing almost all its members. Gary, Darrell, and two other prisoners became determined to rebuild the group as the "ChapelWinds" and make it the best choral and instrumental ensemble possible. Gary as the choir director and over the next few years, the choir grew to twenty plus members. The Chapel Winds performed weekly for masses and were asked to do Cursillos, banquets, graduations, holiday shows, and televised charity benefits and radio shows. Darrell developed into the assistant director, requiring him to play piano and direct. The Chapel Winds became the best group possible within the prison's restrictions.

During this period, music revealed to Darrell one of its most valuable lessons. Music is not about being the best. No one can claim music as his own since music belongs to everyone. Music allows an individual to build skills, reputation, and ego to the heights of heaven. Music is centered on sharing, expressing, and giving part of one's self to an audience and the world. To truly express music, a musician must care about those who will hear their expression. They must care for and respect those they are playing or singing with. The musician must ultimately understand the honor given when they are allowed to speak to others through their music and songs. The musician doesn't have to be the best.

The only qualification is to express honestly and from within one's self when playing or singing. When truthfully sharing experiences and emotions with others, an aesthetic beauty exists that every human being on earth can appreciate and be connected to. Technical skills and proficiency are simply a means to an end for musicians but cannot define who is or is not musically gifted. A 10 year-old singer can achieve more expressive ability than a professional singer who has spent her whole life imitating music. If there is no offering of one's self-contained within the music, he is only playing notes, not creating music.

It took Darrell many years to understand this. However, it was this one simple revelation that changed his life forever. His personal life was ugly, filled with drugs, anger at those who wrongfully incarcerated him, and had false barriers and images erected to keep people away from discovering his insecurities and fears. Darrell was afraid to openly love, care, and share even with those closest t him. In his limited experience, those who weren't strong, tough, and accepted by the "in crowd" were fated to be victims and abused. The strong never show their feelings. The tough don't get scared. Darrel's life at this point was not worth sharing with anybody. He could either change what he detested about his life or give up music, as music would always require a sharing of the true self.

This was not an easy decision. Stopping drug use meant facing reality and having to say "no" to people who accepted him. Giving up his hustles meant there would be no more money to buy the small comforts available in prison. Losing weight meant losing size that could intimate and keep predators away. For Darrell, it was an all or nothing choice. Either change everything or nothing at all. His love for music was strong enough to enable him to quit drugs cold, eliminate the jailhouse hustles from his life, lose about seventy pounds, and even quit smoking. Music became the catalyst for change and also opened up what and who Darrell was meant to be. This revelation caused his true musical salvation.

No one ever knew why the change occurred, even after another twelve years, until this writing. Many people don't understand why there is such a strong connection to music for musicians. To non-musicians or even those who dabble in playing notes or singing, it appears to be a fun past-time or hobby. Hey consider music as something to occupy time and when taken away they can easily move on to the next activity. For others, music is their identity. Music allows them to learn bout themselves and develop respect, compassion, and empathy for others through the safety of musical expression.

Being a member of the choir reinforced the importance of commitment, dedication, integrity and responsibility. If a person commits to doing something musically, it must be done. The preparation and practices require discipline to be ready. Distractions and what a person might rather be doing become secondary. Musicians must be dedicated to the endeavor or not agree to do it. Musicians don't want to let the other members of the group down. Being a member of the choir was the one positive and productive part of Darrell's life that he could take pride in. The experience of being part of something bigger than yourself that touches and affects so many others creates a feeling of happiness and satisfaction that cannot be rivaled. To give of oneself freely with no expectation of a reward or accolades is itself intoxicating and addictive.

For the next 13 years, the music program at SCI-Huntingdon grew and thrived and saved Darrell – and many others – from certain insanity. Darrell grew profoundly as a human being and was a successful and much-appreciated teacher. When he was eventually transferred to Graterford Prison, the music teacher there put him right to work in their program teaching and playing music. Once again, Darrell became a valuable asset to an already successful program.

It seems that just about all good things come to an end. After the cable TV station VH1 filmed a documentary on Graterford's music program, the DOC found another excuse to shut down yet another of the most worthwhile inmate programs that were left. Politicians and other mean-spirited individuals concocted misleading stories about inmate musicians being paid to perform and how they were having too much fun playing music in prison. The end result was that they did away with music in prison. The end result was that they did away with all full-time music teachers. Now they have part-time instructors and the programs are unable to meet the therapeutic needs of all the inmate population. Rules are in place to discourage and limit musical activities. Never mind that there is a plethora of research about the

benefits of learning to sing or play an instrument –
how it increases self-awareness, improves reality
testing and problem-solving skills, develops healthy
verbal and non-verbal communications skills,
decreases impulsivity through practical techniques,
increases responsibility, and allows one to explore
feelings and make positive changes. Prison
administrators have long been aware of the positive
influences and benefits of music on prisoners, but
they face the dilemma in supporting such programs
when the public is misled about them, which is exactly
what happened here.

The major problem facing music and other
such programs is public perception. When media
coverage is focused on music, it concentrates on
sensational scenes instead of the constructive. The
lead-in becomes "Murderer Allowed to Sing and Have
Fun in Prison" instead of "Prisoners Use Choral
Techniques to Express Feelings of Remorse While
Learning to Understand What Caused their Condition
of Confinement." Sensationalism sells. The truth is
hard for most people to accept, especially when it
require humanizing a despised prisoner.

The challenge facing all prisoners and their
families, friends, supporters, advocates and other
musicians is to stay focused on the positive. We must
get more community involvement and support. We
need to find musicians, music educators, and music
mentors who want to be involved with prisoners.
They know the power of music and will make great
volunteers in prison music programs. We need to
encourage groups or organizations to do more studies
on the effects of music in prisoners' lives. The

evidence of music's benefits is there. Get others involved saving the music. VH1 touts their "Save the Music" program but are nowhere in sight now that the sensational story is over. We need to find people who want to promote and use music to help keep prisoners out of jail, not those looking for a quick story or sound bite. Are you that person? Do you know someone who is? Music is a true salvation for many prisoners.

Darrell has been moved to another prison where there are no music programs, but he still teaches music when and where possible. He was fortunate enough to have other writing, art, and educational activities to fill in some of the time music used to fill. These are welcome substitutes but will never receive the love, dedication and commitment music received. Music allowed Darrell to grow, discover truths about himself and others, and saved his sanity and life. He will never stop advocating and fighting to keep music in prisons where it is needed more than ever.

Afterthoughts: The Effects of Writing this Book

Each of the seven core contributors answered the following questions:

- When we first started talking about the book project, do you remember how you felt? What you thought?

- What were your doubts about: yourself? The project?

- What was it like for you to write your story?

- What was the hardest thing for you to write about?

- How did you push through your internal resistance?

- What was the most healing part of doing this work?

- Have your perceptions of yourself changed in any way since doing the work?

- Any new dreams?

- Your criticisms/kudos about the project and the process?

- What do you see as the next step for SageWriters?

Jameel Salahuddin
($930,000)

My initial encounter with Judith Trustone and her Creative Writing course was quite serendipitous in that I simply stumbled upon it one evening. I'll never forget how it happened. I was on my way to a college-level English course held in the prison's education department. As I made my way to the English class, I saw an astonishing sight. From the corner of my eye as I walked past a room, I saw what appeared to be a tiny little woman sitting in a circle with a group of prisoners.

Without pausing, I walked on until the impact of what I'd just seen hit me. I stopped, turned around and walked back for a second glance. Sure enough, there they were, sitting in a circle rather than the usual rows of chairs in the middle of the room. What caught my attention the most was Judith, sitting in a chair with her legs tucked up under her like one of those meditation gurus. She appeared to be almost levitating, and she radiated light. It was like a bright oasis in this dark place.

Amazed, I tapped on the door and asked if I could enter the room. Once inside, I apologized for the interruption and inquired about what kind of a class this was. After being told it was Creative Writing, I then asked if I could have a seat and join in for a moment.

As I sat in the midst of that circle, I listened with fascination as each prisoner in turn read something he had written about fatherhood. Genuinely moved, I was impressed with the depth of feeling and emotion present in the readings. I just happened to have with me a copy of a letter I'd sent to my cousin earlier that day sharing with her memories of my father. I asked Judith if I could read the letter to the group, and she said okay. As I began reading it aloud, I became so caught up in the intensity of what I was sharing that I almost started crying. Although the letter was brief, I feared I wouldn't make it through the reading, as my voice began to crack and my emotions overwhelmed me. When I finished, the room was silent and everyone just sat looking at me, speechless, their own father issues stirred.

I never made it to the English class down the hall.

The Creative Writing class met weekly, and although I had another course on the same evening, I split my time between them. I'd sit in Judith's class for an hour and then go to my English class for the remainder of the evening. In this way, I still managed to get good grades in my college courses as well as hanging out with Judith and her squad.

Prior to meeting Judith, I had never been involved in anything like what I experienced in her class. From her I learned there is much more to the writing process than simply using words in a descriptive way. Under her guidance, we underwent all sorts of meditative and healing exercises long before we got seriously down to the task of writing.

When we first started talking about the possibility of a book project, I, like many in our group, didn't really take the idea seriously. We simply viewed it as wishful thinking. But once we began writing our individual stories, several men dropped out of the group. It's one thing to think or talk about what you've experienced, but when it comes to writing and finding the proper words to convey those experiences to others, it can be difficult, especially when those experiences were painful.

I have always longed for the ability to write. There have even been times when I've sat in a dark cell during the night pleading with God to give me a voice capable of conveying to the world who I am and what I've been through. Yet I had no idea what the process of telling my story would be like. Sitting alone, thinking about and reliving my past was an emotional roller coaster ride. While writing about the happier moments in my life, I was filled with a warm sense of joy. But while writing about the darker times, I plunged into deep bouts of depression. Most difficult was writing about the sexual and physical abuse of my childhood. Long-buried thoughts and memories came to the surface.

There was one occasion, while I was writing about my childhood abuse, that an intense rage began boiling inside me, a rage so strong I thought I would explode. I had to stop writing for several days. I wrote to Judith (she'd been banned from the prison by then) and cussed her out for stirring all this stuff up inside me. I even asked her what was I supposed to do with all this rage? I called her and she gently suggested some techniques for handling the anger.

I stayed in my cell for days, too afraid to come out, fearing I might snap out at someone, anyone. I was forced to examine my past and come to grips with the fact that these abuses were not my fault, and if I wanted to heal and grow, then I had to move beyond the pain and rage.

I did move on, and resumed writing. Having somehow worked my way through the rage, I began to feel a certain lightness in my heart and soul. And my willingness to share my story opened me to a new level of freedom I'd never felt before.

After mailing my story to Judith, I felt a genuine sense of accomplishment. Soon the world would know who I am.

But as the months passed and Judith told us of the many challenges she faced putting this book together, I and many others in the group began to doubt if it would ever be a reality. The whole idea just seemed too good to be true. And, like everything else good that happens in here, nothing positive would come of it.

Then September 11th happened, causing our hopes to plummet. We were sure no publisher would touch us now.

But Judith kept leading the charge, telling us to just keep pressing forward.

Now, almost two years since we first began this book project, it looks like it's finally going to be published. It appears that Judith has pulled off a miracle. I don't even know what to say.

Although neither Judith nor I are at Graterford any longer, my experience in her course has had an incredible impact on my life. Here, in another prison, I spend a lot of time and energy talking with some of the younger prisoners about writing. I even function as an editor for many of them, assisting them in creating short stories and other works.

It seems as if our SageWriters group has grown so much larger than its founding members. The spirit of Judith Trustone and our small group is touching more lives than I ever thought possible.

After 24 years, Jameel was released on parole. He married, had a good job, but is currently back in prison for a parole violation--not notifying his parole officer of a job change.

* * *

Tony Harper
($965,000)

When the topic of the book first came up, I was a bit hesitant to relate my life to outsiders because it would leave my personal experiences open to criticism. Through the course of writing about myself, I learned that we all suffer from what others think of us. Most of my life has been closed to everyone but my family because of the state of the world in which we live. Opening up to strangers, I was afraid of what they'd think about me and my family. What I've learned through writing this book is that there is rain in everyone's life. The point is how we deal with situations.

I really didn't think I had enough knowledge and information to put pen to paper. Life experiences, yes. But as I worked, I taught myself the most important lesson of all; that I am a human being and, if I want to be heard, I will lend myself a voice. Judith just kept encouraging me to write, and that was the best advice.

Writing my story awakened so many painful memories about my young life that it hurt to reflect that far back. When I looked at how my parents raised us, I disliked the way they did it. But after feeling angry for awhile, something else kicked in and I realized that back then children didn't come with an instruction book, and my parents, kids themselves, did the best they knew how to do. I'm grateful that the most important thing my parents taught me was how to love.

Putting my story on paper was a healing process for me. It helped me put both my life and my parents' lives into a form I could understand. But there are some things I can never understand or accept, like why my mother abandoned us to go to raise someone else's children when her own kids had not grown up yet. We are handed so many choices in life; sometimes we make the wrong ones for what we think are the right reasons without considering the outcome.

What helped me push through my resistance was that I kept getting encouragement and came to feel that what I had to say had value.

Now I was seeing myself more as a man with something good to say to the world.

Since writing my story, I have grown more comfortable with who I am as a person. I don't blame myself anymore for the course my life has taken. I have new confidence, and I realize that my lifelong shyness has disappeared. I'm no longer afraid to talk on any subject.

I have new energy to bring about the most important thing, to get on with the rest of my life. I am now a writer.

I've become a much stronger person through my writing.

I can see that most of the SageWriters are eventually going to write their own books, and Judith will have lots of little babies running around the world. They will owe a deep thanks to this special lady who saw that there is more to us than just our labels and numbers.

Peace be with all of us.

* * *

Danny Haggard
($860,000)

Part of me has always dreamed of having a book published. It has been along the lines of fiction/fantasy, so I was a bit apprehensive about a group book. I'll admit I was skeptical but hopeful. The skepticism came mostly from my judging the capabilities of the other inmates involved.

I wasn't sure about how much I was willing to reveal about myself. In the first edition I chose to remain anonymous because of possible retaliation from the Department of Corrections when I'm considered for parole. I had and still have confidence in Judith's abilities and determination. The project as a whole was under question by me because I felt that many of the others involved couldn't or wouldn't pull their own weight.

While I was writing my story, a lot of memories came up for me the more I wrote. Many of my personal experiences were forgotten until I actually started to write. Some of the more painful ones were difficult, but in a way it has helped me to cope in a positive way by writing and revealing them to others.

The hardest thing to write about was the time of my life with Uncle Warren when he sexually abused me. I felt such shame and betrayal. Even though it wasn't an extreme form of abuse, it was a very big turning point in my life. I believe it created in me a deep distrust of people and their true motives.

After I decided to reveal all, it became easier for me. Once the pen started to flow, I was able to write smoothly. I think a writer has to be decisive and know where he or she wants to go. After that, at least for me, it just happened.

Being able to walk through my most painful issues from the past was a healing process for me. It triggered memories, both good and bad.

My perception of myself has changed. My self-esteem has improved. I realize that after writing my story, what happened to me wasn't so bad. It allowed me to compare my relatively small issues with other people's huge ones.

One of my dreams has always been to write a novel. Now I have a better idea of what it takes. I don't have any new dreams as I'm still trying to achieve my old dream of peace of mind.

I wished the students had shown more enthusiasm for the class. When assignments were given, not everyone complied in a timely way. I didn't care for the way this institution conspired against the Creative Writing class and our teacher. Eventually they succeeded in removing both from the grounds.

I'm grateful for the ongoing correspondence with Judith, which has kept me writing, for that kind of support and encouragement can be in short supply in here. Without her drive, determination and organizational skills, none of this would have happened.

I'm a bit skeptical about SageWriters' chances for survival beyond this project. I say this only because of the conditions under which we live. For the most part, most of the members of the group itself are preoccupied with their own problems and lack of liberty. I've displayed this on several occasions, and my situation is minor compared to some of the others. I will be getting out of here someday. I'd like in the future to see a monthly publication by SageWriters consisting of who prisoners are and what they've done to change themselves. Until and unless the public has a better understanding of prisoners as human beings, this will always be a hostile environment for us.

Danny was released on parole but was soon back behind bars.

* * *

Anton Forde/Trevor Mattis
($545,000)

I don't recall exactly how I felt when the book project was first discussed, but I know I was supportive of anything that gives us prisoners a voice.

My only doubts were about revisiting the past. Though my story is always in my head, and I plan an autobiography, writing it was, I don't know, maybe cathartic. I was just hesitant about reliving the past and that moment that brought me here, since I tend to compartmentalize my experiences and rarely visit my pre-incarcerated life.

Nothing was really hard for me to write. The worst of my experiences, that of being charged and convicted for a crime I didn't commit, is a thing I've written about over and over as I litigate my case in my fight to obtain justice.

I liked revisiting my college years. I'm not sure about healing aspects, but I truly appreciate getting the opportunity to show who I am as a person.

My perceptions of myself have not changed, but I think I've become a better writer, though I do procrastinate. I am proud of publishing *Contemplations of a Convict*; I'm working on the second edition right now, as well as a book of poetry.

I have no new dreams; I have a laundry list of old dreams yet untouched.

The next step that I see for SageWriters is taking on the issue of prison reform and contributing a voice to the political and social issues of the day.

My admiration and respect go out to Judith Trustone for her compassion, dedication and tenacity in seeing such an arduous task as the compilation of this book through to the end. Congratulations to all of us SageWriters!

* * *

Muti Ajamu-Osagboro
($825,000)

When the book project began, I felt it was just another project for me. One of perhaps fifteen that I was juggling. It is but a slice of the quadruple-layered cake I will eventually present to the entire world.

Writing "Portrait of Innocence" was deeply spiritual. Another step on the road to cathartic liberation.

I had no doubts about myself. My doubts about Judith were: Will her brainwashed upbringing allow her to accept the ugly truth about the country's judicial system, and just as important, how much of it will she actually present to the public? Could she really grasp the reality of black lives?

The hardest thing for me to write was how the entire system routinely gang-raped the so-called rights that I had, all in a day's work. They didn't even stop to burp.

There was no resistance, just pain. I've told my story thousands of times before, and each time I do, it's less painful. Each time it is cathartic. The funny thing with "Portrait" was that it was the first time I'd written it all out from start to finish and to actually see all the treachery the injustice system has taken me through. It's unreal.

According to their plan, I was supposed to be dead years ago. If I never thought miracles existed before, I now know that my being alive is a miracle. That's what I see every time I look in the mirror...a breathing miracle.

Every time I read my story in its totality it was a healing experience.

I don't have dreams. I have visions, and this is just one page in the book of my life.

I appreciate Judith's willingness to learn, her caring and her kindness. Her ability to come out of her comfort zone and risk being "niggerized." Her willingness to challenge wrongs as she is blessed to understand them.

The next step for SageWriters is whatever we decide.

The revolution will be visualized…in literary excellence.

* * *

Robert "Muhkam" Hagood

($1,175,000 until he died a few years ago)

When the men in our creative writing circle sat down to discuss the possibility of a collective book project, I aligned myself with the group decision as a gesture of support for the group's efforts to extend their horizons of communications with what we prisoners call "The Outside World." I realize now that I should have participated more in these group discussions and paid more attention to what was being agreed to, for at no time had I entertained the possibility of ever being called upon to write about myself. After all, everyone in the SageWriters group knew that my writing skills were limited to the writing of poetry, or so I thought. Also, I was most comfortable with the thought that I would leave the serious writing for the book project to the men who had ambitions to be novelists and playwrights, as well as the academic types who enjoyed endless discourses on the subject of writing styles and which author wrote what a hundred years ago. My thoughts were that I would write what I see, think and feel, and be free from the box of academia. Nevertheless, the time did arrive when I either had to shit or get off the pot. I had to honor my word.

After evaluating my concerns about my own writing ability, there remained a consideration that was like a straight arrow destined to penetrate the core of my being and honoring my word.

During the years of interacting with Judith in our SageWriters group, I developed an intense respect for her as a result of her dedication and loyalty to the prisoners, to prison reform issues and our efforts to maintain human dignity.

Also, when she sent the urgent message, "Come on, Muhkam, I've heard from everyone but you," my thoughts were that although I had been the ninth man called to the plate, there was no way that I was leaving the game without taking my turn at bat. No way!

We've all heard that in the final seconds of life, a drowning man sees his whole life flash before him like a film being projected upon a gigantic movie screen. To my knowledge, the drowning man has never told anyone about this peculiar experience that so many believe to be true.

However, my experience of three decades of imprisonment has resulted in my revisiting the events and circumstances of my life over and over again. Thus the call for me to begin writing about myself was the inevitable revisiting of my sinful past, over and over again.

Writing about myself compelled me to recall memories of my childhood, the escapades of a too curious and fearless teenager, and the young adult who didn't quite find his way to manhood until after he had experienced all of the chastisements of living, and then finally learning the cold, often cruel reality lessons of life.

Aside from the remembrances of the mundane events of my life, there were several pleasant revisits of that most memorable and joyous experience of meeting, knowing and loving the gracious and beautiful Doris Dean Hagood, my beloved wife, God's blessing to my life. She brought me years of comfort, encouragement, love and happiness, until she died of a brain aneurysm on June 28, 1997.

The process of writing for the book carried me to that place where I was no longer talking to someone else about me; rather, Muhkam was talking to Muhkam, re-evaluating, resolving, becoming and perhaps, as Judith always says, "being in beauty."

* * *

Jameel Whitaker
($615,000)

Because I was a part of this project from its very inception, I felt that our writing group (SageWriters) would get authentic exposure. Also, our collective talents would serve to build a bridge between prisoners who are sincere and utilize their time well with citizens who are willing to listen to various shades of a prisoner's mind.

I had no doubts about the book's success; I hope it will gain the necessary momentum needed to open doors for other endeavors like this one. My writing suffered when society's pressures distracted me from working with the same intensity and passion as when I was confined at Graterford. Though in prison your day is dictated by prison officials, one can concentrate more because prisoners are not being bombarded with everyday societal pressures like paying the rent and car repairs.

I pushed myself to write when I fell into a writing slump by thinking about the men I left behind. I knew I had the other SageWriters' votes of confidence and they expected me to stand tall and resolute in the world after serving a lengthy prison sentence.

Submitting my work, usually late, to Judith, who showed so much patience and support with my procrastination episodes was rather healing. My perception of myself always changes when I undergo a difficult challenge and meet it successfully. For me and I'm sure for many, inertia is the true enemy of creativeness.

There is so much opportunity in anyone's life if they can learn to tap into that creative force. I'm still exploring this process. I've had glimpses, however brief, of my own creative genius.

I see some very heavyweight SageWriters coming from Graterford and other prisons.

I thank Judith Trustone for sharing her light with me.

* * *

Judith Trustone

While this is the end of the book, it really is a beginning. With the exciting new technology of print-on-demand publishing there will be room in later editions for many of those whose work was not included, those who promised to write but haven't yet, and for reactions from readers. It is apparent that as a nation we must begin honest conversations minus political posturing and take actions to change this dysfunctional, barbaric, and extremely expensive system. The bottom line is what are we going to do about the injustice created by poverty and racism? With the growing gap between the haves and the have nots, Shadow America becomes larger and darker each year as the prison industry grows and grows like a tough weed, choking the life out of everything and everyone in its path, especially fragile seedlings.

Hopefully at this point the reader has come to realize the tragic waste of the human beings whose voices are heard on these pages, and will do whatever possible to remedy conditions in Shadow America.

Personally, this was a difficult project to complete as I couldn't visit the SageWriters, all mail comes under the eyes of censors and all phone conversations are monitored and recorded. In the group we developed a kind of code so we could talk more freely. For instance, the book was called "Nelly" after Nelly Bly, the nineteenth century journalist from Pennsylvania who got herself admitted to the Belleview mental asylum in New York, spent two weeks there and then got out through the intercession of a colleague. Her book about conditions there was a wake-up call for making American mental asylums more humane.

While reading what the SageWriters wrote was exciting, especially as they grew more confident and assured, I was at times overwhelmed at the responsibility of editing Black English from a white perspective. And their sense of time was quite different from mine. If I asked for immediate responses through the mail I was certain to get them at least three weeks later. Dealing with prison life consumes them and makes them unaware of deadlines or the different kinds of pressures we feel outside the walls. Because of the chronic traumatic stress syndrome from which they all suffer, they tend to be self-absorbed. Yet they all amazed me with their strength and courage; and each, in his own way, has been illuminating. I doubt if I could survive one day of their lives.

On a deep level, my painful awakening to the truth about the criminal justice system shook my view of the rest of the world. Yes, I am more cynical than ever; yet knowing what they've survived and achieved has given me inspiration and an incredible perception of gratitude for the abundance, privileges and freedoms that I have. Whenever I feel weary or sorry for myself, all I have to do is think of my imprisoned "brothers" and "sisters" and I immediately stop my internal whining. There are times when I have a beautiful experience that I yearn to share with them. My capacity for joy has grown, and I am much more patient.

When I travel or shoot a spectacular sunset, I send them pictures. I have a series of "Skyscapes" currently on exhibit that came about when Muti once asked me while I was flying to the west coast to take pictures above the clouds as he'd never been on a plane.

When I eat a succulent mango I wonder if Anton will ever again taste the fruit that grows abundantly in his native land. In a way that's hard to explain, the two years of getting this book together has made us a kind of family – an odd one for sure, but a family none the less.

I have tried as much as is possible under such malevolent scrutiny to share my life, my struggles and my triumphs.

I feel honored to have worked with these prisoners and for having earned their not-easily-won trust. I pray I have given their voices the accuracy and the honesty they deserve.

I fear for the harm they may experience as a result of being openly involved with this project. As soon as I learn of any retaliation against them by guards or administration, the information will be posted on our website, www.SageWriters.org, along with names and numbers of who to call to protest. I will also alert the media.

Just as we were going to press with the first edition I got a call from Jameel Salahuddin, who was terribly upset. It seems he was emptying a waste basket into a larger container when an apple rolled across the floor and then fell five tiers down, splattering at the feet of some guards. Jameel immediately put up his hands and yelled down that it was an accident. Within minutes he was shackled, and while standing and trying to explain, one of the guards picked up an apple and threw it at his chest as hard as he could, almost knocking Jameel over. Demanding medical attention and a chance to write up the guard who injured him, he spotted a lieutenant walking nearby with some men in suits. He meekly called out could he talk to the lieutenant and proceeded to tell what had happened and that he wanted to file a complaint against the guard. Calling the guard a "known hothead," the lieutenant asked Jameel not to file a complaint and that the guards' accusations that he had assaulted them with an apple would also be dropped. So instead of being sent to The Hole for six months or more, Jameel was unshackled and released into his cell. All he was trying to do was clean his "house." He could have been badly beaten like Anton was. Or had years added to his time.

Such is the daily life of terrorism in our prisons.

Let us join together to shine a light into Shadow America and create a new system that gets rid of poverty, treats, trains and rehabilitates, a healing system that brings out the best in all who enter. If half the folks in prison were released tomorrow with no threat to the community as the experts state, imagine what **$23 billion** could do for rehabilitation, treatment and training. We need to explore becoming more of a social democracy rather than the arrogant empire the rest of the world is coming to despise. Ending poverty and ending mass incarceration and changing prisons needs to be declared a national emergency.

Chapter Five

Things You Can Do Right Now

"Never doubt that a small group of thoughtful committed citizens can change the world. Indeed, it's the only thing that ever has."

Margaret Mead

The resources and recommended reading listed in this book are but a small sample of what's out there. Go to your library, get on the internet and explore the world of alternatives to this terrible system. Educate yourself, and as you learn, educate those around you, especially when you hear someone saying something that in no way reflects the reality of prison life, like: "They're all getting a free college education, and I have to work hard to pay for my kids to go to college." Or "They should lock them all up and throw away the key!" And one of the most common, that prisons are like "country clubs." According to inmates, the series "Oz" on HBO in no way presents a true picture of prison life.

Most importantly, visit your closest maximum security prison and become a volunteer.

TWELVE THINGS YOU CAN DO TODAY

1) Write to any or all of the SageWriters whose stories have touched your heart. Offer your support in whatever way is appropriate. (We can forward your letters to them.)

2) Identify activist groups in your state or region and join the one that most appeals to you (see Resources at the end of this chapter).

3) If you're a member of a church, synagogue or mosque, find out if your institution has a prison ministry. If not, start one.

4) Volunteer to teach/mentor an inmate through local programs (see Resources).

5) Sign up to write to four recommended inmates. This will give you a wider perspective on the issues than just writing to one.

6) Find out your state's laws on mandatory sentencing, the death penalty, life sentencing and aftercare services. If you don't like what you learn, speak out – to politicians, the press, the clergy. Get active.

7) Make generous contributions to organizations like the Prison Society, the ACLU and Amnesty International that are working to improve conditions in Shadow America.

8) Speak out when someone makes a joke about rape in prison. Make the truth known.

9) If you're a lawyer, contact Muti, Anton, Tony and the others and help to get them out of there!

10) Write and e-mail letters to television crime shows that portray prison rape, prosecutorial misconduct and inaccurate pictures of prison life as acceptable.

11) Begin ongoing conversations with local and federal politicians about your concerns about the waste of your tax dollar and the destruction of the human spirit and lack of treatment and rehabilitation that characterize our current system.

12) Hold ALL prisoners, but especially those in this book, in your prayers and meditations, so they may survive the physical, mental, emotional and spiritual bites the beast tries to tear daily from their troubled beings.

To contact Sagewriters Publishing:

Box 215 Swarthmore, PA 19081

www.Trustonekindness.com

Judith.Trustone.Wordpress.com

info@Trustonekindness.com

See "How To Create A Kindness Circle" and an interview of Judith Trustone by best-selling Chicken Soul author, Jack Canfield on Youtube

Please send us your reviews or post them on Amazon.

Thank you. And may you always
BE IN BEAUTY!

Made in the USA
Columbia, SC
29 November 2017